Homeland Security Handbook
for Citizens and Public Officials

Homeland Security Handbook for Citizens and Public Officials

Edited by Roger L. Kemp

McFarland & Company, Inc., Publishers
Jefferson, North Carolina, and London

Grateful acknowledgment is made to the following
organizations and publishers for granting permission to reprint
the material contained in this volume: A. J. Parrino & Associates,
American Red Cross, American Society for Public Administration,
American Society of Civil Engineers, *Fire Engineering*, Heldon
Publishing Company, *Homeland Defense Journal*, International
Association of Chiefs of Police, KMD Media LLC, Massachusetts
Municipal Association, National Fire Protection Association,
National Sheriffs' Association, Pennwell Publishing Company,
PRIMEDIA Magazines & Media Inc.,
the Council of State Governments.

LIBRARY OF CONGRESS CATALOGUING-IN-PUBLICATION DATA

Homeland security handbook for citizens and public officials /
edited by Roger L. Kemp
p.   cm.
Includes index.

ISBN 0-7864-2432-X (softcover : 50# alkaline paper)

1. Emergency management — United States.
2. Terrorism — United States — Prevention.
3. Civil defense — United States.
4. National security — United States.
I. Kemp, Roger L.
HV551.3.H675   2006   363.325'70973 — dc22   2006001523

British Library cataloguing data are available

On the cover: Eagle ©2006 Photodisc; Flag ©2006 Comstock Images

Manufactured in the United States of America

McFarland & Company, Inc., Publishers
Box 611, Jefferson, North Carolina 28640
www.mcfarlandpub.com

For my mother, *Eva*

TABLE OF CONTENTS

Part III
The Future of Homeland Security

PREFACE

The world was shocked on September 11, 2001, when foreign terrorists used commercial airplanes owned by United States airline companies in a well-planned attack on the *Pentagon* next to our nation's capitol, and the *World Trade Center* towers located in New York City. The loss of life caused by this terrorist attack was the largest to take place on American soil since the Civil War. In total, nearly 3,000 people died from all walks of life, including police officers, fire fighters, other emergency personnel, as well as citizens in general.

Since this tragedy, all levels of government — the federal, state, county, as well as municipal — national organizations, as well as citizens and taxpayers in general, have undertaken numerous initiatives to see that such an incident does not take place again on American soil. Citizens and public officials alike, throughout the country, have taken steps to enhance the emergency preparation and response programs at all levels of government, not-for-profit organizations, as well as the private sector.

Specifically, all of these initiatives and programs focus on one or more of the primary four phases of emergency management. These phases include mitigation, preparedness, response, and recovery, which are briefly explained below. These four phases include the combined programs and activities of all levels of government, national organizations, as well as the general public. The goal of all of these efforts is to limit the loss of life and property during a crisis, such as one brought about by a man-made or natural disaster.

- *Mitigation*— Includes activities that eliminate or reduce the chance of occurrence or the effects of a disaster. While governments and citizens cannot prevent disasters, measures can be taken to minimize their impact.
- *Preparedness*— The next phase of emergency management is preparedness. It includes planning how to respond when an emergency or disaster occurs, and working to marshal the required resources to respond in a timely and effective manner.
- *Response*— Response is the third phase of emergency management and covers the period during and immediately following a disaster. During this phase, public officials, sometimes assisted by citizen volunteers, provide emergency assistance to victims of the event and try to reduce the likelihood of further damage.
- *Recovery*— Recovery is the final phase of the emergency management cycle. This phase continues until all systems return to near-normal operations. Short-term recovery restores vital life-support operations. The long-term recovery, which may go on for months or even years, includes measures to reduce the future likelihood of another disaster.

This volume documents numerous homeland security initiatives, or best practices, from throughout the nation. All of these efforts have taken place since September 11, 2001, a timeframe of only four years. The major programs examined in this volume include the following:

1

- Access Control to Buildings
- Air Transportation Safeguards
- Automated Public Notification Systems
- Building Design Safeguards
- Citizen Volunteerism
- Communications During Emergencies
- Disaster Preparedness Guidelines
- Dispatch Center Services
- Early Warning Systems
- Emergency Response Planning
- Entrepreneurial Resources
- Evacuation Procedures
- Fatalities Management
- Federal Government and its Agencies
- Geographic Information Systems
- Infrastructure Assessment and Protection
- Multi–Government Agency Cooperation
- Municipal Public Safety Departments
- Mutual Aid Agreements
- Personal Identification Systems
- Private Sector Cooperation and Support
- Public and Private Healthcare Systems
- Risk and Vulnerability Assessment

The examples in this book have been taken from all four levels of government, as well as respected national not-for-profit organizations. In total, the homeland security practices reflected in this study come from eleven municipal governments, six county governments, ten state governments, eight federal agencies and commissions, and ten national not-for-profit organizations. These cities, counties, states, federal agencies and commissions, and not-for-profit organizations, are highlighted below.

- *Cities*— Austin, Texas; Boca Raton, Florida; Bowling Green, Kentucky; Fremont, California; Lima, Ohio; Los Angeles, California; New York, New York; Olathe, Kansas; Palm Beach, Florida; Rowlett, Texas; and San Jose, California.
- *Counties*— Allen County, Ohio; Fairfield County, Virginia; Johnson County, Kansas; Los Angeles County, California, Orange County, California; and Stafford County, Virginia.

- *States*— California, Florida, Georgia, Kentucky, Massachusetts, New York, Ohio, Missouri, Washington, and Virginia.
- *Federal Agencies and Commissions*— Department of Homeland Security, Department of Justice, Federal Aviation Administration, Federal Emergency Management Agency, Immigration and Naturalization Service, Office of the White House, President's Homeland Security Advisory Council, and the Presidential Commission on Critical Infrastructure Protection.
- *Not-for-Profit Organizations*— American Public Works Association, American Red Cross, American Society of Civil Engineers, International Association of Emergency Managers, International Conference of Police Chaplains, National Fallen Fire Fighters Foundation, National Fire Protection Association, National League of Cities, National Sheriffs' Association, and the Public Safety Communications Officials Association.

This volume is divided into three sections for ease of reference. The first section introduces readers to this new subject, "homeland security." The second section and, by design, the longest includes numerous case studies, or best practices, on how citizens and public officials are developing new homeland security practices. Section three focuses on the future of homeland security during the coming years. Several appendices are included in the last section of this volume that highlight important information in this new subject area. Based upon this conceptual schema, the four primary sections of this work are briefly highlighted below.

- *Introduction to Homeland Security*— This chapter examines how our nation, since World War II, has gone from civil defense, to emergency management, to the evolving field of homeland security. This introductory chapter will reveal how the present resembles the past, particularly the post-war years when our public officials and citizens focused their efforts on civil defense. The nation's focus on homeland security will likely continue for many years to come.

- *Homeland Security for Citizens and Public Officials*— The policies, plans, and programs of numerous cities, counties, states, federal agencies and commissions, and not-for-profit organizations, are examined in this section. The best practices presented in this section, as mentioned above, include eleven cities, six counties, ten states, eight federal agencies and commissions, and ten nationally respected not-for-profit organizations. Chapters are arranged in alphabetical order based on best practices in the field of homeland security.
- *The Future of Homeland Security*— This section examines the future of homeland security, focusing on the civil liberties, and trends evolving in the new field of homeland security. Some Americans, citizens and public officials alike, are now starting to reexamine the proper balance between protecting public safety and safeguarding individual civil liberties. Government officials are now reexamining some policies that protect the public at the expense of the loss of individual civil liberties. The proper balance between homeland security practices and civil liberties will no doubt be debated for many years to come.
- *Appendices*— Several appendices are included in this volume, including a listing of homeland security acronyms, a guide to homeland security Internet resources, and the American Red Cross's homeland security advisory system recommendations. Lastly, contact information for the Federal Emergency Management Agency's regional offices, and contact information for all state offices and agencies of emergency management, is listed by region and state. Emphasis has been placed on places that citizens and public officials can go to for additional information in the field of homeland security.

The case studies, or best practices, examined in this volume are typically applied in a piecemeal and incremental fashion by citizens, public officials, as well as representatives of not-for-profit organizations. For the most part, everyone is doing their own thing relative to his or her own community, government, or organization. Most citizens and public officials do not have the time to find out what their neighbors are doing, let alone what citizens and public officials in other levels of government, and national organizations throughout the country, are doing in this field. For this reason, the case studies selected for this reference volume represent an important codification of knowledge in the homeland security field.

This reference work assembles, for the first time, materials based on a national literature search, and makes this information available to citizens and public officials throughout the United States. The goal of this volume is to help educate citizens and public officials on how to best use these state-of-the-art homeland security practices to help protect their own neighborhoods in cities and towns throughout the country.

Spurred to action by the events of September 11, 2001, citizens, public officials, their governments, and many not-for-profit organizations developed the practices described in this volume. These practices will continue to evolve in cities, counties, states, the federal government, as well as national organizations, in response to citizen expectations and directives at the federal level from the new Cabinet-level Department of Homeland Security. For this reason, other volumes of this nature will have to be developed in the future to continue to spread the word about the evolving best practices in this field.

Lastly, I would like to personally thank representatives from the following national professional associations, not-for-profit organizations, and publishers, for granting me permission to reprint the material contained in this volume. Professional associations include the American Society for Public Administration, the American Society of Civil Engineers, the International Association of Chiefs of Police, the Massachusetts Municipal Association, the National Sheriffs' Association, and the Council of State Governments. Not-for-profit organizations include the American Red Cross and the National Fire Protection Association. Publishers include A. J. Parrino & Associates, *Fire Engineering*, Hendon Publishing Company, *Homeland Defense Journal*, KMD Media, LLC, Pennwell Publishing Company, and PRIMEDIA Magazines & Media Inc.

Roger L. Kemp, PhD
City of Vallejo
California
Spring 2006

Part I
Introduction to Homeland Security

CHAPTER 1

CIVIL DEFENSE, EMERGENCY MANAGEMENT, AND HOMELAND SECURITY

David Wagman

On Sept. 10, 2001, the Los Angeles Emergency Preparedness Department held a bioterrorism training exercise, one of several disaster drills the agency regularly holds. The reporters who covered the exercise on that Monday could have fit into a telephone booth, recalls Ellis Stanley, the department's general manager.

Today, similar training exercises are media circuses wherever they are held. The attention marks one of the subtle, yet fundamental, shifts in how emergency management goes about its business in the post–Sept. 11 world.

The heightened emphasis on preparing to deal with terrorist threats since Sept. 11 is returning emergency management to its roots in the Civil Defense days of the '40s, '50s and '60s. During those years, Civil Defense efforts involved community vigilance and local preparation to guard against the perceived threat of foreign invasion. As worry over that threat waned, emergency management focused more on natural disaster planning and recovery. That focus was codified with the creation of the Federal Emergency Management Agency (FEMA) in 1979.

The Pope and Timothy McVeigh

The first World Trade Center attack in February 1993 and security efforts to protect Pope John Paul II during his visit to the United States later that year, however, prompted a nearly decade-long effort by emergency managers to make terrorist attacks a part of their disaster planning regimen. The sense of urgency grew after the 1995 Oklahoma City and 1996 Olympic Park bombings, and the 1995 sarin nerve gas attack on the Tokyo subway. The September 2001 attacks in New York City and Washington, D.C., closed the circle, bringing civil defense and terrorism planning once again to the forefront of emergency management planning.

"We're back to where we started," Stanley says.

Well, almost. For one thing, today's terrorist threats are technologically more sophisticated and more difficult to anticipate than those of a generation ago. Where Civil Defense wardens of the '60s might have stood watch on a beach on a dark night to guard against commandos landing in a rubber boat,

Originally published as "There and Back Again," *Homeland Protection*, Vol. 1, No. 1, July/August 2002. Published by A. J. Parrino & Associates, Western Springs, Illinois. Reprinted with permission of the publisher.

emergency management teams today plan for and train to respond to terrorism that might come in many different forms, from chemical or biological to nuclear. In a worrisome twist on the rubber raft scenario, for example, emergency managers today must think about the possibility of a nuclear device being packed into a cargo container and loaded onto a ship sailing for a U.S. harbor.

The task of guarding against such a varied menu of threats requires a level of coordination and cooperation that eclipses anything necessary for natural disaster planning. "In the past, our planning was for contingencies we knew a lot about," says Bob Andrews, president of the International Association of Emergency Managers (IAEM) and head of the Clark County, Nev., emergency management department. Tornadoes, hurricanes and floods have predictable seasons and lend themselves to early preparation.

Not so terrorism, which is most effective when it plays on unknown whens, wheres and hows. "We now have to focus on an unknown equation," Andrews says.

New Ties to Law Enforcement

In their quest to deal with those unknowns, emergency managers have a tool, law enforcement, that they lack in dealing with natural disasters. "There's no crime in a flood; there's no investigation or intelligence gathering," says Bob Brooks, who heads up Colorado's emergency management effort as director of the state's Department of Local Affairs. Since Sept. 11, criminal law enforcement and investigation functions have increasingly become part of the emergency management strategy, another fundamental shift in the emergency management system.

"We have a heightened need to work with public safety," Brooks says. His department has staff members assigned to work with the Colorado Bureau of Investigation, which, in turn, has direct links to the FBI.

In the fall of 2001, Gov. Bill Owens created a state office to parallel the newly created federal Homeland Security office; Brooks has assigned staff to that office as well.

"If a building falls down, it doesn't matter if it was caused by a bomb, an earthquake or a tornado," Brooks says. "If it was caused by a terrorist, then the added element is the crime scene investigation. It's the same response training, but supplemented by law enforcement."

The Communications Quandary

Yet even as emergency management evolves to incorporate the threat of terrorism, some things remain constant, notably communications problems. Those problems extend to communications at all levels, whether between emergency agencies that respond to a disaster, or among entities competing for grant money.

"Where every mission fails is in communication," says Mike Fagel, an emergency management director in suburban Chicago and a member of the Illinois Terrorism Task Force.

For Stanley, the communication issue comes down to interoperability: the ability of fire, police, EMS and other teams to talk with one another at the scene of a disaster. Emergency agencies tend to buy their own communications equipment, and much of it doesn't work across agency boundaries. Consequently, communications can break down, hindering emergency response efforts.

Emergency managers are looking to the Federal Communications Commission (FCC) to create a public safety band spectrum that would facilitate interagency communication. However, they realize that the cost of creating a single communication system accessible by all local emergency response units will be steep. In Los Angeles alone, the price tag for changing all fire department radios could run as high as $50 million, Stanley says.

Improving communication between local emergency response departments and state and federal agencies could be tougher still because of the array of agencies involved in terrorism response. For example, since Sept. 11, emergency managers have begun working more closely with local hospitals and healthcare providers, says Marcus Aurelius, emergency management coordinator for Phoenix and co-chair of IAEM's terrorism subcommittee.

Local laws also are being reviewed to clarify everything from line of succession (if local leaders are incapacitated) to who is authorized to impose a quarantine. Efforts also are under way to address potential vulnerabilities in local utilities and pipelines.

Additionally, emergency managers are working with local businesses to help them understand how to survive a terrorist attack, Aurelius says. Realizing the importance of post-attack economic continuity, they're developing ways to help local businesspeople learn how to maintain their businesses after an incident, as well as how to plan for and recover from a disaster.

Budget Issues

Lack of funding for emergency management remains a serious issue, with the recent economic downturn squeezing budgets even as the public expects higher levels of preparation. Part of the problem is that Congress had focused its spending priorities on school violence rather than on terrorism, says Karen Cobuluis, a spokeswoman for the National Emergency Management Association, which focuses on statewide response issues. To adjust to the post–Sept. 11 world, Congress has had to reshuffle its budget priorities.

... President Bush and Congress have promised billions of dollars for homeland defense .... Stanley cautions that even after the money becomes available, local emergency managers will need to apply for and compete

with other agencies for funds. The money also will likely be earmarked for specific items such as equipment or training.

But specifying exactly how the money can be spent can cause problems, Aurelius says, comparing the situation to a car buyer who's forced to use specific funds for various parts: He can buy tires only with money from a certain pot and must use a separate source of cash to buy the horn.

Emergency management lobbying groups are working to convince Congress of the efficacy of funding entire programs, rather than creating a piecemeal approach. "Congress needs to think how money is allocated at the local level," Aurelius says.

Groups like the National Emergency Management Association (NEMA) also are watching to see how the federal money is allocated. If it's tagged for disbursement generally through the Department of Justice (DOJ), then municipal police and fire organizations stand to benefit the most. If the money is dispersed more through FEMA, it's likely to be targeted at statewide terrorism planning efforts.

Cobuluis prefers the latter scenario. "Cities don't always coordinate with one another on their purchases," she says, arguing that states could better make the spending decisions that benefit multiple jurisdictions.

"A Lively Period"

Still, emergency managers like to point out that the first response to a terrorist attack is almost always a local one. "All disasters are local; that's the byword we have to remember," says Fagel.

In Colorado, where Brooks' agency provides $120 million a year in grants, the focus is on helping local emergency managers prepare for and respond to disasters, including terrorism. "In a disaster, the response is at a local level when fire, police and ambulance crews work on their own for at least the first few hours," Brooks says. "When they need more help, our folks go in and make immediate connections."

In that sense, the concept of all-hazard disaster planning seems even more relevant than ever. When emergency response crews turn on their sirens and head to a disaster, they need the same level of preparation whether the disaster is caused by nature or, as Aurelius says, by "some bizarre man-created incident."

The process of shoring up homeland defense can bolster the strategies needed to deal with natural disasters, says IAEM's Andrews. A communication system that fosters interoperability, for example, is useful regardless of the nature of a disaster. "We need to develop in a manner that bridges both worlds," he says.

Being an emergency manager on Sept. 12, 2001, wasn't the same as being one on Sept. 10. Since Sept. 11, the job requires emergency managers to continue to plan for and be able to respond to natural disasters, even as they plan for bigger catastrophes.

Emergency planning remains uneven across the country, an indication that it reflects local needs, budget priorities and politics. Regions that are routinely affected by natural disasters are better prepared to respond to a terrorist threat than are "disaster-deficient" parts of the country, Aurelius says. Additionally, areas that have existing regional emergency planning boards are likely to be better able to handle difficult coordination issues if only because they have a core of people who know one another.

Finally, the challenge of embracing national goals and programs related to homeland security and making them work at the local level remains. Sept. 11 spawned a sea change in the concept of emergency management, and the pace of change has yet to slow down. "It is," says Aurelius in a classic understatement, "a lively period."

Part II
Homeland Security for Citizens and Public Officials

CHAPTER 2

ACCESS CONTROL SYSTEMS IMPROVE BUILDING SECURITY

Jacqueline Emigh

Like other state governments, Washington State faces an increasing barrage of security threats from irate citizens and terrorist groups. To help head off these threats, officials of Washington's Department of Social and Human Services (DSHS) have installed photo ID access control systems at 70 percent of their facilities statewide. E. Robert "Spike" Millman, though, doesn't think current precautions are quite enough. He wants to take security to the hilt, giving all DSHS offices throughout the state protection through interchangeable access control.

"The northwest is a wonderful and beautiful place, but we have our distractions. Washington State is home to a number of potential security threats. It is also a northwest transportation hub accessible to international threat elements," say Millman, security manager for the DSHS, an agency that employs more than 18,000 people in more than 250 offices and institutions statewide.

"I am a one-man traveling medicine show of security, safety, emergency management, and employee preparedness," says Millman, a 16-year DSHS veteran. Before moving into security, Millman served as a building manager, auditor, consultant, social worker, and internal affairs investigator for the agency.

Beyond the hazards posed by anti-government and international terrorism, Millman worries that ordinary citizens might carry out threats of violence. "The DSHS is very vulnerable, because we serve so many different types of clients," he says. "Parents of children served by our Children's Administration office (for example) can become upset if their children are moved into foster care. Meanwhile, our Community Services office has been reducing the rolls of welfare recipients."

As security manager of DSHS headquarters in Olympia in 1988, Millman oversaw the installation of the building's first photo ID system. "In January of 1999, we started to bring things statewide," he recalls. Now, Washington State's DSHS has distributed a grand total of about 7,000 photo ID access badges.

Millman has much bigger goals in mind, though. Beyond extending photo ID

Originally published as "Photo I.D. and Beyond," *Government Security*, Vol. 1, No. 1, April 2002. Published by PRIME-DIA Magazines & Media Inc., Overland Park, KS. Reprinted with permission of the publisher.

access control to all DSHS sites, he foresees a uniform system. Under a proposal from Millman now being considered by the agency, badges issued in one DSHS location could be used interchangeably in any other DSHS office.

The agency has already instituted a statewide color-coding system to denote specific access privileges. Vendors, for example, are outfitted with orange-colored badges. Visitors' badges come in two different color schemes: Hot pink badges provide visitors with building wide access and bright yellow badges require visitors to have an escort.

According to Millman, what's most needed right now is the statewide installation of access control devices that are able to read both proximity and bar code photo IDs.

Some DSHS offices are now using proximity cards, while others are using bar code IDs. Although some offices have issued cards that use both technologies, others still rely on older magnetic stripe card technology. "We've been trying to eliminate mag stripe, but we haven't been able to do so entirely yet, due to economic factors," Millman says.

A uniform system would also help ease waiting lines in DSHS buildings for ID card distribution. People would need only to obtain one ID card that would grant access to all DSHS offices with the appropriate access rights, he says.

"One photo ID/access badge could access many different systems, provided each local office granted access. The computer at the local office would be able to control the access system as well as the levels of employee access," Millman says.

Millman's proposal also calls for a centralized budget and purchasing process. All planned or future access control systems would need approval from the DSHS security manager. Currently, the agency is using access control systems from Galaxy, Westinghouse (now NexWatch) and Northern Computers.

"Right now, however, the proposal is on hold. Some people are in favor of it, and

some are not," Millman says.

Some DSHS offices have already installed motion sensor devices and "customer-friendly" glass barriers in reception areas. "The glass barrier prevents someone from jumping over the counter. At the same time, it can help reduce the spread of viral germs," says Millman, who is also a member of the Washington State Committee on Terrorism, as well as a state agency liaison to the state's Military Department.

In a proposed security manual, Millman identifies other possible future precautions such as the installation of panic alert buttons and microphones in DSHS offices. "Panic alert buttons in the receptionist area and interview rooms would either go directly to a security alarm monitoring company, or trigger a blue strobe light installed away from the reception area, but visible to other employees," he says.

Panic alert lights in interview rooms would also trigger lights in the hallway, flashing on and off directly above the door to identify the room that is in danger.

The panic lights would also activate listen-in microphones. "The microphones would be monitored by a security alarm company, which would advise local law enforcement as to the nature of the problem, and whether any weapons are involved," Millman says.

Millman is looking toward eliminating the current use of keypad locks on doors as well. "These codes are easily observed and obtained by lobby visitors and clients. The codes need to be changed whenever any employee resigns, retires, transfers, or is terminated," he says, but points out that codes are rarely changed in that circumstance.

Millman readily admits, however, that security devices alone are not enough. He envisions development of a comprehensive emergency preparedness plan, with frequent practice through emergency drills. Topics covered would include procedures for events such as "fires, earthquakes, evacuations, terrorism, bomb threats, assaults, clients yelling threats or brandishing a weapon, workplace violence and medical emergencies."

Above all else, employee cooperation is essential, according to Millman. "You can have all the security devices in the world, but employee cooperation and involvement will still be needed. Employee training and continuing education are paramount to the success of any security system."

CHAPTER 3

AIR TRANSPORTATION, IMPOVED SAFEGUARDS, AND HOMELAND SECURITY

Dan Cook

There will be no going back to the days when a traveler dutifully passed through a metal detector deliberately set at the lowest possible setting so screeners wouldn't have to be bothered with using hand-held wands. Ten years ago, a distracted screener conversing with a pretty young colleague impatiently waved me and my laptop computer through the detector. By contrast, on a recent trip from San Francisco, I repeatedly set off the detector and subsequent wand frisks by Transportation Security Administration (TSA) personnel. Off with the Nikes! Off with the belt! The offending object? Ironically, it was a staple on my airline ticket.

The collection of security measures presently in place or contemplated may well be the staple that secures the future of international air transportation. At stake is nothing less than the industry itself, according to at least one of its spokesmen. Some details of new security programs have begun to emerge, while others remain, for obvious reasons, undisclosed.

One other thing is certain: The implementation of these programs will require megadollars, amounts far in excess of the budgets of TSA and the Department of Homeland Security (DHS).

The US-VISIT Program

The US-VISIT program, for which a contract is expected to be awarded in the near future, would employ a network of computerized databases designed to track visitors to the United States long before their actual arrival. Called by some a "virtual borders" program and by others a serious assault on privacy and personal liberty, DHS believes it will significantly improve its ability to monitor who is entering the country at more than 300 land, sea and air border-crossing checkpoints.

The rub? The *New York Times* and other newspapers reported on May 24 that the program's implementation costs would total more than $15 billion. And, according to one aviation security expert, it is totally unnecessary — and in its ultimate form will be watered down from its initial conception.

Originally published as "Seeking Safety in the Skies," *HSToday*, Vol. 1, No. 3, July 2004. Published by KMD Media, LLC, McLean, VA. Reprinted with permission of the publisher.

"TSA essentially is an agency that's dissolving, and quickly," according to Andrew Thomas, a professor of international business at the University of Akron, where he lectures on a number of aviation-related topics. "I think that was evident during the holidays when they had those major alerts and the warning about the flights that might be hijacked while flying into the country. If you remember, that wasn't coming from TSA, it was coming from DHS, and what you're seeing is a movement within the federal government to make TSA a kind of secondary player."

Thomas, author of *Aviation Insecurity: The New Challenges of Air Travel*, published by Prometheus in 2003, and *Air Rage: Crisis in the Skies*, which, coincidentally, was published on Sept. 11, 2001, by the same publisher, said TSA is becoming marginalized.

"They've done a terrible job in many ways," Thomas said. "GAO reports and TSA's own reports that have been released to the media, as well as other assessments, just show that they have not done a very good job in terms of all they were empowered to do."

The Visa Waiver Program

DHS Secretary Tom Ridge has called aviation security "one of the areas of [DHS's] greatest concern." In testimony before the House Judiciary Committee on April 21, Ridge called for revisions to the Visa Waiver Program (VWP), under which citizens of 27 participating countries are allowed to travel to the United States for 90 days or less without a visa. He said it creates a "potentially significant gap," because VWP users can avoid visa security checks at US consulates abroad.

Under legislation effective next Oct. 26, VWP countries must implement a program to issue their nationals tamper-resistant, machine-readable passports that incorporate biometric and document authentication identifiers that comply with International Civil Aviation Organization (ICAO) standards. The law will require visitors to present these new passports if they were issued on or after that date. Passengers with non-biometric passports issued after Oct. 26 will need a visa.

As might be expected, the American Civil Liberties Union (ACLU) has weighed in, arguing that the setting of such a standard would "needlessly impinge on privacy and other human rights." It added that there is "no need to rush into implementing such standards" before exploring "minimally intrusive alternatives [that] may be just as effective in providing security and reducing fraud." Such a standard, according to the ACLU, "would inevitably be used to create a system of global tracking and surveillance of travelers."

Barry Steinhardt, director of ACLU's technology and liberty program, released the text of a March 30 letter to ICAO by the London-based advocacy group Privacy International and signed by the ACLU and other human rights and civil liberties organizations. It warned that enactment of such a measure might tempt some ICAO signatories to establish a "surveillance regime" by claiming ICAO compliance for draconian laws that would not win political approval at home.

"We call that 'policy laundering,'" Steinhardt said in statement accompanying the letter. "The US government knows that the American people will never go for a national ID card or a national database of every American's fingerprints and photographs, but this proposal, if approved, will allow the United States to claim that large steps toward those policies are necessary to comply with international standards."

CAPPS II

Among the measures DHS hopes to adopt is a security tool called the Computer Assisted Passenger Prescreening System II

(CAPPS II), some details of which were announced at a March 17 hearing of the House Transportation and Infrastructure Aviation Subcommittee by acting TSA Administrator David M. Stone.

Its purpose is to determine which passengers should undergo additional scrutiny prior to boarding by conducting "risk assessments." This assessment would include passenger name record from the airline, which includes name, address, phone number, date of birth and the flight number and itinerary information for a passenger.

Again, the ACLU said the program poses severe threats to personal privacy and basic civil liberties. And the US General Accounting Office (GAO), the investigative arm of Congress, voiced additional concerns.

"It is a deeply significant step for the nation's airlines to begin feeding ... details of Americans' travel records to the government for CAPPS II," the ACLU's Steinhardt said in a statement issued after Stone's testimony. "It's a sign of things to come with a program that is simply incompatible with privacy and fairness for travelers."

"Imagine a travel system where everyone is a suspect — based upon secret information they can't review, let alone dispute — that's CAPPS II," added LaShawn Y. Warren, an ACLU legislative counsel. "Even after admitting that they are uncertain about the accuracy of the databases the CAPPS II system will use, TSA still plans to rely on this information to assess air passengers' risk levels, which could mean detention or, worse, land some passengers in jail."

Norman J. Rabkin, managing director of the GAO's Homeland Security and Justice Division, presented a report at the hearing highly critical of the program.

"Key activities ... have been delayed, and the Transportation Security Administration has not yet completed important system planning activities, including ... testing and developing initial increments of CAPPS II," the report said. This is due to delays in ob-

taining passenger data from air carriers because of privacy concerns, the report said, adding that TSA also has not identified specific system functions, the schedule for delivery and estimated costs.

Further, it also has not completely addressed seven of the eight issues identified by Congress relative to the program. As of Jan. 1, only one — the establishment of an internal oversight board — has been completely addressed. Other issues, including ensuring the accuracy of data used by CAPPS II, stress testing, preventing unauthorized access to the system, and addressing privacy concerns remain unresolved, according to the GAO.

It identified three additional challenges, including the development of international cooperation needed to obtain passenger data, the possible expansion of the program's mission beyond its original purpose and assurance that identity theft cannot be used to negate the system's security benefits.

James May, president and CEO of the Air Transport Association (ATA), also expressed some reservations. "While the promise of CAPPS II is impressive, many significant issues ... remain unresolved. Any final judgment ... must await resolution of those issues," May told the aviation subcommittee. "Favorable resolution ... will require [it] to meet three basic tests." May said CAPPS II must be efficient, economical and protective of passenger privacy rights.

"Acceptance ... will largely depend on the government generating public confidence ... in the legitimacy of the system. Importantly, however, public acceptance will also depend on ... avoiding CAPPS II–related delays during the reservation and airport check-in processes. CAPPS II cannot be seen as contributing to the 'hassle factor.'

"Achieving these objectives is imperative," May warned. "If they are not realized, the public could come to regard CAPPS II with suspicion or hostility. All of us in the commercial aviation community have a stake in this outcome; if the public rejects CAPPS

II, the very real risk could emerge that travelers will forgo the use of air transportation."

Stuart Matthews, president and CEO of the Flight Safety Foundation (FSF), told *HSToday* that the FAA, for its part, is prepared for and to date has reacted appropriately to the terrorism threat.

"However, it does concern me that, as presently proposed, funding for the agency will be reduced in the next financial year. The rationale is that there will be organizational and other changes that will make it more efficient," he said. "I hope that is right, because I would not like to see a major accident occurring that might be blamed in part on the FAA's inability to provide appropriate oversight or services due to a reduced level of financial resources."

Added Darryl Jenkins, a visiting professor at Embry-Riddle Aeronautical University and a well-respected Washington, DC, aviation authority: "The direction is for more and more money. These issues cannot be addressed without committing too large a portion of our gross domestic product to aviation security."

As to whether CAPPS II will be implemented as envisioned or will be watered down, Jenkins, who was a member of the Executive Committee of the White House Conference on Aviation Safety and Security several years ago, called it "better than a kick in the pants, but it's no silver bullet. When it comes to legislating on matters of personal privacy, it's very scary; very scary stuff."

The University of Akron's Thomas said the predecessor program, CAPPS I, was effective, but predicted that CAPPS II will be weakened by demands from federal officials.

"What everybody needs to remember is that CAPPS I worked; it did profile nine of the 19 hijackers on 9/11," he said. "But ... the problem was training. There were no protocols in place for these people to be checked except for their luggage that they had sent through, which very few of the [hijackers] had. So the security protocols and the training weren't up to snuff. Again, we can institute all of these new technologies, but if we don't have these very human elements — like training, like recognition on the part of the individuals involved in these processes — the technology is pretty much wasted, he said.

"A lot of people have doubts about it, but I think at the end of the day you're going to see a very watered-down version of it," Thomas added. "In principle, I think it's a good idea, but ... until we get the human element working, including the training and the assessment of that training, it just does not give us what we really need. We miss the human domain here, and that's critical. The threat [to aviation safety] is human ... not technology. The way you're going to fight this stuff is with good, human interaction, and that starts with training."

Congressional Action

On May 6, Rep. Ed Markey (D-Mass.), senior member of the House Select Committee on Homeland Security, along with 31 co-sponsors introduced new legislation, HR 4312, designed to patch existing holes in the infrastructure. The so-called Safe Passengers and Lading in Aviation for the National Enhancement of Security Act (Safe PLANES Act) of 2004 consists of 14 steps designed to strengthen existing measures.

"In the wake of [Sept. 11], this country has made a multibillion-dollar investment in aviation security, yet security gaps remain," said Rep. Jim Turner (D–Texas), ranking minority member of the House Select Committee, upon the bill's introduction. "We need to make sure our skies are as safe as they can be so Americans never have to relive that tragic day and to make sure that our valuable security dollars are spent as wisely as they can be."

The bill is currently in the House Transportation and Infrastructure Committee and had not been acted upon at press time.

As is the case with other programs under

FIGURE 1
The Safe PLANES Act of 2004 would:

— Require a study of the necessary TSA screening workforce size, and DHS certification that security levels will be maintained if airports are allowed to opt-out of TSA screening. The measure would list criteria by which TSA will evaluate applications;

— Require that priority be given to airports that are not screening 100 percent of checked baggage in determining which airports should receive federal assistance. It also would remove the matching of bags to passengers as an acceptable alternative when electronic baggage screening is unavailable, leaving physical and canine inspection as allowed options;

— Require a report on the research and development underway for technologies, including its maturity and planned deployment schedule. It would require TSA to update the standards used to certify detection equipment, and DHS to establish and begin implementing within 120 days a program to fully inspect all cargo carried on passenger aircraft;

— Require TSA to complete a known shipper database by April 1, 2005.

— Require DHS to set a security standard for federal law-enforcement officers to meet before serving as alternate air marshals, and direct the agency to work with foreign governments to coordinate air marshal training, procedures and information-sharing;

— Require hardened cockpits for all passenger and cargo aircraft flying over the United States and require regulations for daily aircraft searches for weapons and other prohibited items and funds for training of flight crews and others;

— Direct DHS to provide flight crews with appropriate in-flight communication devices and to report on implementation of previous statutory requirements for perimeter security and access control, and that all airport workers go through screening and require more in-depth background checks for airport workers accessing secure areas;

— Require a detailed report on deployment options after the completion of the man-portable air defense systems (MANPADS) countermeasure study and diplomatic and international programs to reduce the MANPADS threat.

---

way, the Safe PLANES Act would take money — and lots of it.

"When we talk about air-cargo security — because the supply chain is so broad and so globalized — the amount of money to secure the air cargo on commercial aircraft will be billions and billions of dollars. Those are Carl Sagan–type numbers," said Andrew Thomas. "I just don't know where TSA is going to get the money for any of this stuff. The air cargo, the antimissile systems that they're spending a couple of million to research — these test programs — all sound good, but if you're going to implement something, you're talking a ton of money."

Still, the debate on balance between

personal privacy and security continues and will be subject to ongoing modification. Both Jenkins and Thomas believe that many compromises will be made before an improved air security program is in place to which all parties can agree.

"I assume that one will be found and will also be ignored," Jenkins told *HS Today*. "Nobody just reacts; if they under-reacted before, they have under-reacted this time. Let's just say that I'm kind of skeptical that a good answer will be found," he concluded.

Thomas said aviation security could be made seamless and unobtrusive if done with the right training.

"The problem is that training is not

sexy. Nobody gets elected; nobody makes great proclamations about how wonderful the training program is at TSA. There's a lot of value for politicians and bureaucrats to point and say, 'Look; we're doing this new computerized system. It's going to identify the terrorists for us. We're doing this new air cargo database that we're creating.'

"There's a lot of political capital ... gained in that. But when you institute a training program that's rigorous, ongoing, but you can't put it on television and most people don't understand it, don't really care about it, then there's not a lot of return on the investment from a political perspective."

Jenkins and Thomas disagree with the concerns about the potential effect of increased passenger "hassle" and hostility against air transportation expressed by ATA's James May.

"[T]here are always people who will need to fly and will, but it has been devastating to short-haul travel in airplanes," Jenkins said, downplaying May's warning.

"If people aren't flying, we have some serious economic issues in this country; everything we've done is [designed] to get people traveling again," added Thomas. "When we get to the summertime, it's going to be a real problem around the country. We're going to have to [either] offset the 'hassle factor' by reducing the effectiveness of security or try to increase the level of security and create more hassle."

Seeking Solutions

What should the government do — or not do — to avert the impingement of added security on the bottom lines of the air carriers? The secret may lie in some of the provisions of the Safe PLANES Act.

"It wasn't the checkpoints on 9/11 that caused the breakdown; that was the big mythology that came out of 9/11, that bad screening ... allowed 9/11 to take place," said Thomas. "It had nothing to do with 9/11; it was the cabin, the cockpit door, lax security in the cabin, no flight-attendant training on hijacking.... Those were the security breakdowns."

In fact, Thomas believes that certain constituencies, including the airlines, capitalized on the events of 9/11. The airlines, he alleges, never wanted to be in the security business in the first place, and saw the terrorist attacks as an opportunity to turn that over to the government.

"They had the political capital and the will of the American people behind them and they were able execute that," he concluded.

Note

HR 4312 (the Safe Passengers and Lading in Aviation for the National Enhancement of Security Act) is also known as the "Safe PLANES Act."

CHAPTER 4

AMERICAN RED CROSS DISASTER PREPAREDNESS GUIDELINES

Marsha J. Evans

Devastating acts, such as the terrorist attacks on the World Trade Center and the Pentagon, have left many concerned about the possibility of future incidents in the United States and their potential impact. They have raised uncertainty about what might happen next, increasing stress levels. Nevertheless, there are things you can do to prepare for the unexpected and reduce the stress that you may feel now and later should another emergency arise. Taking preparatory action can reassure you and your children that you can exert a measure of control even in the face of such events.

What You Can Do to Prepare

Finding out what can happen is the first step. Once you have determined the events possible and their potential in your community, it is important that you discuss them with your family or household. Develop a disaster plan together.

1. Create an emergency communications plan.

Choose an out-of-town contact your family or household will call or e-mail to check on each other should a disaster occur. Your selected contact should live far enough away that they are unlikely to be directly affected by the same event, and they should know they are the chosen contact. Make sure every household member has that contact's, and each other's, e-mail addresses and telephone numbers (home, work, pager and cell). Leave these contact numbers at your children's schools, if you have children, and at your workplace. Your family should know that if telephones are not working, they need to be patient and try again later or try e-mail. Many people flood the telephone lines when emergencies happen but e-mail can sometimes get through when calls don't.

2. Establish a meeting place.

Having a predetermined meeting place away from your home will save time and minimize confusion should your home be affected or the area evacuated. You may even want to make arrangements to stay with a family member or friend in case of an emer-

---

Originally published as "Terrorism: Preparing for the Unexpected," *Brochure A1366*, American Red Cross, Washington, D.C., October 2001. Reprinted with permission of the publisher.

gency. Be sure to include any pets in these plans, since pets are not permitted in shelters and some hotels will not accept them.

3. Assemble a disaster supplies kit.

If you need to evacuate your home or are asked to "shelter in place," having some essential supplies on hand will make you and your family more comfortable —

- Prepare a disaster supplies kit in an easy-to-carry container such as a duffel bag or small plastic trash can.
- Include "special needs" items for any household member (infant formula or items for people with disabilities or older people), first aid supplies (including prescription medications), a change of clothing for each person, a sleeping bag or bedroll for each, a battery powered radio or television and extra batteries, food, bottled water and tools.
- It is also a good idea to include some cash and copies of important family documents (birth certificates, passports and licenses) in your kit.

Copies of essential documents — like powers of attorney, birth and marriage certificates, insurance policies, life insurance beneficiary designations and a copy of your will — should also be kept in a safe location outside your home. A safe deposit box or the home of a friend or family member who lives out of town is a good choice.

For more complete instructions, ask your local Red Cross chapter for the brochure titled *Your Family Disaster Supplies Kit* (stock number A4463).

4. Check on the school emergency plan of any school-age children you may have.

You need to know if they will keep children at school until a parent or designated adult can pick them up or send them home on their own. Be sure that the school has updated information about how to reach parents and responsible caregivers to arrange for pickup. And, ask what type of authorization the school may require to release a child to someone you designate, if you are not able to pick up your child. During times of emergency the school telephones may be overwhelmed with calls.

For more information on putting together a disaster plan, request a copy of the brochure titled *Your Family Disaster Plan* (A4466)* from your local American Red Cross chapter. You may also want to request a copy of *Before Disaster Strikes... How to Make Sure You're Financially Prepared* (A5075)* for specific information on what you can do now to protect your assets.

If Disaster Strikes

- Remain calm and be patient.
- Follow the advice of local emergency officials.
- Listen to your radio or television for news and instructions.
- If the disaster occurs near you, check for injuries. Give first aid and get help for seriously injured people.
- If the disaster occurs near your home while you are there, check for damage using a flashlight. Do not light matches or candles or turn on electrical switches. Check for fires, fire hazards and other household hazards. Sniff for gas leaks, starting at the water heater. If you smell gas or suspect a leak, turn off the main gas valve, open windows, and get everyone outside quickly.
- Shut off any other damaged utilities.
- Confine or secure your pets.
- Call your family contact — do not use the telephone again unless it is a life-threatening emergency.
- Check on your neighbors, especially those living alone, elderly or disabled.

A Word on What Could Happen

As we learned from the events of September 11, 2001, the following things can happen after a terrorist attack:

- There can be significant numbers of casualties and/or damage to buildings and the infrastructure. So employers need up-to-date information about any medical needs you may have and on how to contact your designated beneficiaries.
- Heavy law enforcement involvement at local, state and federal levels follows a terrorist attack due to the event's criminal nature.
- Health and mental health resources in the affected communities can be strained to their limits, maybe even overwhelmed.
- Extensive media coverage, strong public fear and international implications and consequences can continue for a prolonged period.
- Workplaces and schools may be closed, and there may be restrictions on domestic and international travel.
- You and your family or household may have to evacuate an area, avoiding roads blocked for your safety.
- Clean-up make take many months.

EVACUATION

If local authorities ask you to leave your home, they have a good reason to make this request, and you should heed the advice immediately. Listen to your radio or TV, follow the instructions of local emergency officials and keep these simple tips in mind —

- Wear long-sleeved shirts, long pants and sturdy shoes so you can be protected as much as possible.
- Take your disaster supplies kit.
- Take your pets with you; do not leave them behind. Because pets are not permitted in public shelters, follow your plan to go to a relative's or friend's home, or find a "pet-friendly" hotel.
- Lock your home.
- Use travel routes specified by local authorities — don't use shortcuts because certain areas may be impassable or dangerous.
- Stay away from downed power lines.

Listen to local authorities. They will provide you with the most accurate information specific to an event in your area. Staying tuned to local radio and television, and following their instructions is your safest choice.

If you're sure you have time:

- Call your family contact to tell them where you are going and when you expect to arrive.
- Shut off water and electricity before leaving, if instructed to do so. Leave natural gas service ON unless local officials advise you otherwise. You may need gas for heating and cooking, and only a professional can restore gas service in your home once it's been turned off. In a disaster situation it could take weeks for a professional to respond.

SHELTER IN PLACE

If you are advised by local officials to "shelter in place," what they mean is for you to remain inside your home or office and protect yourself there. Close and lock all windows and exterior doors. Turn off all fans, heating and air conditioning systems. Close the fireplace damper. Get your disaster supplies kit, and make sure the radio is working. Go to an interior room without windows that's above ground level. In the case of a chemical threat, an above-ground location is preferable because some chemicals are heavier than air, and may seep into basements even if the windows are closed. Using duct tape, seal all cracks around the door and any vents into the room. Keep listening to your radio or television until you are told all is safe or you are told to evacuate. Local officials may call for evacuation in specific areas at greatest risk in your community.

ADDITIONAL POSITIVE STEPS YOU CAN TAKE

Raw, unedited footage of terrorism events and people's reaction to those events can be very upsetting, especially to children. We do not recommend that children watch television news reports about such events, especially if the news reports show images over and over again about the same incident. Young children do not realize that it is repeated video footage, and think the event is happening again and again. Adults may also need to give themselves a break from watching disturbing footage. However, listening to local radio and television reports will provide you with the most accurate information from responsible governmental authorities on what's happening and what actions you will need to take. So you may want to make some arrangements to take turns listening to the news with other adult members of your household.

Another useful preparation includes learning some basic first aid. To enroll in a first aid and AED/CPR course, contact your local American Red Cross chapter. In an emergency situation, you need to tend to your own well-being first and then consider first aid for others immediately around you, including possibly assisting injured people to evacuate a building if necessary.

People who may have come into contact with a biological or chemical agent may need to go through a decontamination procedure and receive medial attention. Listen to the advice of local officials on the radio or television to determine what steps you will need to take to protect yourself and your family. As emergency services will likely be overwhelmed, only call 9-1-1 about life-threatening emergencies.

First Aid Primer

If you encounter someone who is injured, apply the emergency action steps: **Check-Call-Care. Check** the scene to make sure it is safe for you to approach. Then check the victim for unconsciousness and life-threatening conditions. Someone who has a life-threatening condition, such as not breathing or severe bleeding, requires immediate care by trained responders and may required treatment by medical professionals. **Call** out for help. There are some steps that you can take, however, to **care** for someone who is hurt, but whose injuries are not life threatening.

CONTROL BLEEDING

- Cover the wound with a dressing, and press firmly against the wound (direct pressure).
- Elevate the injured area above the level of the heart if you do not suspect that the victim has a broken bone.
- Cover the dressing with a roller bandage.
- If the bleeding does not stop:
  — Apply additional dressing and bandages.
  — Use a pressure point to squeeze the artery against the bone.
- Provide care for shock.

CARE FOR SHOCK

- Keep the victim from getting chilled or overheated.
- Elevate the legs about 12 inches (if broken bones are not suspected).
- Do not give food or drink to the victim.

TEND BURNS

- Stop the burning by cooling the burn with large amounts of water.
- Cover the burn with dry, clean dressings or cloth.

CARE FOR INJURIES TO MUSCLES, BONES AND JOINTS

- Rest the injured part.
- Apply ice or a cold pack to control swelling and reduce pain.
- Avoid any movement or activity that causes pain.
- If you must move the victim because the scene is becoming unsafe, try to immobilize the injured part to keep it from moving.

Be Aware of Biological/ Radiological Exposure

- Listen to local radio and television reports for the most accurate information from responsible governmental and medical authorities on what's happening and what actions you will need to take.
- The Web sites referenced at the end of this brochure can give you more information on how to protect yourself from exposure to biological or radiological hazards.

Reduce Any Care Risks

The risk of getting a disease while giving first aid is extremely rare. However, to reduce the risk even further:

- Avoid direct contact with blood and other body fluids.
- Use protective equipment, such as disposable gloves and breathing barriers.
- Whenever possible, thoroughly wash your hands with soap and water immediately after giving care.

It is important to be prepared for an emergency and to know how to give emergency care.

More Information

All of these recommendations make good sense, regardless of the potential problem. For more information on how to get ready for disaster and be safe when disaster strikes, or to register for a first aid and AED/CPR course, please contact your local American Red Cross chapter. You can find it in your telephone directory under "American Red Cross" or through our home page at **www.redcross.org** under "your local chapter."

For information about your community's specific plans for response to disasters and other emergencies, contact your local office of emergency management.

For information on what a business can do to protect its employees and customers as well as develop business continuity plans, see "**www.redcross.org/services/disaster/bepre pared**" or request a copy of the *Emergency Management Guide for Business and Industry* and/or *Preparing Your Business for the Unthinkable* from your local American Red Cross chapter.

Chapter 5

Automated Public Notification Systems Enhance Communications with Citizens

Gary Raymer and *Rick Wimberly*

Automated notification systems, formerly considered an expensive luxury for larger urban agencies, are now becoming standard equipment for police departments and public safety organizations of all sizes. No longer do first responders need to rely on time-consuming and labor-intensive phone trees, which often fail to deliver detailed and useful information during emergency situations. Moreover, manual phone trees limit the number of participating agencies in the call lineup, narrowing notification and response capabilities.

In the wake of September 11, high-speed notification systems also are used more frequently for nonemergency communications. They can serve as a community outreach tool, ensuring better communication with businesses and residents. And the systems can be used with neighboring agencies to ensure a seamless approach on countywide or regional levels.

When such systems were still relatively new to smaller law enforcement agencies,

Kentucky's Bowling Green Police Department — which currently has 96 sworn officers — acquired an automated high-speed notification system. The department found that activation was as simple as placing a phone call or pushing a computer key and that notification times in emergency situations were significantly shortened. The department also discovered that the system could be used for numerous proactive police and community notifications involving schools, hospitals, nursing homes, banks and pharmacies.

Police departments across the region, as well as state and federal agencies, also tapped into the Bowling Green Police Department's system for true cross-jurisdictional use. Sharing costs among participating agencies, the department reduced its own expenses yet became an essential informational hub for the region. The department now receives numerous invitations to share information about its experience and expertise in the implementation of this technology. This chapter provides

Originally published as "Obtaining and Using High-Speed Notification Technology in a Cross-Jurisdictional Setting." Reprinted from *The Police Chief*, Vol. LXIX, No. 6, June 2002. Published by the International Association of Chiefs of Police, Alexandria, VA. Reprinted with permission of the publisher.

an overview of one department's use of its high-speed notification technology in a cross-jurisdictional setting.

The Setting

The city of Bowling Green is located along Interstate 65 in southern Kentucky, approximately 110 miles south of Louisville and 65 miles north of Nashville, Tennessee. With a resident population of 50,000, Bowling Green is a metropolitan hub for a predominately rural surrounding area.

The city draws 200,000 commuters daily for recreation, employment, and healthcare. Students and faculty at Western Kentucky University make up 16,000 of those commuters. Interstate 65, a major north-south corridor, intersects the city, as does the L&N Railroad — both known to carry heavy commercial traffic with subsequent spill hazards.

The area is routinely plagued by severe weather, as it lies in a tornado-prone region of the southeast. Moreover, Bowling Green is home to 36 hazmat sites, including GM's Corvette manufacturing plant and Holley Automotive, maker of racecar carburetors and fuel injection systems.

The Shortcomings of a Traditional Notification System

In 1976 the Bowling Green Police Department created a neighborhood watch program, which now involves about 70 watch groups. The program relied on manual call trees to alert its top members who, in turn, made calls to the other participants. Callouts included those about lost children, burglary suspects, as well as man-made and natural disasters.

The manual call trees caused uncertainty when group members needed to relay updated information. Apart from quarterly

face-to-face meetings and occasional alerts, no regular communication channels existed to check the status of the neighborhood watch groups. Additionally, team recalls and police call-outs were performed manually, generating concern about response time, the conveying of incident-specific information or potentially life-saving instruction.

To address these community concerns, a crime prevention officer of the Bowling Green Police Department began looking for a way to improve the neighborhood watch program, to provide for immediate relay of information to the participants. High-speed notification technology was determined to be the best solution for fast, accurate communication to enhance community policing efforts, as well as to ensure the quick response of department personnel.

Evaluation of Systems

In early 1997 the police department evaluated several high-speed notification systems in search of one that could meet the growing demands of both the department and the community. The department required a solution that could provide automation of all emergency and nonemergency communication procedures with immediate verification of call receipt.

The research found that while some providers offered a basic notification system with limited or expensive add-on features, other companies had the ability to modify their technology to meet the department's site-specific needs, as well as those of the surrounding communities. Equally as important to department officials preparing to purchase this technology was the providing company's references, commitment to customer support, and dedication to regular system upgrades.

With high-speed notification technology fast becoming an essential component of both routine and emergency communications for law enforcement, the department was more easily able to secure funding through a grant from the U.S. Department of Justice. The Bowling Green Police Department received competitive bids from three providers. The agency preferred the Microsoft Windows operating system, so that ruled out companies that used DOS-based technology.

The department ultimately purchased the software and hardware for a high-speed notification system and GIS mapping interface. Additional costs included minimal support fees, software upgrades, and the installation of additional phone lines.

Planning

With the grant in hand in October, and the installation of the new system planned for December 1997, the department did the necessary groundwork for pre-implementation. Recognizing that the department's 15 dispatchers were already working under an existing operational system, planners decided that the new equipment would be housed in the crime prevention office. This location would provide dispatchers physical or remote access during system training. As part of the training process, scenarios for possible call-out situations were created.

Survey forms, easily modified for basic roster information such as phone numbers and other personnel data, were created. The department used these forms to survey its police force, as well as neighborhood watch groups, fire departments, banks, emergency medical services and others. As the integration of the high-speed notification technology began, the department created a time-line and implementation plan. The department described the plan as "Crawl, walk, and run."

Implementation

Within the timeline and implementation plan, basic system functions were identified and established. Initially a severe weather threat scenario was created. The original phone tree contact list had 33 people on it. The new system permitted an expansion to 147, adding key contacts such as schools, utility companies, other law enforcement agencies, day care centers, hospitals, and even the media.

Satisfied with the results, the department created numerous call-out scenarios and included other agencies in the communications plan. Allowed to access the equipment, these agencies quickly determined that they could enhance their own emergency notifications using the notification system.

System Details

The Bowling Green Police Department employs the following scenario templates for the timely, accurate delivery of information:

• Simple delivery — all participants called and information conveyed
• Simple delivery with response — all participants called and their response(s) entered through touch-tone phone dialing
• Secure delivery — all participants called and information given upon entry of a valid identification code
• Secure delivery with response — all participants called, information delivered upon entry of a valid identification code, and their responses logged through touch-tone phone

Uses

The first real test of the system came when a tornado roared through Arkansas, Tennessee, and Kentucky, causing widespread damage in the Bowling Green area. When the police department received word of a tornado that touched down in south Warren County, it quickly alerted other local law enforcement agencies, the National Weather Service, hospitals, schools, daycare centers, and the media. Each party was notified twice in less than nine minutes. While softball-sized hail damaged 11,000 roofs and pounded 3,000 cars, personal injuries were kept to a minimum because of the advance notice of the approaching storm front.

The Bowling Green Police Department also routinely uses the notification system to cut down on criminal activity. Located near the Tennessee state line, Bowling Green is a prime target for criminals who prey upon the city and then flee back across the border. One perpetrator, a woman from Murfreesboro, Tennessee, attracted the attention of bank officials after attempting to open an account with a suspicious $14,800 check. When the transaction was questioned, she abruptly left the bank and went to another.

The bank notified police, who used the system to send out an alert. A third bank called within a minute to report that the woman was in its lobby. Police officers quickly apprehended the woman, who was in possession of eight counterfeit checks and had planned to open accounts in various banks, withdraw cash, and flee with the money.

The system was also used to locate and capture a Tennessee woman who had stolen prescription pads and was attempting to purchase drugs from Bowling Green pharmacies.

By issuing alerts and warnings, the department is able to quickly apprehend crime suspects and ensure public safety during emergencies. Companies victimized by crime receive subsequent notifications, relaying the police department's progress in ongoing investigations. The system is also used to alert other businesses in the affected area, enabling them to take necessary precautions against such criminal activity.

FIGURE 1
City of Bowling Green Police Department Recommendations High-Speed Notification Systems

The Bowling Green Police Department recommends that other departments contemplating implementation of a high-speed notification system take the following steps to ensure smooth installation and operation:

Before Implementation

- Ensure that top managers and commanders are fully committed to the project.
- Size up the environment early by identifying and understanding the unique aspects of the technology and what success it can create.
- Determine constraints and areas of conflict and deal with all present contradictions by creating a shared need.
- Consider rapid implementation with multiple project phases. Simple scenarios and smaller groups are a great way to start.
- For best results, start training within the department before the start of onsite implementation.

During Implementation

- Use basic system functions quickly to ensure rapid success for buy-in from both the department and the community.
- Model the results of successful scenarios by replicating call-flows in similar situations.
- Use the system to address the needs of those requiring public safety and crime-prevention information on the front end.

Using the System Across Jurisdictions

The Bowling Green Police Department has allowed other departments and agencies, including those outside Warren County, to send their own alerts through Bowling Green's notification system or to activate many of the more than 100 scenarios created in the past five years.

The privately owned emergency medical service (EMS) in Bowling Green uses the notification system to call off-duty ambulance personnel. The Bowling Green Fire Department, the Emergency Operations Center, area schools, and the regional jail also use the system to send out a variety of alerts. The multijurisdictional I-65 Drug Interdiction Taskforce, along with law enforcement agencies along the 145-mile stretch between Nashville and Louisville, uses the system to stop drug trafficking.

Most recently, the U.S. Attorney's Office for the Western District of Kentucky set up an antiterrorist taskforce after September 11, to include the Bowling Green Police Department as well as federal, state, and local law enforcement agencies. After U.S. Attorney General John Ashcroft suggested the creation of phone trees for the various regional taskforces, the Bowling Green Police Department took the next step and automated its own taskforce notifications. During a test in March 2002, more than 90 taskforce members were contacted within six minutes. Like EMS, the antiterrorist taskforce can activate the system remotely by touch-tone phone, putting the call-out into immediate action.

With several users having secure access to the system, priority levels must be assigned to the various notifications. When nonemergency scenarios are running, they can be automatically paused to allow emergency alerts and notifications to take precedence. The nonemergency scenarios automatically resume upon call-out completion. All of these notifications can be accommodated under the system's default settings or set manually as needed.

The Bowling Green Police Department further tested the system's capabilities by creating a mock disaster, with five different emergency scenarios successfully running at the same time.

High-speed notification technology has clearly demonstrated its relevance as an effective communications tool, enabling law enforcement to quickly and accurately connect with other agencies, counties and communities-at-risk. Such technology warrants serious consideration for agencies striving toward optimization of resources, effective information flow and management at all levels. A high-speed notification system can be a very powerful tool for law enforcement, allowing department personnel to work smarter, not harder.

CHAPTER 6

BUILDING DESIGN IMPROVES PUBLIC SAFETY

Joseph F. Russo

A recent PBS series entitled "Building Big" chronicled the history of building high-rise structures around the world. Famous successes and dangerous blunders are part of the story. In addition to a history lesson, the viewer gets a sense of the evolutionary process that brought building construction from heavyweight, brick, mortar, and reinforced concrete to the lightweight metal deck, glass skin, and steel of modern high-rise structures. That trend has become more widespread, as can be seen at much smaller building projects.

A survey of any fire company's response area will likely reveal several new and renovated buildings in various stages of construction. An examination of these buildings is sure to be a thought-provoking experience. A revolution is now in full swing in the residential and commercial construction industries. Attempting to understand the change is an ongoing process, and a necessary one, for any fire service professional interested in staying alive inside a fire building. Knowing how buildings are put together will help you to understand how and why they come apart in a fire.

Lightweight Construction Components

- *Trusses.* The trusses may be of wood or metal. Their quick failure in fires has been well documented around the country. Prefabricated off site, they are only as good as the manufacturer's quality controls and the construction crew's skill in installing them. Municipalities have rejected some trusses as defective because of improper gaps or missing glue. Weather and rough handling affect trusses, and trusses must be properly installed to be able to bear the designed loads. In recent years, buildings under construction have collapsed when a load was placed on an improperly supported area (Middleton Street, Brooklyn, New York, Nov. 23, 1999, for example). In another part of that borough, a strong gust of wind blew down a partially constructed frame building.
- *Metal or "C" joist.* This cold-rolled steel building product is favored partly because it does not add to the fire load. But remember, *fire resistive does not mean failure-proof.* The main concern when encountering a metal joist is the lack of mass. Metal

Originally published as "Become an Advocate for Safer Buildings," *Fire Engineering*, Vol. 155, No. 3, March 2002. Published by Pennwell Publishing Company, Tulsa, OK. Reprinted with permission of the publisher.

joists, like conventional steel I-beams, fail when a critical temperature is reached. If not properly enclosed and protected from fire, the failure can occur in minutes. Ribbons of twisted metal joists were observed at a Bronx taxpayer fire and again at a multiple-alarm fire in a row of wood-frame dwellings in Brooklyn. It's worth noting that both incidents did not involve new construction: they were renovations or additions to existing buildings.

- *Combination of components.* Typically, combinations of materials are used in lightweight construction. In one example, cold-rolled steel "C" joists are used to support engineered wood trusses and plywood I-beans. In another instance, peaked-roof trusses, held together with metal plate connections (MPC truss), rest on 2 × 4 studded walls. There are many variations. Another common practice combines brick and block exterior walls with lightweight trusses or metal floor joists.
- *Renovations.* These include adding stories or pushing walls out to the property line, which creates structures in which old-style framing and new lightweight materials exist side by side.

When you see a new building being erected or an older one under renovation, stop to examine which materials and construction methods are being used. Be curious, or be surprised by a building with a failure time for which you are not prepared. Experience has shown that lightweight building materials must be installed with great attention to detail. Shoddy construction techniques can be deadly. Weak connection points or poor or nonexistent fire stopping can have disastrous consequences in a fire.

Firefighters of the 1960s and 1970s owe a debt of gratitude to the designers that crafted the building codes of the earlier years. The use of full-dimension lumber in the hands of skilled laborers and craftsmen, coupled with diligent inspections, resulted in well-constructed buildings with structural elements that contained much more mass and which, therefore, were more resistant to collapse. This made it possible for firefighters to engage in interior firefighting operations for longer periods of time.

Now, many buildings are more than a hundred years old and are near the end of their life expectancy. Many are under massive renovation and present a similar set of problems as newly constructed structures. Among these are the vast amount of materials, held together with glue and gang nails (metal plate fasteners), that are above a firefighter's head and shoddy, rushed construction.

Current and future generations of firefighters need to be aware of which older structures have undergone renovation and have incorporated in them new lightweight materials and construction methods. These structures are more likely to collapse early in firefighting operations.

- *Premanufactured housing.* This construction method produces entire buildings that have been welded and screwed together in a factory, much like mobile home construction, and dropped on foundations. They are present at various locations around the country. When the exterior is completed, it becomes impossible to identify these metal-frame buildings. The only way to identify them and document their hazards for preplanning purposes is to inspect them at the construction site.

Affordability is the excuse commonly given to gain approval for these new construction methods, but increased profit and outright greed are often the overriding motives.

What the Fire Service Can Do

The fire service should do more than merely "sound the alarm." We should also collect scientific data that will back up our demand for better-built structures. Fire departments around the country — better yet, around the world — must begin to build a database that incorporates every instance of the failure of a building product. Details about the failure should be recorded on the fire report, and the incident should be brought to the attention of the safety chief. A simple universal report form could be used to record the data. These anecdotal records will become the foundation of the evidence that can be used to force change.

Sharing information is also important. In the summer of 1998, during a fire in a high-rise multiple dwelling in Brooklyn, plastic wire molding in the public hallway melted and began dropping on firefighters. This molding, which holds coaxial cable wires, is commonly used in the telecommunications industry. This molding can present hazards for firefighters battling a fire in any jurisdiction. Sharing this type of information can save firefighters' lives. Identifying patterns and trends can alert firefighters before a disaster occurs. There is presently no existing effective network by which fire departments can share such information.

Fire departments must have access to technical expertise. One way to do this is develop a relationship with universities that have strong architectural and engineering programs for the purposes of keeping up to date with new construction trends and materials and researching questionable conditions observed at a building site. This type of an alliance would also help the fire department to learn the appropriate terminology for construction features and other construction-related terms so that the fire service will be able to explain its position in a more professional manner.

The building industry is a powerful lobby with unlimited funds. It may take the united action of the entire fire service to make our voice heard on this issue.

We must be proactive so that we can avert tragedies. Fighting fires in buildings of lightweight construction calls for an adjustment of tactics. We need better methods for identifying the hazards involved and strategies for making more efficient use of hose streams so that personnel will be kept out of areas with unstable floors and roofs. The rules of the game have changed. A room-and-contents fire calls for an aggressive interior attack, but when fire involves the lightweight structural components or when the fire has hold of the structure's combustible concealed spaces, our fireground tactics must be adjusted or changed to a safer method of firefighting.

The building material and construction industries are aware of our concerns about lightweight building products. An article in *Builder* magazine (October, 1999) characterizes the objections of the firefighters in a quote from Ken Grundahl of the Wood Truss Council of America: "The problem is that you've got the fire service out there with emotion on their side, and they'll play that to the hilt. Over here in the industry, we don't have emotion. We have facts on our side. And they don't have the same appeal."

In essence, he is claiming that the fire service's argument is an emotional one that has more appeal than actual facts and that the industry's information is based on scientific testing. But critics have declared the 80-year-old ASTME E119 testing standard used to test construction components invalid for today's hotter fires fueled by plastics and synthetics.

Documenting, communicating, and networking are not enough. The intention is not to become adversaries of the building industry; it is to become advocates for our profession. We should write more articles, attend more conferences, read more journals, and network with other professionals. We have a unique opportunity during this period of rapid change in the building industry to have input that will affect the lives of firefighters for generations to come. The pen of history continues to write. How will it evaluate our actions or inactions during this period of the largest building boom in recent history? What will firefighters of future generations say about what took place on our watch?

CHAPTER 7

COMMUNICATIONS AMONG FIRST RESPONDERS

Roger Williams

The New York City Police Department has tackled its share of disasters, but nothing compares to the challenges these men and women faced on September 11, 2001, when the World Trade Center towers collapsed as the result of a terrorist attack. In the aftermath of this disaster, which cost the lives of scores of New York's finest First Responders and public safety officers in rescue and recovery efforts, the city's emergency officials began searching for a way to improve the interoperability of their communications systems.

In analyzing the disaster, officials recognized the communications problems that made this scene so difficult to manage. Literally hundreds of officers reported to the area from different departments, cities and states. Each emergency response team brought its own set of radios, which worked on a single frequency, thus leaving the radio networks incompatible and powerless for interagency communication. In many critical response situations, different agencies communicated as best they could, sometimes resorting to handwritten instructions passed along by runners. This virtual Tower of Babel system left lifesavers unable to communicate effectively, with insufficient accuracy and speed of delivery for crisis response.

System Interoperability

Communications interoperability is defined as the ability for two or more parties to exchange information, when and where needed, even when disparate communications systems are involved. To achieve this interoperability for public safety radio communications, JPS Communications designed its ACU-1000 to offer crossband radio interconnect capability at the flip of a switch.

The unit enables emergency officials to speak to one another using their own radios, whether VHF, UHF or 800 MHz. It also connects phone or cellular calls to a handheld radio when necessary. The ability to use existing radio equipment to achieve interagency communication saves time and resources, which are especially critical in life threatening situations.

The ACU-1000 is transportable (configured as the TRP-1000) for quick communication set-up in the field for emergency response teams. Specialized controller software features icons for each network, enabling the ACU to provide agencies complete control over all communication within each agency or between them. Suitable for high frequency, land mobile radio and SATCOM systems,

Originally published as "New York City on the Rise," *LAW and ORDER*, Vol. 50, No. 9, September 2002. Published by Hendon Publishing Company, Deerfield, IL. Reprinted with permission of the publisher.

the unit can be utilized in a number of applications requiring fast, accurate connections to available on scene communications resources, therefore eliminating the need for runners, message relays or specialized radios.

Communications Needs

In the past, there were few alternatives to the relaying of information between agencies at an emergency response scene. Using conventional radio technology, "the only way officers could speak was on the 800 MHz ALERT (Agency Liaison Emergency Radio Trunk) disaster channel, but only if they had 800 MHz radio systems programmed with the DoITT (Department of Information Technology and Telecommunications ALERT Subfleet). If not, they had to get one from the Office of Emergency Management (OEM)," explained Stuart Goldstein, communications coordinator for the NYPD's TARU (Technical Assistance Response Unit). These types of equipment struggles were not conducive to response efforts in time-sensitive situations.

Recognizing the need to improve communications, the Department of Justice supplied the New York City OEM with TRP-1000s as part of a national grant. One unit was placed in TARU's Investigative Response Vehicle (IRV) Mobile Field Command Post, with one stationary unit in a secure location. OEM organized an ACU committee, which included NYPD TARU communications specialists and representatives of the OEM Watch Command to oversee the testing and implementation of the system. After an initial period of installation and training, the TARU team programmed all possible radio frequencies in the ACU-1000 and began testing radio transmissions in a variety of situations.

Putting It to the Test

Acting in a high level of alert as part of the homeland defense strategy adopted by the country during its time of record, TARU implemented the ACU-1000 at high-profile events involving large groups of people or groups of well-known public officials.

When the NYPD TARU first began testing the ACU-1000 system, bureau chiefs questioned whether the system would be able to communicate with all significant response personnel at a moment's notice. A Yankee-Mets game was selected as a beta-test venue for the system. Fire, police, radiation control, Department of Health, New York City Emergency Management and officers from other departments were represented at the June 2002 game. TARU Communications Coordinator Goldstein directed each of the participating groups to a designated frequency in accordance with their radio type.

"I hit the switch and asked the NYPD police chief to call the fire chief. In no time everyone was lit up and the chief was amazed," Goldstein remarked. Having this system in place at the sporting event allowed each of the agencies to communicate within and across their departments, along with all other agencies in the event that a suspicious package or device was found.

Without any further adjustments by the radio operator, each group was linked to the critical information with great success, Goldstein explained. "Now the ACU-1000 system is being requested by everyone. There is nothing out there that can respond to communications interoperability problems at a scene like this system, it's portable and you can operate it at 12 volts, so you can run it even if there's only a car battery for power."

Challenging Environments

The NYPD's most extensive practical test of the ACU-1000/TRP-1000 came in

June 13, 2002, when the unit was used to facilitate underground communication. In cities like New York, the subway and train systems pose a major challenge for communication systems. Underground tunnels, hundreds of feet below ground, add significant obstacles for radio waves to penetrate, making belowground communications an impenetrable problem that even 800 MHz radio could not solve. With a reconfigured communications system more than seven years away, law enforcement needed to be prepared for any difficulties in the interim.

Having witnessed the benefits of JPS's interoperability system in other applications, the NYPD's TARU (as part of the ACU committee) tested the ACU-1000's capabilities against the imposing physical barrier of the East River Tunnel. Testers lowered three radios attached to cables, called umbilical cords, through the tunnel's emergency escape hatches nearly 150 feet below ground. Radio One was designated for a UHF NYPD Tactical channel, Radio Two for a VHF FDNY tactical channel and Radio Three served the Amtrak personnel. Each radio operated on its own network to facilitate communication within the agency, but also enabled transmissions between agencies when necessary.

To test the strength of the system, a group of officers boarded a train heading away from the umbilical cord attached to the three radios. After activating the ACU, officers in the tunnel transmitted and received messages clearly from testers at ground level, and in some cases officers picked up a clear signal as far as 2,500 feet away from the umbilical cord, depending on the curves of the tunnel. Communication between groups above and below ground was equally successful.

"This subway capability is going to be a lifesaver all around the U.S.," Goldstein observed. The ACU system proved its worth as a quick, dependable solution to interoperability using established radio technology.

Supporting Every Angle

Reliable, high-performance communication systems are critical to public safety agencies if they are to properly respond and protect citizens. Even in non-critical situations, simple disruptions in communication can greatly inhibit public safety effectiveness. "That's another reason why I like the ACU-1000 system," Goldstein explained. "When power outages occur and radios won't function, the ACU can also be used as a back-up communications system. We knew this system facilitated interagency communication, but we didn't know about its effectiveness below-ground or as a back-up system."

"With the ACU, you show up at the scene with your own radio on your side and talk to every other agency present at the site. You can take one of these systems and put it in your communications center. If you lose power at the center, you just plug it up to a generator and you are up and running again. There are so many possibilities," Goldstein added.

Going Forward

The NYPD's TARU Unit and ACU Committee hope to find more applications for the JPS unit in the future. Currently, the ACU committee is testing the interoperability system as a means to alleviate the communications complications associated with high-rise buildings, a problem common in many large U.S. cities. After the 9/11 attacks, it became clear that no weak links in the nation's public safety communications systems could be overlooked. Continued testing will ensure that communications interoperability is the driving force to a secure solution.

Five to 10 years from now, Goldstein believes the ACU-1000 will be implemented as a back-up system in every major communications center, and additional units will be put into operation as more grants are awarded for public safety communications systems upgrades. Since September 11, communications equipment has become a necessity, not an option.

A year after the September 11 attacks, public safety officials have answered the call to action with their commitment to finding and implementing communications interoperability solutions as a means to improve response efforts and decrease casualties. Having tested and benefitted from the ACU-1000 system in a range of scenarios, NYPD TARU's Communications Coordinator Stuart Goldstein argued, "The system works so well, I am getting phone calls from every-where asking me to tell them about the ACU system. There have been no negative results with this unit."

With New York City public safety officers putting their lives on the line each day in service to their community, it offers much-needed peace of mind and precious seconds in which to take action in an emergency.

"Having communications system interoperability isn't going to prevent terrorism," Goldstein explained, "but should something happen again, it lets us work together efficiently to save time, and more importantly, to save lives."

Chapter 8

Community Emergency Response Teams Provide Vital Emergency Services

Colin A. Campbell

What a difference a couple of years can make, especially once attention and funding are focused on something.

In late 2001, there were about 170 community emergency response teams in 28 U.S. states and territories. Then, in his January 2002 State of the Union address, President Bush announced the formation of the Citizen Corps Council. Since then, the number of CERTS has skyrocketed to 1,200 teams in 54 states and territories.

Sam Isenberger, the CERT program manager for FEMA's Emergency Management Institute, Emmitsburgh, Md., attributes the increase to a number of reasons. "For one," he says, "the grant money gave the CERT program the momentum that it needed." Congress made $5 million available for CERTS in the 2002 supplemental appropriations bill.

In addition, Isenberger says, for years, "response agencies across the country have been looking for ways to involve citizens, and CERT gave them a way to do this. After 9-11, citizens were looking for a way to be better prepared and contribute to the community, and the match was made."

Frank Lucier agrees. The former San Francisco Fire Department lieutenant, who ran the CERT there, says emergency managers are discovering that CERTS are a great way to connect with the public. "I see more and more emergency managers involved in CERTS" he says, adding that police departments are also more likely to be involved these days.

Although CERT didn't receive any federal funding in fiscal 2003, the seeds were there and programs continued to multiply. For fiscal 2004, Congress appropriated $40 million for the Citizen Corps Council, though that umbrella now includes Neighborhood Watch, Volunteers in Police Service and the Medical Reserve Corps in addition to CERT. In other words, the pot of funding has been growing, but so has the number of potential applicants. The CCC has requested $45 million for fiscal 2005.

In the meantime, FEMA continues to support CERT with training materials, a CERT Web site and train-the-trainer courses at the EMI and at the state and regional levels. Interested jurisdictions and CERTS should

Originally published as "CERT's Growth Spurt," *Homeland Protection Professional*," Vol. 3, No. 6, July 2004. Published by A. J. Parrino & Associates, Western Springs, Illinois. Reprinted with permission of the publisher.

contact their state emergency management agencies or their local CCC representatives.

The Origins of CERT

In the mid–1980s the idea for community response teams had grown from the need to better prepare California residents for that state's frequent earthquakes. Los Angeles sent investigative teams to Japan and Mexico in 1985 to study how those countries prepared for and responded to earthquakes.

In Japan, the Los Angeles team found that the government had trained entire neighborhoods to respond to one consequence of an earthquake. These single-function neighborhood teams were trained in either fire suppression, light search and rescue, first aid or evacuation.

Later in 1985, following the devastating earthquake in Mexico City that killed more than 10,000 people, Los Angeles dispatched another investigative team. That group found that "Mexico City had no training program for citizens prior to the disaster." However, the team's report said, "large groups of volunteers organized themselves and performed light search and rescue operations." Those volunteers saved more than 800 lives, but lost more than 100 of their own number.

"The lessons learned in Mexico City," the Los Angeles CERT Web site <www.cert-la.com> says, "strongly indicated that a plan to train volunteers to help themselves and others, and become an adjunct to government response was needed as an essential part of overall preparedness, survival and recovery."

In a pilot program the following year, the City of Los Angeles Fire Department trained 30 members of a Neighborhood Watch program in one neighborhood. Rather than form a Japanese-style single-function team, the department decided on a multifunctional volunteer team trained in basic fire suppression, light search and rescue, and first

aid. That first team was a great success, but a tight city budget limited expansion of the program.

In 1987, shaken literally and figuratively by the Whittier Narrows earthquake, Los Angeles formed a disaster preparedness unit in the fire department. One of the unit's objectives was to "develop, train and maintain a network of Community Emergency Response Teams." That was the real start of the program.

CERT got a big boost from FEMA in 1993, when the agency made the concept and program available to communities nationwide. With help from the City of Los Angeles Fire Department, EMI added to the CERT materials and made them applicable to all hazards. The Citizens Corps Council took over as CERT's umbrella organization in 2002, and, as we've seen, the program has flourished.

A Variety of Starting Points

Jurisdictions have had different reasons for starting CERT programs. Like Los Angeles, many communities on the West coast formed CERTS because they wanted to be better prepared for earthquakes.

For example, in Fremont, Calif., the after-action reports from the Northridge and Loma Prieta earthquakes showed that the public safety services had been overloaded and 911 calls had to be prioritized. "This indicated to us a need to get the citizens involved," says Div. Chief Vic Valdes of the Fremont Fire Department.

Rowlett, Texas, is a suburb of Dallas with a mostly residential population of 50,000. The city's fire and rescue department formed a team in spring 2001 because of the need for citizen support of first responders during long-term emergency incidents. Basically, the team would set up a rehab site, give firefighters fluids and snacks, and take blood pressures and similarly assist the police department at large incidents.

Later, the city's first actual CERT team was trained by a group of ham radio operators sent to the National Fire Academy for a train-the-trainer course. The pre-existing team, now called CERT Relief, was rolled in as a subgroup of the CERT, with its members gradually receiving full CERT training.

The CERT in Olathe, Kan., also had its origins in a group of ham radio operators, who had functioned previously as storm spotters. (Olathe's surrounding county, Johnson County, had formed a CERT in 1998 after studying teams on the East and West Coasts.) The city graduated its first team in March 2001.

Fairfax County, Va., took a neighborhood approach to CERT, says Chief Michael Neuhard of the county's fire and rescue department. "After 9-11," he says, "it was apparent that in times of large-scale community disasters, first response agencies were pushed to extreme limits. Fairfax County wants to leverage the community, more specifically the citizens, to help in response to disasters."

The county has "a fundamental belief that citizens have a need to respond to a disaster," he adds, which is evident in the tremendous response from citizens who want the training.

One of Fairfax County's CERT groups is in the Town of Herndon, where the team grew from the police department's Citizens Support Team. "The town thought CERT would be a nice complement to the police unit," says Hal Singer, Herndon's CERT coordinator and a member of the police support team.

This arrangement requires the CERT to grow, he explains. "If an incident occurs, the police will want its support unit, thus depleting the number of members available to CERT, so the decision has been made to expand the CERT group."

Recruiting

CERT organizations have a variety of both traditional and non-traditional marketing techniques to recruit new members.

Rowlett, for example, used the shotgun approach, with booths at public events, articles and advertisements about CERT in the local newspapers, a flyer in the water bill, and a presentation before the city council, which was videotaped for later broadcast on the city's cable-access tv channel. Chief Larry Wright of the Rowlett Fire Rescue Department says the water bill flyer received the most response, though not necessarily the most recruits. The city has a goal of 175–200 CERT members, with 107 now trained.

The emergency management coordinator in Olathe, Rita Hoffman, says the initial CERT recruitment efforts were targeted at emergency service families "to get them involved in and allow them to plant the seeds about the benefits of CERT training."

She says the city then piloted a course to a neighborhood group, business, the school district, a church group and a county government agency. "CERT is also being promoted to city employees," she adds, "with the goal of slowly building a cadre of CERT–trained city employees."

Fairfax County also has used a variety of approaches, including the Virginia emergency management, Citizens Corps Council and Volunteer Fairfax Web sites, a flurry of initial publicity in local newspapers, and word of mouth.

In addition, the fire and rescue department's CERT coordinator, Bob Mizer, made a presentation to the county's Federation of Community Associations. Mizer says the county now has four teams with a total of 62 trained members, including the first community association-based CERT, in the Canterbury Woods section, where 20 citizens were trained this past winter. The department's goal is 2,000 CERT members in 100 teams, affiliated with every fire station in the county.

Herndon's recruiting effort featured a brochure, which was placed in libraries, the visitors center, popular restaurants and anywhere else it would be visible. In addition, Singer created a PowerPoint presentation for the town's cable-access tv channel and a mailbox on yahoo.com.

Fremont focused on community-based organizations, faith-based groups, ham radio operators and the Red Cross. The Freemont CERT has a current strength of 2,000, but the goal is an ambitious 21,000. Valdes says, "10% of the city's population of 210,000 committed to the same level of training would mean the city is well prepared."

Training

One common shortcoming with CERTs, says Lucier, is that people don't understand that "the generic FEMA training" is intended to be customized at the local level.

"We have to customize this for our own community," he emphasizes, based on local threats, resources, topography and demographics. "People are going to have to start adding other skills, different skills for different hazards," such as sandbagging for floods and knowledge of wildland fire behavior and reporting.

As it happens, the jurisdictions interviewed for this article use the standard FEMA CERT training course, but tweaked the curriculum to accommodate their own situations. For example, Olathe added a unit on fire department operations and responsibilities. That unit includes a "show-and-tell" session during which the fire department demonstrated its specialized equipment to the trainees.

Fremont uses the standard FEMA course, but has added an emphasis on earthquakes because a major fault runs right through the city. Valdes says the city has also developed an additional curriculum, "Personal Emergency Preparedness," that CERT members will teach to the citizens.

As with their marketing efforts, local CERTS are using both traditional and non-traditional techniques to conduct refresher training and are using refresher training to try to hang on to their members. Johnson County conducted a countywide CERT Rodeo to allow members to come back and refresh their training. The team is also doing the obligatory disaster drill and several in-depth training sessions that focus on specific skills.

Hoffman says the Olathe team wants to improve its radio communications, so it's working up a communications class. In addition, the Olathe CERT will be conducting training on how to deal with animals during a disaster.

Fairfax County is looking for ways to keep the teams engaged, according to Neuhard, so it will be conducting mass-casualty drills and open houses at fire stations, among other activities. "It is important to emphasize that CERT skills can be used every day," Neuhard says, "because CERT members are a force multiplier for everyday incidents, such as someone collapsing on the street, not just for disasters." The county will also sponsor a refresher day every year, which will be a combination of classroom instruction and hands-on training.

Herndon is planning to hold refresher training at least three times a year, in addition to joint training and disaster drills with other CERTs in Fairfax County.

Rowlett's fire and rescue chief, Larry Wright, thinks "retention is going to be a big problem. How do we keep them interested?" Accordingly, he plans to use the CERT for more than just disasters and terrorism incidents. Rowlett will deploy its team for community events and has scheduled more in-depth training, for example, a 40-hour EMS class. (A publication called "Starting and Maintaining a CERT Program" is available on the FEMA Web site.)

Organization and Funding

With roughly 12 members, plus 35 on the waiting list for training, the Herndon CERT is a fledgling organization. While the team is part of the Fairfax County CERT network, it also operates independently, securing its own funding, as does the Canterbury Woods team. Both are assembling and submitting grant applications to such organizations as Home Depot and Wal-Mart, which have funds available for local emergency response efforts, and both are exploring the possibility of securing non-profit status.

Herndon has put together a list of equipment necessary for the team, but said its ultimate goal is a covered trailer with generators, bullhorns, binoculars and a host of other equipment.

The Rowlett Fire Rescue Department split the city into nine zones divided by natural barriers. Each zone has a team leader and a calling tree for quick activation of the members in that zone. Members are charged with being intimately familiar with their neighborhoods and are expected to be self-sufficient for 72 hours.

Rowlett's CERT has received a Citizens Corps Council grant and achieved 501(c)(3) status, which Wright says is very important because the team is eligible for donations. The team has received contributions from Wal-Mart and the local women's club, and will be seeking corporate donations in the near future.

Fremont is divided into six districts, each of which has a coordinator, assistant coordinator and communications officer. Each district also has a preparedness container, containing first aid equipment, backboards, stretchers, ham radios, tables, vests, sledgehammers, pry bars, charts and forms, as well as other necessary equipment. The citywide CERT leadership team and the district coordinators make up an informal executive committee.

Valdes says the Fremont CERT was funded initially from the city's general funds, but after local jurisdictions nationwide faced serious budget shortfalls, the team had to seek other sources of revenue. Like Rowlett, Fremont has received a CCC grant and, like Rowlett's, the Fremont CERT has received donations from local charitable organizations.

In Olathe, the city used a FEMA Project Impact grant to get its CERT started, but now relies on CCC grants. Olathe's goal is 1,100 team members. Hoffman is working with the GIS department to pinpoint where the 400 current CERT members are situated, so the program can pinpoint future training to fill in the geographic blanks.

CERT/Fire Department Relations

During a recent CERT training class in an unnamed jurisdiction, the instructor was asked what the career firefighters had been told about CERT. The answer was, "Nothing yet!" This highlights one aspect of CERT, which must be handled with caution.

"This is an interesting challenge that fire departments need to work very carefully with," says Valdes, who hastens to add that it isn't a problem in Fremont. "The majority of the fire department staff understand the value of the CERT program and work with it."

In Rowlett, the CERT Relief program paved the way, says Wright. "Police officers and firefighters early on recognized the support the CERT can give at large-scale incidents and disasters."

Olathe and Johnson County came up with an interesting solution to initial resistance to CERT. CERT organizers approached the fire chiefs' association in Johnson County and were not well received initially. As noted above, the organizers then reached out to emergency services families to get them involved. When the organizers next approached the county fire chiefs' association, a deputy chief's wife came to speak on behalf of CERT.

In Boca Raton, Fla., where the CERT organization has 330 members, CERT has initiated a program to train firefighters about the team's responsibilities and operations. In addition, team members are invited to breakfasts at the fire stations in their areas.

Fairfax County Fire and Rescue started by telling battalion chiefs about CERT during battalion chiefs' meetings. Then Bob Mizer, the CERT coordinator, started having conversations with station captains. This spring, the department issued a bulletin to all stations and divisions, notifying them that the first CERT class had graduated and that CERTs would "function as a citizen arm of the Fire and Rescue Department."

The bulletin went on to describe the training and the roles the teams can adopt: "In addition to disaster roles, the CERT program can provide community service by having the teams perform non-emergency public service duties during community events or assisting with smoke detector installation and other public safety initiatives.

"In the event of a large-scale disaster where our response is limited, the Fire and Rescue Department will depend on the established CERT to assist in operations. It is anticipated that the Incident Commander will utilize the CERT Leader/Incident Commander as a section or branch leader as appropriate."

The memo called the working relationship between the team and its community fire station "the key to the success of the CERT program." The department plans to introduce the CERTs to their neighborhood fire stations at evening meetings "to ensure that the staff knows the teams in their area and are familiar with the CERT's capabilities and training."

Demonstrated Usefulness

FEMA's Sam Isenberger thinks that CERT is "accomplishing what it was meant to accomplish, involving people in the community." He points to recent CERT deployments as evidence of this, including wildfires in Arizona and California, Hurricane Isabel in Virginia, storm clean-up in Kansas and flooding in Washington.

Some of the CERTs mentioned in this article have already deployed. In 2002, the Olathe CERT was activated during an ice storm to help the needy and assist people who just couldn't deal with the debris. The following year, the team was activated after a series of tornadoes, again to help with debris removal.

The Fremont CERT has been activated several times during periods of heavy rain. The city's street maintenance department usually becomes overrun with blocked street drains, and the CERT members have helped clear the drains, thus helping to avoid a near disaster, says Valdes.

The Herndon team was deployed to a large town festival. CERT members helped the fire department staff the first aid tent and performed other duties.

Valdes calls CERT a "program that connects the government to the community and helps build that critical relationship. It's a great program, it makes sense and it's good for the community."

Looking Ahead

What's ahead for CERT? Everyone agrees that growth is the number-one priority, while number two is ironing out the inconsistencies among CERT programs around the country.

A new resource on the FEMA Web site should help with both these priorities. The resource is a Web-based independent study program called "Introduction to Community Emergency Response Teams."

The program will introduce people to the CERT concept and materials and prepare them for classroom training. For members who have already completed the CERT training, the study will reinforce concepts learned in the classroom. When the program is completed, participants will receive a certificate. The program is available at <http://training.fema.gov/EMIWeb/cert/>.

Finally, in an article on his community preparedness Web site, the Connection <www.naem.com/connection.html>, Lucier makes an interesting suggestion for changing the disaster preparedness culture of the United States. He would like to change the culture "from one of depending on everyday 911 emergency response to one of self-sufficiency and active response and assistance following a disaster...

"Cultural change in this country has always begun with the children. In the future, CERT training should be part of the education program in the schools. Then and only then will we be truly prepared as a nation."

CHAPTER 9

COMMUNITY VOLUNTEERS AS HOMELAND SECURITY STAKEHOLDERS

Stephen McGrail

The tragedies of September 11, 2001, led to many changes in our lives. Emergency management in Massachusetts, however, has not experienced dramatic, widespread changes primarily because much of the all-hazard training, planning and drilling at the state and local levels was not in need of serious modifications. The Massachusetts Emergency Management Agency had been presenting Terrorism/Weapons of Mass Destruction training for first responders since 1995. MEMA had also asked municipalities to evaluate their potential vulnerability before the events of two years ago. Terrorism annexes have been included in state and local Comprehensive Emergency Management plans since 1999. The training and drilling of those plans, particularly with a terrorism scenario/component, has been occurring for many years.

There have been many positive changes, however. September 11 produced a renaissance of interest by municipal officials in emergency management and Comprehensive Emergency Management plans. Communication between all levels of government —

local, state and federal — has greatly improved. Cooperation and coordination among all of the agencies and organizations that have a stake in the protection of Massachusetts residents is much more apparent. The stakeholders are frequently sitting at the same table, finding solutions to problems that face us. Funds from the federal government are being well utilized to ensure safety. Ironically, some of the best programs funded through federal dollars have been in motion for a number of years. MEMA has coordinated a $10 million Department of Justice grant for the purchase of nearly one hundred mobile decontamination trailers, the use of which is being coordinated by hospitals and local fire departments statewide. The Justice Department grant has also been used for the purchase and dissemination to local officials of hundreds of 800 MHz radios and supporting transmission equipment to ensure communication during multi-jurisdictional events anywhere in Massachusetts.

Originally published as "Preparedness Efforts Offer Opportunities for Volunteers," *Municipal Advocate*, Vol. 20, No. 3, Fall 2003. Published by the Massachusetts Municipal Association, Boston, MA. Reprinted with permission of the publisher.

Citizen Volunteers

The events of September 11 have also motivated many individuals to assist others and to help strengthen their communities. The federal government created the Citizen Corps in 2002 and called on Americans to engage in volunteer service. The mission of the Citizen Corps is to make communities safer and better prepared to respond to threats of terrorism, crime, public health issues, and disasters by engaging individuals in emergency preparedness and response through education, training, and volunteer service. In addition to tapping into the Citizen Corps offers opportunities to individuals with special skills and interests, such as the Medical Reserve Corps, Neighborhood Watch, and Volunteers in Police Service. The Community Emergency Response Teams program (CERT) focuses on training for volunteers. The intent is to have community-based volunteer groups work in concert with public safety agencies and local officials to effectively respond to any threats to public health and safety.

Citizen Corps/CERT Team coordinators, under the direction of MEMA, are supporting more than 130 Massachusetts communities in managing a 2002 federal grant designated for Citizen Corps and CERT activities. Additionally, the Federal Emergency Management Agency has approved Massachusetts' grant application for 2003 for more than $290,000, targeted for CERT activities within communities. These federal dollars can be used to start a CERT program or to expand an existing program by funding training or equipment and supplies. Local grant requests are evaluated by the Massachusetts State Citizen Corps Council, which includes representatives of dozens of organizations from the business sector, education, emergency management, fire services, law enforcement, public health, human services, municipal and regional government, and volunteer agencies. The State Council has identified needs and has developed a statewide strategy for increasing first responder and volunteer collaboration.

CERT is a grassroots-training program that can be implemented by local governments and emergency response agencies. The goal of the CERT program is to train volunteers who will first care for their family and neighbors and then offer assistance to the community within a controlled environment. Emergency services cannot meet all immediate needs during some events, especially if there's little or no warning, such as in the case of an earthquake, tornado or terrorist event. Citizens in the area of the event are the most immediate source of help to others and will often spontaneously try to respond. CERT training prepares community members for this role of citizen-responder. The twenty-hour program includes training in disaster preparedness, fire suppression, basic disaster medical operations, light search and rescue, disaster psychology, team organization, and terrorism. Training usually concludes with a disaster simulation in which participants practice the skills they have learned. After completing the training, community members become partners with emergency management and part of the response capability for their area.

Developing a CERT team in your community provides a greater sense of security, responsibility and personal control. It helps build community pride and promotes risk reduction and good preparedness practices. Most of all, CERT prepares us for helping our friends and neighbors in a crisis, allowing first responders to address the most critical needs.

For more information, contact Massachusetts Citizens Corps Council Coordinator Ken Tacelli at ken.tacelli@state.ma.us. For an overview of the national program, visit www.citizencorps.gov.

FIGURE 1
How the Public Can Help After a Disaster

When disaster strikes, people everywhere want to help those in need. To ensure that this compassion and generosity are put to good use, the media can highlight these facts:

- Financial aid is an immediate need of disaster victims. Financial contributions should be made through a recognized voluntary organization to help ensure that contributions are put to their intended use.

- Before donating food or clothing, the public should wait for instructions from local officials. Immediately after a disaster, relief workers usually don't have time or facilities to set up distribution channels, and too often these items go to waste.

- Volunteers should go through a recognized voluntary agency such as the American Red Cross or Salvation Army. They know what is needed and are prepared to deal with the need. Local emergency services officials also coordinate volunteer efforts for helping in disasters.

- Organizations and community groups wishing to donate items should first contact local officials, the American Red Cross, or Salvation Army to find out what is needed and where to send it. Be prepared to deliver the items to one place, tell officials when you'll be there, and provide for transportation and unloading.

CHAPTER 10

COORDINATION BETWEEN THE PUBLIC AND PRIVATE SECTORS IN THE FIELD OF HOMELAND SECURITY

Thomas Ridge

The nature of American society and the structure of American governance make it impossible to achieve the goal of a secure homeland through federal Executive Branch action alone. The Administration's approach to homeland security is based on the principles of shared responsibility and partnership with the Congress, state and local governments, the private sector, and the American people.

The Department of Homeland Security will coordinate, simplify, and where appropriate consolidate government relations on its issues for America's state and local agencies. It will coordinate federal homeland security programs and information with state and local officials.

The Department will give state and local officials one primary contact instead of many, and will give these officials one contact when it comes to matters related to training, equipment, planning, exercises and other critical homeland security needs. It will manage federal grant programs for enhanc-

ing the preparedness of firefighters, police, and emergency medical personnel. It will set standards for state and local preparedness activities and equipment to ensure that these funds are spent according to good statewide and regional plans. To fulfill these preparedness missions, the Department of Homeland Security will incorporate the Department of Justice's Office of Domestic Preparedness, the Federal Bureau of Investigation's National Domestic Preparedness Office, and the Federal Emergency Management Agency's Office of National Preparedness.

United States Secret Service

The primary mission of the United States Secret Service is to protect the President, Vice President, and other national leaders. The Service also contributes its specialized protective expertise to planning for events of national significance (National Special Security Events). In addition, the Service

---

Originally published as "State, Local, and Private Sector Coordination," *Department of Homeland Security*, Washington, D.C., November 2002.

combats counterfeiting, cyber-crime, identity fraud, and access device fraud, all closely tied to the terrorist threat. Under the President's proposal, the Secret Service will report directly to the Secretary of Homeland Security. While the Service will remain intact and not be merged with any other Department function, the Service's unique and highly specialized expertise will complement the core mission of the new Department.

Non-Homeland Security Functions

The Department of Homeland Security will have a number of functions that are not directly related to securing the homeland against terrorism. By incorporating the emergency management mission of FEMA, it will be responsible for natural disasters. Through the Coast Guard, it will be responsible for search and rescue and other maritime functions. By incorporating the INS, it will be responsible for immigration and naturalization services. Through the Secret Service, it will be responsible for fighting counterfeiters. And by incorporating the Customs Service it will be responsible for stopping drug smuggling.

The New Department Will Improve Efficiency Without Growing Government

The Department of Homeland Security must be an agile, fast-paced, and responsive organization that takes advantage of 21st-century technology and management techniques to meet a 21st-century threat.

The creation of a Department of Homeland Security will not "grow" government. The new Department will be funded within the total monies requested by the President in his FY 2003 budget already before Congress for the existing components. The cost

of the new elements (such as the threat analysis unit and the state, local, and private sector coordination functions), as well as department-wide management and administration units, can be funded from savings achieved by eliminating redundancies inherent in the current structure.

Going forward, increased resources may be required to meet emerging challenges, but by minimizing duplication of effort and lack of coordination we can ensure that any growth is limited to what is absolutely required. By combining and integrating functions that are currently fragmented, the Department of Homeland Security will:

- **Enhance operational efficiencies** in field units with overlapping missions. For example, the deployment of a cross-trained work force will provide more cost efficient inspection activities at the ports of entry than exist today with three separate units. Integration will allow for a more productive workforce at the agent level and elimination of parallel overhead structures in the field, as well as at headquarters.

- **Reduce redundant information technology spending.** Development of a single enterprise architecture for the department will result in elimination of the suboptimized, duplicative, and poorly coordinated systems that are prevalent in government today. There will be rational prioritization of projects necessary to fund homeland security missions based on an overall assessment of requirements rather than a tendency to fund all good ideas beneficial to a separate unit's individual needs even if similar systems are already in place elsewhere.

- **Effective management of research and development spending** will be facilitated by central control of research and development funding based, again, on overall homeland security priorities.

- **Better asset utilization** will be gained through consolidation and joint, comprehensive capital planning, procurement, and maintenance. This will pertain to boats, vehicles, and planes, as well as property management.

- **Consolidated, streamlined grant making** will promote targeted, effective programs at the state and local level, stretching the federal dollar further than is possible in the environment of multiple funding sources with sometimes overlapping missions.

In order to respond to rapidly changing conditions, the Secretary will need to have great latitude in re-deploying resources, both human and financial. The Secretary will have broad reorganizational authority in order to enhance operational effectiveness, as needed. Moreover, the President will request for the Department significant flexibility in hiring processes, compensation systems and practices, and performance management to recruit, retain, and develop a motivated, high-performance and accountable workforce. When a job needs to be done the Department should be able to fill it promptly, at a fair compensation level, and with the right person. Likewise, employees should receive recognition for their achievements, but in cases when performance falls short, should be held accountable. Finally, the new Department will have flexible procurement policies to encourage innovation and rapid development and operation of critical technologies vital to securing the homeland.

Planning, Transition, and Implementation Process

The implementation process for the new Department has already begun. During this period, the Department will maintain vigilance and continue to coordinate the other federal agencies involved in homeland security. Until the Department of Homeland Security becomes fully operational, the proposed Department's designated components will continue to operate under existing chains of command.

The formal transition process began once Congress approved the President's proposal and the President signed the bill into law. Under the President's plan, the new Department was established on January 1, 2003, with integration of some components occurring over a longer period of time. To avoid gaps in leadership coverage, the President's proposal contemplates that appointees who have already been confirmed by the Senate would be able to transfer to new positions without a second confirmation process.

CHAPTER 11

CRITICAL INFRASTRUCTURE ASSESSMENT AND HOMELAND SECURITY

American Society of Civil Engineers

While the security of our nation's critical infrastructure has improved since September 11, 2001, the information needed to accurately assess its status is not readily available to engineering professionals. This information is needed to better design, build and operate the nation's critical infrastructure in more secure ways. Security performance standards, measures and indices need to be developed, and funding must be focused on all critical infrastructure sectors, beyond aviation.

Background

Protecting assets against security risks has always been a priority for the owners and operators of the nation's critical infrastructure. However, before the attacks of September 11, 2001, most efforts were focused on isolated, relatively minor infractions such as vandalism, and not on high-profile, high-consequence attacks by well-organized terrorist groups. Now, a different kind of protection is needed, involving counter-terrorism (e.g., intelligence gathering, analy-

sis, strategies, and tactics) and anti-terrorism (e.g., hardening of infrastructure through the use of surveillance systems, barriers, and operating procedures). An "all hazards" approach is warranted, with the inclusion of these new malevolent threats added to the list of hazards that our critical infrastructure must be prepared to endure and survive.

Conditions

There are numerous challenges to securing the nation's infrastructure. Beyond the enormous cost implications of security measures in all sectors, there is the fundamental difficulty of coordinating efforts across infrastructure sectors, jurisdictional boundaries, and geographic locations. Issues related to differences in equipment standards are solvable with sound engineering practices, but resolving differences in chains of command and cultural attitudes is much more complex and difficult. Information sharing is critical — but what information should be shared, and with whom? There is also the challenge

---

Originally published as "Infrastructure (I)," *Infrastructure Report Card 2005*, American Society of Civil Engineers, Reston, VA, 2005. Reprinted with permission of the publisher.

of developing a thorough and comprehensive national response to terrorism against the backdrop of a deep-rooted desire of all Americans to preserve the basic constitutional freedoms that we hold dear, including the freedom of speech and assembly, and the right to be secure against unreasonable searches and seizures. Perhaps the most disturbing challenge is the difficulty in measuring progress. Is the absence of a large-scale attack the consequence of effective counter-measures, or simply the period of time between planned attacks? Regardless of the answer to this question, it is important to invest in protecting our infrastructure against these new threats, for without the additional layers of security, the occurrence and consequences of attacks would surely be more frequent and greater in scale.

Actions Taken

The Homeland Security Act of 2002 established a new Department of Homeland Security (DHS). The Information Analysis and Infrastructure Protection (IAIP) Directorate within the DHS developed the requirements for a National Critical Infrastructure Protection (CIP) Program. The vision for the National CIP Program was initially communicated through the July 2002 "National Strategy for Homeland Security." In February 2003, the President issued more specific strategies for physical protection of critical infrastructure and key resources and for the protection of cyberspace. In December 2003, the President issued Homeland Security Presidential Directive 7 (HSPD-7) to further direct and strengthen the CIP effort.

More recently, in February 2004, DHS launched its Protected Critical Infrastructure Information (PCII) Program. The PCII Program enables the private sector to voluntarily submit infrastructure information to the federal government to assist the nation in reducing its vulnerability to terrorist attacks.

To help develop ways of better protecting our critical infrastructures and to help minimize vulnerabilities, DHS established Information Sharing and Analysis Centers (ISACs) to allow critical sectors to share information and work together.

DHS also has led the development of the National Response Plan (NRP), which consolidates and reconciles multiple national-level incident-response plans into a single, focused, universally understood strategy. This effort includes the development of a new catastrophic incident response protocol that will greatly accelerate the delivery of critical federal assistance to domestic venues suffering from a mass casualty/mass evacuation incident.

In addition, DHS initiated the National Incident Management System (NIMS) and established the NIMS Integration Center, which ensures that federal, state, and local governments, and private-sector organizations, are all using the same criteria to prepare for, prevent, respond to, and recover from a terrorist attack or other major disaster.

Several information-sharing vehicles exist today that did not exist before September 11, 2001. The Homeland Security Information Network, which is available in all 50 states, makes threat-related information available to law enforcement and emergency managers, as well as to private-sector stakeholders through a web-based system.

The Customs-Trade Partnership Against Terrorism (C-TPAT) is a joint government-business initiative to build cooperative relationships that strengthen overall supply chain and border security. C-TPAT recognizes that U.S. Customs and Border Protection (CBP) can provide the highest level of security only through close cooperation with the ultimate owners of the supply chain: importers, carriers, brokers, warehouse operators, manufacturers, border infrastructure crossing facilities, and operators, and asks businesses to ensure the integrity of their security practices and communicate their security guidelines to business partners within the supply chain.

The Public Health Security and Bioterrorism Preparedness and Response Act of 2002 (the Bioterrorism Act), which President Bush signed into law June 12, 2002, addresses the enhancement of controls on dangerous biological agents and toxins, protecting the safety and security of food and drug supply, and drinking water security and safety.

The Federal Transit Administration spearheaded efforts after September 11 to prepare for future attacks by focusing on three areas: (1) training all transit employees and supervisors, (2) improving emergency preparedness, and (3) increasing public awareness of security issues.

Recognizing the critical importance of the security of our nation's water infrastructure — particularly in the post–September 11 environment — ASCE, the American Water Works Association (AWWA) and the Water Environment Federation (WEF), with a grant from the U.S. Environmental Protection Agency (EPA), developed a set of three security guidance documents addressing the design of online contaminant monitoring systems, and the physical security enhancements of drinking water, wastewater and stormwater infrastructure systems. The voluntary guidelines aim to assist drinking water and wastewater utilities in mitigating system vulnerabilities to man-made threats through the design, construction, operation, and maintenance of both new and existing systems of all sizes.

Professional organizations and public agencies formed The Infrastructure Security Partnership (TISP) as a forum for U.S.-based public and private sector non-profit organizations to collaborate on issues related to the security of the nation's built environment, including protection from both natural and man-made disasters. TISP acts as a national asset, facilitating dialogue on physical infrastructure security, by leveraging members' technical expertise and research and development capabilities in the design and construction industries. TISP offers extensive opportunities to its members and sponsors through its forums, education and training opportunities, communication and outreach mechanisms, and networking opportunities. TISP membership currently includes more than 180 organizations and agencies, reach more than two million individuals and firms involved in the planning, design, construction, and operation of the nation's built infrastructure.

The National Commission on Terrorist Attacks Upon the United States (also known as the 9/11 Commission), an independent, bipartisan commission created by congressional legislation and the signature of President Bush in late 2002, was chartered to prepare a full and complete account of the circumstances surrounding the September 11, 2001, terrorist attacks, including preparedness for and the immediate response to the attacks. The Commission was also mandated to provide recommendations designed to guard against future attacks. On July 22, 2004, the Commission released its public report.

Funding

The 2005 budget request of $40.2 billion for homeland security is $9 billion (29%) more than the 2003 level, and $20.4 billion more than the 2001 level, an increase of 103% over the 2001 level of homeland security funding. The vast majority of this funding is slated for airport screening and deployment of existing technologies. The Government Accountability Office (GAO) has published numerous reports recommending more attention to vulnerabilities other than air travel, and a broader, more coordinated, and better-managed program of research and development of new technologies.

Since September 11, 2001, most critical infrastructure owners and operators have conducted preliminary vulnerability assessments of their facilities, and have updated and modified their security procedures to enhance deterrence, protection, response, and recovery. In addition, training exercises and drills have been conducted with employees and contractors, and public outreach programs have been implemented at health, medical and research facilities; energy plants; water facilities; employment centers; public and private schools; and on public transportation systems, including bridges, tunnels, highways, and public transit. Industry has also invested heavily in protecting supply chains and the transport of hazardous materials.

Collectively, these steps have certainly improved the security of our nation's critical infrastructure systems since September 11, 2001; however, enormous challenges remain. Overcoming them will require a steadfast willingness to acknowledge the threats, think "outside the box," and to work with other sectors of the economy and professional disciplines. Sacrifices must be made in deference to a coordinated, integrated, and comprehensive public/private effort to prevent, protect, respond to, and recover from terrorist attacks. The security of our critical infrastructures, key resources, and our people depends on it.

Policy Options

America must design, build, and operate critical infrastructure by incorporating security as part of an "all hazards" approach. We must increase investment at all levels of government, and then spend that money wisely, leveraging the use of standards and protocols to enable interoperability between and among systems.

Congress must provide adequate funding to meet current infrastructure needs, and must include enough funding for research and development. Public and private partnerships must be forged, and professional and competitive differences must be managed, to ensure collective improvement in the security of the nation's infrastructures.

Specific recommendations supported by ASCE:

- Making information more readily available to professionals who can use the knowledge to better design, build, and operate critical infrastructures in more secure ways
- Continuing to conduct periodic vulnerability assessments in all infrastructure sectors
- Continuing to implement plans for security improvements, including education, training, exercise, and drills
- Increasing funding for long-term infrastructure security research efforts at the national level
- Establishing a federal, multi-year capital budget for critical infrastructure protection
- Encouraging the use of life-cycle cost analysis principles to evaluate the total costs of projects
- Supporting the Infrastructure Security Professional Advisory Network (I-SPAN) goals of bringing together state and local homeland security offices, other state and local government officials, and TISP member organizations, to review and assess needs for public-private sector collaboration, and to address infrastructure protection and recovery from natural and man-made disasters through robust partnerships at the sub-national level

Note

The information to prepare this report was obtained from nearly 40 governmental and nonprofit organization websites from throughout the nation, including various reports prepared by the American Society of Civil Engineers (ASCE). For a complete listing of these, primarily internet, resources, refer to ASCE's website (www.asce.org/reportcard/2005/page.cfm?id=32&printer=1).

CHAPTER 12

DEPARTMENT OF HOMELAND SECURITY: ITS PROPOSED STRUCTURE AND OPERATIONS

Thomas Ridge

The President's most important job is to protect and defend the American People. Since September 11, all levels of government have cooperated like never before to strengthen aviation and border security, stockpile more medicines to defend against bioterrorism, improve information sharing among our intelligence agencies, and deploy more resources and personnel to protect our critical infrastructure.

The changing nature of the threats facing America requires a new government structure to protect against invisible enemies that can strike with a wide variety of weapons. Today no one single government agency has homeland security as its primary mission. *In fact, responsibilities for homeland security are dispersed among more than 100 different government organizations.* America needs a single, unified homeland security structure that will improve protection against today's threats and be flexible enough to help meet the unknown threats of the future.

The President proposes to create a new Department of Homeland Security, the most significant transformation of the U.S. government in over a half-century by largely transforming and realigning the current confusing patchwork of government activities into a single department whose primary mission is to protect our homeland. The creation of a Department of Homeland Security is one more key step in the President's national strategy for homeland security.

Immediately after last fall's attack, the President took decisive steps to protect America — from hardening cockpits and stockpiling vaccines to tightening our borders. The President used his maximum legal authority to establish the White House Office of Homeland Security and the Homeland Security Council to ensure that our federal response and protection efforts were coordinated and effective. The President also directed Homeland Security Advisor Tom Ridge to study the federal government as a whole to determine if the current structure allows us to meet the threats of today while anticipating the unknown threats of tomorrow. After careful study of the current structure — coupled with the experience gained since September 11 and new information we

Originally published as "Executive Summary," *The Department of Homeland Security*, Office of the White House, Washington, D.C., December 2002.

have learned about our enemies while fighting a war — the President concluded that our nation needs a more unified homeland security structure. In designing the new Department, the Administration considered a number of homeland security organizational proposals that have emerged from outside studies, commissions, and Members of Congress.

The Department of Homeland Security *would make Americans safer* because our nation would have:

• One department whose primary mission is to protect the American homeland;
• One department to secure our borders, transportation sector, ports, and critical infrastructure;
• One department to synthesize and analyze homeland security intelligence from multiple sources;
• One department to coordinate communications with state and local governments, private industry, and the American people about threats and preparedness;
• One department to coordinate our efforts to protect the American people against bioterrorism and other weapons of mass destruction;
• One department to help train and equip for first responders;
• One department to manage federal emergency response activities; and
• More security officers in the field working to stop terrorists and fewer resources in Washington managing duplicative and redundant activities that drain critical homeland security resources.

The Organization of the Department of Homeland Security

The department of Homeland Security would have a clear and efficient organizational structure with four divisions:

• Border and Transportation Security
• Emergency Preparedness and Response
• Chemical, Biological, Radiological and Nuclear Countermeasures
• Information Analysis and Infrastructure Protection

Border and Transportation Security

The Department would unify authority over major federal security operations related to our borders, territorial waters, and transportation systems. It would assume responsibility for operational assets of the Coast Guard, Customs Service, Immigration and Naturalization Service and Border Patrol, the Animal and Plant Health Inspection Service of the Department of Agriculture, and the recently created Transportation Security Administration — allowing a single government entity to manage entry into the United States. It would ensure that all aspects of border control, including the issuing of visas, are informed by a central information-sharing clearinghouse and compatible databases.

Emergency Preparedness and Response

The Department would oversee federal government assistance in the domestic disaster preparedness training of first responders and would coordinate the government's disaster response efforts. FEMA would become a central component of the Department of Homeland Security, and the new Department would administer the grant programs for firefighters, police, and emergency personnel currently managed by FEMA, the Department of Justice, and the Department of Health and Human Services. The Department would also manage such critical response assets as the Nuclear Emergency Search Team (Department of Energy) and the National Pharmaceutical Stockpile (Health and Human Services). Finally, the Department would integrate the federal interagency emergency response plans into a single, comprehensive, government-wide plan, and ensure that all response personnel have the equipment and capability to communicate with each other as necessary.

Chemical, Biological, Radiological and Nuclear Countermeasures

The Department of Homeland Security would lead the federal government's efforts in preparing for and responding to the full range of terrorist threats involving weapons of mass destruction. To do this, the Department would set national policy and establish guidelines for state and local governments. It would direct exercises and drills for federal, state, and local chemical, biological, radiological, and nuclear (CBRN) attack response teams and plans. The result of this effort would be to consolidate and synchronize the disparate efforts of multiple federal agencies currently scattered across several departments. This would create a single office whose primary mission is the critical task of protecting the United States from catastrophic terrorism.

Chemical, Biological, Radiological and Nuclear Terrorism. The Department would be the lead agency preparing for and responding to chemical, biological, radiological, and nuclear terrorism, including agroterrorism. The Department would unify three of America's premier centers of excellence in this field, including the Lawrence Livermore National Laboratory (Department of Energy). The Department would also manage national efforts to develop diagnostics, vaccines, antibodies, antidotes, and other countermeasures.

Science and Technology. In the war against terrorism, America's vast science and technology base provides us with a key advantage. The Department would press this advantage with a national research and development enterprise for homeland security comparable in emphasis and scope to that which has supported the national security community for more than fifty years. The new Department would consolidate and prioritize the disparate homeland security related research and development programs currently scattered throughout the Executive Branch. It would also assist state and local public safety agencies by evaluating equipment and setting standards.

Information Analysis and Infrastructure Protection

Intelligence and Threat Analysis. The Department would fuse and analyze intelligence and other information pertaining to threats to the homeland from multiple sources — including the CIA, NSA, FBI, INS, DEA, DOE, Customs, DOT and data gleaned from other organizations. The Department would merge under one roof the capability to identify and assess current and future threats to the homeland, map those threats against our current vulnerabilities, issue timely warnings, and immediately take or effect appropriate preventive and protective action. An important partner with the Department's intelligence and threat analysis division will be the newly formed FBI Office of Intelligence. The new FBI and CIA reforms will provide critical analysis and information to the new Department.

Protecting America's Critical Infrastructure. The Department would be responsible for comprehensively evaluating the vulnerabilities of America's critical infrastructure, including food and water systems, agriculture, health systems and emergency services, information and telecommunications, banking and finance, energy (electrical, nuclear, gas and oil, dams), transportation (air, road, rail, ports, waterways), the chemical and defense industries, postal and shipping entities, and national monuments and icons. Working closely with state and local officials, other federal agencies, and the private sector, the Department would help ensure that proper steps are taken to protect high-risk targets.

Other Key Components

State/Local Government & Private Sector Coordination. The Department would consolidate and streamline relations with the federal government for America's state and local governments. The new Department would contain an intergovernmental affairs office to coordinate federal homeland security programs with state and local officials. This new Department would give state and local officials one primary contact instead of many when it comes to matters related to training, equipment, planning, and other critical needs such as emergency response.

Secret Service. The Department would incorporate the Secret Service, which would report directly to the Secretary. The Secret Service would remain intact and its primary mission will remain the protection of the President and other government leaders. The Secret Service would also continue to provide security for designated national events, as it did for the recent Olympics and the Super Bowl.

The White House Office of Homeland Security and the Homeland Security Council. The White House Office of Homeland Security and the Homeland Security Council will continue to play a key role, advising the President and coordinating a vastly simplified interagency process.

Non–Homeland Security Functions. The new Department would have a number of functions that are not directly related to securing the homeland against terrorism. For instance, through FEMA, it would be responsible for mitigating the effects of natural disasters. Through the Coast Guard, it would be responsible for search and rescue and other maritime functions. Several other border functions, such as drug interdiction operations and naturalization, would also be performed by the new Department.

Interim Steps

The President — using the maximum legal authority available to him — created the Office of Homeland Security and the Homeland Security Council in the weeks following the attack on America as an immediate step to secure the homeland. Since then, the government has strengthened aviation and border security, stockpiled more medicines to defend against bioterrorism, improved information sharing among our intelligence agencies, and deployed more resources and personnel to protect our critical infrastructure.

The White House Office of Homeland Security will continue to coordinate the federal government's homeland security efforts and to advise the President on a comprehensive Homeland Security strategy. The current components of our homeland security structure will continue to function as normal and there will be no gaps in protection as planning for the new Department moves forward.

Preliminary planning for the new Department has already begun. The formal transition would begin once Congress acts on the President's proposal and the President signs it into law. The President calls on Congress to establish the new Department by the close of their current session — with full integration of the constituent parts occurring over a phased-in period.

Specific Examples of How the New Department Will Make America Safer

EXAMPLE: REMOVING BARRIERS TO EFFICIENT BORDER SECURITY

Currently, when a ship enters a U.S. port, Customs, INS, the Coast Guard, the U.S. Department of Agriculture, and others have overlapping jurisdictions over pieces of the arriving ship. Customs has jurisdiction over the goods aboard the ship. INS has jurisdiction over the people on the ship. The Coast Guard has jurisdiction over the ship while it is at sea. Even the Department of Agriculture has jurisdiction over certain cargoes. Although the Coast Guard does have the authority to act as an agent for these other organizations and assert jurisdiction over the entire vessel, in practice the system has not worked as well as it could to prevent the illegal entry of potential terrorists and instruments of terror.

Consider this scenario: if the Coast Guard stops a ship at sea for inspection and finds there are illegal immigrants on the ship, the Coast Guard relies on the INS to enforce U.S. immigration law and prevent their entry. If the Coast Guard finds potentially dangerous cargo, it relies on Customs to seize the dangerous cargo. Unfortunately, these organizations may not always share information with each other as rapidly as necessary.

So, instead of arresting potential terrorists and seizing dangerous cargo at sea, our current structure can allow these terrorists to enter our ports and potentially sneak into our society. The system might also allow the dangerous cargo to actually enter our ports and threaten American lives.

Under the President's proposal, the ship, the potentially dangerous people, and the dangerous cargo would be seized at sea by one Department that has no question about either its mission or its authority to prevent them from reaching our shores.

EXAMPLE: PROTECTING OUR NATION'S CRITICAL INFRASTRUCTURE

Nearly five million Americans live within a five mile radius of the most hazardous chemical facilities in the nation. Right now there is no single agency in the government whose core mission is to protect against and respond to an attack on one of these major facilities.

Consider the current homeland security apparatus facing a non-citizen that intends to enter our nation and attack one of our chemical facilities. At our border, INS, Customs, Border Patrol, the Coast Guard, and others share jurisdiction over preventing this person's entry. These government organizations may or may not share information, which makes it possible that this potential terrorist might slip through the cracks.

Currently, at least twelve different government entities oversee the protection of our critical infrastructure. These many government entities may or may not share all information, and state and local governments must work with twelve separate contacts just to help protect their local infrastructure.

Under the President's proposal, the same Department that analyzes intelligence data on the potential terrorist who wants to attack the chemical plant would also be the same Department that can simultaneously alert our border security operatives, alert all of our hazardous materials facilities to ensure that they are prepared to meet this specific new threat from this specific terrorist, and alert all of the affected communities.

EXAMPLE: COMMUNICATING TO THE AMERICAN PEOPLE

Currently, if a chemical or biological attack were to occur, Americans could receive warnings and health care information from a long list of government organizations, including HHS, FEMA, EPA, GSA, FBI, DOJ, OSHA, OPM, USPS, DOD, USAM-

RIID, and the Surgeon General not to mention a cacophony of state and local agencies.

There is currently no single organization with operational responsibility that could communicate with the American people in a clear, concise, and consistent voice.

Consider another recent example. Information was provided to local law enforcement entities by multiple U.S. government organizations about potential threats to the Brooklyn Bridge, apartment complexes, shopping malls, the Statue of Liberty, subways and public transit systems, our oil and gas infrastructure, and our financial system.

Under the President's proposal, a single government Department would communicate with the American people about a chemical or biological attack. The new Department would also be the organization that coordinates provision of specific threat information to local law enforcement and sets the national threat level. The new Department would ensure that law enforcement entities — and the public — receive clear and concise information from their national government. Citizens would also have one Department telling them what actions — if any — they must take for their safety and security.

EXAMPLE: INTELLIGENCE SHARING AND COMPREHENSIVE THREAT ANALYSIS

Multiple intelligence agencies analyze their individual data, but no single government entity exists to conduct a comprehensive analysis of all incoming intelligence information and other key data regarding terrorism in the United States. There is no central clearinghouse to collect and analyze the data and look for potential trends.

Under the President's proposal, the new Department would contain a unit whose sole mission is to assemble, fuse, and analyze relevant intelligence data from government sources, including CIA, NSA, FBI, INS, DEA, DOE, Customs, and DOT, and data gleaned from other organizations and public

sources. With this big-picture view, the Department would be more likely to spot trends and would be able to direct resources at a moment's notice to help thwart a terrorist attack.

EXAMPLE: DISTRIBUTION OF KEY PHARMACEUTICALS

Potassium Iodide (KI) is a drug that helps prevent thyroid cancer in the event of exposure to radiation. The drug must be taken within hours of exposure for maximum effectiveness.

Currently, if you live within a ten-mile radius of a nuclear power facility, the distribution of Potassium Iodide is regulated by the Nuclear Regulatory Commission (NRC). The NRC is responsible for getting people this crucial drug, even though the NRC's actual mission is to license nuclear facilities, not provide emergency supplies to the greater population. Outside the ten-mile radius of the nuclear facility, the Federal Emergency Management Agency (FEMA) is responsible for regulating the distribution of Potassium Iodide. The Department of Health and Human Services controls the national pharmaceutical stockpiles that are to be sent rapidly into emergencies. And other government agencies would control evacuation of the emergency zone. To make matters even more confusing, if you happen to live within a ten-mile radius of a nuclear weapons facility, the Department of Energy controls the distribution of the Potassium Iodide.

In the event of radiation exposure, states must currently work with three separate government organizations to distribute critical pharmaceuticals, organizations whose jurisdictions are divided by an invisible ten-mile border. Consider this possible scenario: the NRC and the state decide to distribute Potassium Iodide to everyone within the ten-mile radius. FEMA, however, disagrees with the state and decides against distributing the drug outside the ten-mile radius. In the middle of the NRC, FEMA and state decision process, the state and local governments decide to begin an evacuation. In the ensuing chaos, many exposed individuals might not receive the critical drugs they need.

Under the President's proposal, one Department would be responsible for distributing Potassium Iodide to citizens exposed — no matter where they live. There would no longer be an artificial ten-mile barrier to treatment. This same single Department would also be responsible for coordination with state and local officials on immediate evacuation from the emergency zone.

Brief History of Government Reorganization

History teaches us that critical security challenges require clear lines of responsibility and the unified effort of the U.S. government. History also teaches us that new challenges require new organizational structures.

For example, prior to 1945, America's armed forces were inefficiently structured with separate War and Navy Departments and disconnected intelligence units. There were no formal mechanisms for cooperation. After World War II, the onset of the Cold War required consolidation and reorganization of America's national security apparatus to accomplish the new missions at hand.

America needed a national security establishment designed to prevent another attack like Pearl Harbor, to mobilize national resources for an enduring conflict, and to do so in a way that protected America's values and ideals. In December 1945, only months after America's decisive victory in World War II, President Harry Truman asked Congress to combine the War and Navy Departments into a single Department of Defense. President Truman declared, "it is now time to take stock to discard obsolete organizational forms and to provide for the future the soundest, most effective and most economical kind of structure for our armed forces of which this most powerful Nation is capable. I urge this as the best means of keeping the peace."

President Truman's goals were achieved with the National Security Act of 1947 and subsequent amendments in 1949 and 1958. The legislation consolidated the separate military departments into the Department of Defense with a civilian secretary solely in charge, established a Central Intelligence Agency to coordinate all foreign intelligence collection and analysis, and created the National Security Council in the White House to coordinate all foreign and defense policy efforts.

This reorganization of America's national security establishment was crucial to overcoming the enormous threat we faced in the Cold War and holds important lessons for our approach to the terrorist threat we face today.

Note

The Department of Homeland Security is the newest federal agency in the past one-half century. Its current Secretary, Thomas Ridge, was sworn into office on January 24, 2003. The reorganization of existing federal agencies into this newest federal department is still a work in progress. It will no doubt take many years for this federal agency to evolve to its final organizational form. For this reason, the editor thought it important to provide an overview of the President's proposal regarding the structure and operations of this important federal government agency. The information for this chapter was obtained from the Office of the White House website (http://www.white house.gov/).

CHAPTER 13

DISPATCH CENTER SERVICES AND EMERGENCY RESPONSES

Randall D. Larson

There was a lot of attention paid to the challenges and tragedies that faced our first responders on Sept. 11, but very little attention was given to the dispatchers who worked diligently and consistently behind the scenes. In many instances, they were the last to hear the voices of civilians trapped in the World Trade Center, calling from cell phones on hijacked airliners, and the rescuers who were lost in the collapse of the towers.

When the Department of Justice developed the Domestic Preparedness Program in 1998, they made sure to include 911 dispatchers in that training. This made sense, recognizing that our nation's emergency telecommunicators are the ones who will most likely receive the first notice of a terrorist or WMD event, and they are the ones who will be at the center of coordinating and integrating the response to ongoing homeland security concerns.

"America's 911 communications personnel represent the *first* first responder to each and every type of emergency situation imaginable," says Robert Martin, executive director of the National Academies of Emergency Dispatch. "Not only can good information in the 911 dispatch center help to spot early patterns or warning signs of possible terrorist

activities, but properly trained and certified dispatchers can also provide immediate assistance in the way of giving practical advice to callers."

With the encouragement of Attorney General Ashcroft and the Bush Administration, Neighborhood Watch organizations are beginning to proliferate, undoubtedly resulting in an increase in calls to local 911 centers.

"Seeing a lot of our national figureheads including our President directing people to call 911 when they feel something is suspicious, it's obvious that we are America's first-line phone call," says Kevin Willett, senior instructor for Public Safety Training Consultants, a national trainer of 911 dispatchers. "We have to be prepared and we have to know where to refer calls and how to handle them appropriately."

"It's important that the dispatcher is well trained to pick up the clues that will indicate that this is an event that might have much greater consequences to the community, whether it's terrorism caused or not," adds Dr. Frances Edwards-Winslow, director of the San Jose (Calif.) Office of Emergency Services.

Last February, the Association of Public Safety Communications Officials — Interna-

Originally published as "It Starts in Dispatch," *Homeland Protection Professional*, Vol. 1, No. 1, July/August 2002. Published by A. J. Parrino & Associates, Western Springs, Illinois. Reprinted with permission of the publisher.

tional (APCO) launched a Homeland Security Task Force in response to the demands placed on public safety communications in the aftermath of Sept. 11. The Task Force identified six critical homeland security issues demanding primary attention by dispatch centers:

1. **Security** for dispatch centers, communications systems, and infrastructure.
2. **Survivability and redundancy** of dispatch centers and communications systems.
3. **Interoperability** of radio systems.
4. **Impact of public safety operations** on communications centers. How does the response to major incidents impact dispatch operations?
5. Focus on **training** and the needs of tele-communicators/dispatchers
6. Focus on **equipment and infrastructure**. How can dispatch partner with the private sector to create better technology?

APCO also hopes to increase awareness about the funding needs of local 911 and communication centers. "It is hoped that the information gathered will be of assistance not only in regards to homeland security, but also as a means of improving the reliability of day-to-day operations," says Barry Furey, communications director for Knox County, Tenn., and chair of the APCO Homeland Security Task Force.

Communications Center Security

911 and dispatch administrators need to look carefully at their own premise security to ensure they aren't susceptible to sabotage or intrusion. Maintaining a dispatch center's security and survivability in the event of an attack is paramount to a response agency's ability to respond against terrorism.

The University of Wisconsin at Madison, for example, put a live security camera on the building's air intake and ordered a supply of gas masks as a contingency against a chemical attack on the facility.

Other centers have also stockpiled supplies and beefed up security measures. "Dispatch agencies need to be secure not only against terrorism, but also for more conventional kinds of criminal activity," says Tony Harrison, a dispatch instructor with The Public Safety Group. "I know several dispatch centers that could be taken out of order with a single pipe bomb, because all the phone lines enter the facility at one location and the phone box is above ground."

The Columbia 9-1-1 Communications District in St. Helens, Ore., recently revised its facility security policy. The central administrative area is no longer open to the public during business hours, and all entry is screened by on-duty personnel. Additional external cameras and monitors were installed, as well as expanded capacity to monitor those camera views.

"We are no longer offering tours and visits from the public," explains Sally J. Jones, the district's administrator. "Our physical address was removed from our Web site, and only our Post Office Box is published now. As an agency, we also participated in developing a statewide procedure for handling homeland security messages distribution."

Redundancy is also a necessity, especially for facilities as vital as communications centers. Yet budgets rarely allow such a major expense as a back-up facility, especially one that, in the eyes of local politicians, might never be used.

Nonetheless, there are solutions. For example, Milwaukee's communications director came up with a way to justify developing a back-up 911 site by setting it up as a primary dispatch training site. The equipment is constantly being used and therefore tested, and it gets 911 trainers off-site and able to train hands-on without being on top of the people actually working. Partnering with neighboring agencies to be each other's back-up call receipt and dispatch site is another way to accommodate redundancy on limited budgets.

Interoperability

The ability to communicate not only with your own resources but also with those of your neighboring agencies will also be vital during any homeland security plan. If a WMD or terrorist event does happen in your community, you'll most likely require the assistance of neighboring jurisdictions to mitigate the incident, not to mention the federal responders that will begin swarming in.

Speaking to the Senate Communications Subcommittee on March 6, 2002, APCO president Glen Nash reminded congress that, especially with the new homeland security responsibilities being placed on state and local public safety agencies, "the need for effective radio communications is heightened even more..." and that "there will be even greater demand for public safety [radio] spectrum." What is needed are adequate radio channels with adequate radio coverage, including a combined approach with interoperability between all public safety agencies and support entities. Solutions can be costly and long-term, but must be thought out now. At the same time, workable solutions can be found through short-term means.

A report on public safety communications during the attack on the Pentagon, issued in February by the Public Safety Wireless Network, concluded that, to link agencies during a major incident, planning, training and asset management are more urgently needed than sophisticated technology. The group noted that at the Pentagon, a lack of SOPS, politics, and turf battles prevented the implementation of available technical solutions.

How agencies communicate, and the daily habits they get into, will most likely predicate how they will (or won't) communicate in response to a major disaster. "It seems that most agencies wait until something happens and then they look at interoperability," says Tony Harrison of The Public Safety Group. "The most important aspect is that if they aren't doing it on a daily basis, they're not going to do it during a disaster." The inability to properly communicate with outside personnel who are working the same incident not only hampers effective operations, but can lead to a serious breach in responder safety.

Tactical Dispatchers

Another component of homeland security that was developed around the same time as the Domestic Preparedness program was Metropolitan Medical Task Forces, an EMS equivalent of FEMA's Urban Search & Rescue task forces that are deployed to aid victims of building collapse. Many of the large cities that created MMTFs included communications as an important component of those teams.

The San Jose (Calif.) Fire Department, for example, maintains among its staff a rapid-response team of specially trained and equipped dispatchers who will deploy with a communications vehicle to establish communications, resource accountability and documentation at an incident's command post. Noting the effectiveness of this kind of team on fires and rescues, San Jose's MMTF quickly brought the Incident Dispatch Team into its response parameters.

"When the MMTF responds into the field, communication is a real key safety issue," says Edwards-Winslow. "By being able to take along incident dispatchers, we have a high level of confidence that the people who are handling our message traffic are well aware of the situation we're working in and can provide us with the highest level of cooperation and support."

Cincinnati also included communications personnel when it developed a Metropolitan Medical Response System. "Communications personnel possess the skills and forethought needed in this type of disaster," says Lisa Knapp, communications supervisor for the Cincinnati Fire Department. "They are used to multi-tasking, they are masters in the Incident Command System and radio communications, they know who and where to call for resources needed, they are consistently reviewing and creating emergency procedures for all types of disasters."

"The dispatchers bring a different perspective to the table than a first responder or an emergency manager," says Edwards-Winslow, "and it's another perspective that's really crucial in developing a full response that has safety at its core."

Dispatcher Training

Perhaps the most important component of any homeland security program is the quality of training given the dispatchers responsible for it. As the preliminary link between the public and the response organization, dispatchers must be intimately familiar with department response policies and protocols, current events, current stages of alert, and related warnings that the public may be calling in about. A thorough familiarity with current events, especially as they pertain to homeland security, is vital if an agency's dispatchers are going to prevent panic and reassure its public of an agency's ability to respond to and handle terrorist activities.

"When people call and have questions or begin to describe their symptoms, dispatchers who are well-trained may pick up on clues that may be hard for someone else to recognize," says Edwards-Winslow. "If the dispatcher recognizes the symptoms, it can be a real safety factor for the first responders."

Most 911 and dispatch centers seem to be left to produce this training on their own, with limited budgets, and with limited

know-how. Coordination on the statewide, if not federal, level can be a valuable component to insure appropriate and standardized training. In Oregon, for example, the state Office of Emergency Management along with the Oregon Department of Public Safety Standards and Training has initiated and developed statewide targeted training for dispatch personnel specific to domestic terrorism.

Protocols and Post-dispatch Instructions

Some 911 centers have developed cardsets with specific questions to aid their dispatchers in asking the right kinds of questions for unusual situations, especially in the aftermath of Sept. 11, when suddenly all the paradigms changed and dispatchers realized they had to be prepared to receive calls from passengers on board hijacked aircraft or people trapped in burning high-rises.

The Palm Beach (Fla.) Communications Center developed a comprehensive flow-chart protocol to handle suspicious package or exposure calls. These guidelines include key questions on identifying what makes the package suspicious, addresses caller and scene safety issues, as well as instructions for what the caller should do.

Dispatchers at the Seminole County (Fla.) Department of Public Safety got together and developed a bound cardset, modeled after the popular medical protocol systems already in place in many dispatch centers. The cards allow dispatchers to ask questions designed for specific situations such as biological agent exposure, suspicious mail, calls from aircraft. The cardset also includes important phone numbers for notification and referral.

"Interrogation aids help dispatchers tremendously," says Joe LeBlanc, senior coordinator for Seminole County DPS. "It will help responding agencies and it will help dispatchers to get a better understanding of the actual problem, and it generally helps the caller when the call-taker is calm and collected and has a series of questions that are asked in a logical sequence."

One way to increase homeland security and ensure the availability of immediate patient care is to provide targeted training for 911 communications center personnel. Any center equipped to receive emergency medical calls should have its call-takers trained and certified as Emergency Medical Dispatchers, specifically trained to use a certified medical reference system or protocol to provide appropriate and immediate patient care advice over the phone.

"The EMD will know how to send the right thing(s), in the right way, at the right time, in the right configuration," says Robert Martin, Executive Director of the National Academies of Emergency Dispatch, certifier of dispatch protocol systems for police, fire, and EMS. "In this time of great expectations, but limited funds and severely strained resources, being able to do this effectively is paramount in establishing a solid foundation of early access to this country's emergency response system."

Networking

Perhaps the most important aspect for any agency to embrace is networking. Communication between different 911 centers is a vital component of preparations for any kind of scenario, not only homeland security. Just as different law enforcement agencies need to network to discern connections between seemingly unrelated activities, 911 dispatchers also need to be aware of warning signs detected by their neighboring agencies.

"The more that agencies at the local, state, and federal levels can network and share ideas and brainstorm on solutions, the better off we'll be in the long run," says LeBlanc. "The worst thing that can happen is to be parochial about something like that and develop something totally in the dark and not get ideas from other people in your field."

CHAPTER 14

EARLY WARNING GROUP RESULTS FROM PUBLIC-PRIVATE COOPERATION

Anne Louise Bannon

In Los Angeles County, the key to staying one step ahead of terrorists is simple: relationships.

LA County Sheriff's Sgt. John Sullivan, one of the founders of the county's Terrorism Early Warning Group, says it: "The important thing is that it's a network organization."

Supervisory Special Agent Bob Kellison, of the FBI's LA office, says it, too. "It's important when you respond to [an event] that you know this person by their first name."

And so does Capt. Richard Diaz of the LA County Fire Department: "When something happens, I would know this person and that person would know me. You would have that comfort factor, which makes it a lot easier."

In short, when things are literally blowing up, local agencies can respond a lot faster when one of the county's fire battalion chiefs already knows the city police chief as well as the local health department head and the agents from the nearest FBI office. And they all know the battalion chief and each other.

A Vast Arena for Cooperation

And if that were all the TEW were about, that would be significant enough. But the group does a lot more than just provide a way for everybody to get to know everybody else. It also collects and disseminates information among all the various agencies in the county and provides analysis and synthesis of various forms of intelligence.

The focus is on intelligence and on consequence management planning, says Sullivan. "Basically, we only provide actionable or analyzed information," he explains. "We also issue white papers. We do threat assessment and build target folders. We build playbooks. We don't just pass information around. We analyze information and determine what courses of action are viable and then put that out."

The members include an amalgam of city, county, state and federal agencies, plus a few private organizations, including think tank Rand Corp. The Los Angeles Police Department is part of the core, as is the U.S. Coast Guard. A variety of local agencies also participate. "Basically, every public safety

Originally published as "California Teaming," *Homeland Protection Professional*, Vol. 1, No. 3, November/December 2002. Published by A. J. Parrino & Associates, Western Springs, Illinois. Reprinted with permission of the publisher.

agency in Southern California has a seat at the table," says Sullivan

The TEW also coordinates with two Joint Terrorism Task Forces in the area (one based in Los Angeles, the other in Long Beach), both of which are primarily investigative in focus, Sullivan says.

If getting this kind of interagency cooperation seems like a miracle, consider the following stats on LA County. It covers 4,081 square miles, ranging from skyscraper cityscapes to wilderness with deer, coyotes, bears and mountain lions. While 65% of the county is unincorporated, there are 88 different cities, which have their own police departments or contract with the LA County Sheriff's Department to provide law enforcement. The population of just over 9.8 million is not only among the world's most culturally diverse, a huge portion of it doesn't speak English.

But Southern California has long had an excellent reputation for emergency response agencies that work well together, which is understandable. Earthquakes and brush fires, the two most common large-scale emergencies here, do tend to cross multiple jurisdictional lines. In addition, the extensive freeway system is particularly conducive to highspeed chases, which almost always cross city and county lines. In short, agencies in LA County are already used to working with each other.

In fact, Kellison says that was in part why the TEW was able to happen. "In Southern California, we had the advantage where the local agencies work very well together," he says. "It was the result of working relationships.

In addition, much of the county leadership began to realize that they couldn't ignore the danger. There was the 1993 bombing of the World Trade Center and the Oklahoma City bombing of the Murrah Federal Building in 1995, plus other incidents all over the world.

Still, Sullivan says, it took some effort to bring together all the various responders to form the TEW. He and his then partner, Deputy Larry Richards, had been trying to put something together for several years prior to 1996.

"At that time," Sullivan says, "it was all an informal, ad hoc activity," and the TEW group, formed in October 1996, initially received no funding at all. The group met monthly to exchange information and go over possible scenarios.

"It's something that everybody recognized was necessary," says Kellison.

The TEW has been activated four times since it was set up. The first was during a series of anthrax hoaxes throughout the county in 1998. Kellison says it took a little time for everyone to work out the protocols, but by the fourth or fifth incident, which took place at a federal bankruptcy court in the San Fernando Valley, everyone was working together, and Kellison says that the FBI did get a prosecution out of it.

The group got a second workout in 1999, as part of a joint federal-local WMD exercise called "Westwind," which simulated a chemical attack at an air show. And while the Y2K transition proved to be an anticlimax, the TEW was activated and running, and was again during the 2000 Democratic National Convention in Los Angeles.

Activations and Evolution

Even in the mid–'90s, it was getting a lot harder to stay in denial about terrorism, says Sullivan. "We started to discern an acceleration of global terrorism."

Ongoing Challenges

Sullivan acknowledges that getting such interagency cooperation can be challenging at times. "You're fighting a culture of denial," he says, "and a number of entrenched bureaucracies that traditionally don't work together. You're building new skill sets. It's typical of negotiating any other organizational change, but while there are difficulties, it's incredibly rewarding."

While Diaz was involved only off and on for the first few years of the TEW, he knew it was a good idea. "From the beginning I could see the importance of the TEW," he says, "all the different agencies working together. When something like this event or that happens, everyone's going to be there. The goal is going to be the same goal, trying to determine what the substance is and trying to determine who did it." For the past two years, he's been involved full-time.

Whenever people get together, there's the possibility for conflict and personality clashes, but Diaz says that so far, there haven't been any turf battles. "That's the whole idea behind it," he says. "Everybody needs to work together and not be concerned about their own little area."

Diaz explains that while he does have to take information from the group to his supervisors to get potential action approved, having the group's backing helps get faster approval. Nor is it just a simple matter of him going to the group, then reporting back to his superiors and they work out a plan.

"We will all gather and discuss," he says. "It looks like this event is going to occur. What needs are there from everybody? We're not just taking information and going someplace and thinking about it."

He also says that when things get more speculative, having the group there can be helpful. "That's where everybody working together is beneficial," he says. "I may think something is completely ridiculous, and someone can say, 'Oh, now, that could actually happen.'"

Flexibility and Growth

Describing what the TEW does before, during and after an incident is difficult, be-

cause the group's work varies with each incident. "We've evolved," Sullivan says, "so that as the threat evolved, we've been able to morph."

And each incident is different. While Y2K and the DNC were ripe for targeting, they were both foreseeable events, so the group does some speculative brainstorming.

"We try not to 'What if?' things to death," Diaz says. "We try to keep things as realistic as possible, and yet balance the reality that something else could happen."

The big change for the TEW came in the wake of 9-11. Where the group had been somewhat informal before, after the attacks on New York City and the Pentagon, the LA County supervisors decided to provide the group with a $1.8 million annual budget. The TEW still meets monthly, but several of the core agencies assigned personnel to the group fulltime. There are a sheriff's deputy working forensic intelligence support, a criminalist working two days a week and a data systems analyst, with about 20 people total assigned at least part-time to the group.

"We now have a baseline cadre from which to build," Sullivan says. "We've got a scalable model that can be applied with limited resources and that can be expanded as resources become available."

He does want additional funding and plans to actively seek federal grant funds. The problem is that there aren't any grant vehicles that specifically address what the group does. If anything, federal grants tend to focus on equipment purchases.

One of Sullivan's specific goals for the TEW is to move more heavily into "deep indications and warning," that is, into trying to access terrorist intentions and plans as early as possible. Doing so will put more of a premium on data-mining tools, because of the drastically increased number of leads and indicators.

FIGURE 1
Who Belongs to the TEW

The Los Angeles County Terrorism Early Warning Group is a genuinely diverse and broad-based group. Here's just a partial list of the agencies represented on it.

- Los Angeles Police Department
- Los Angeles City Fire Department
- Los Angeles County Sheriff's Department
- Los Angeles County Fire Department
- Los Angeles County Coroner
- Los Angeles County District Attorney
- Los Angeles County Office of Public Safety (the police agency for county offices, hospitals and parks)
- FBI Los Angeles field office
- Glendale (Calif.) Police Department
- Glendale (Calif.) Fire Department
- Long Beach (Calif.) Police Deparment
- Long Beach (Calif.) Fire Department
- Pasadena (Calif.) Police Department
- Pasadena (Calif.) Fire Department
- U.S. Customs Service
- U.S. Naval Criminal Investigative Service
- California Highway Patrol
- Los Angeles International Airport Police
- Los Angeles International Airport Fire Department
- U.S. Coast Guard
- Federal Aviation Administration Security
- FAA Federal Air Marshals
- Transportation Security Administration
- Union Pacific Railroad police
- Federal Protective Service (General Services Admin.)
- U.S. Department of Veterans Affairs police

A Broadly Useful Concept

For communities considering a similar joint effort, Sullivan, Kellison and Diaz all agree that **laying the groundwork and developing the relationships is crucial.**

"I would suggest that they first off start at their level and try and get one voice," Diaz says. "The whole intent is that everyone's thinking along the same line. It's a matter of getting to know your counterparts in the other agencies. At least start having some sort of gathering, meetings, of having these individuals together."

Planning is also very important, including command issues. "One of the questions that was settled early on was who's in charge," Kellison says, and the result was that the TEW actually decided that no one agency would be in charge.

"When we handle these things, we set up a unified command," Kellison explains. "We work jointly with the command to deal with all of these things. The more you know beforehand, the better you can respond to something."

Another core issue is sharing information. "We established a good foundation, but obviously things change," Kellison says. "You always learn new things. You're constantly gaining new facts and you're constantly responding to those facts. All of us early on in the TEW recognized the need to share information with the first responders and the medical folks."

Finally, it's essential to make sure that the group can prosper despite the inevitable turnover among key personnel. The TEW was founded by specific people who had a vision of what they wanted to accomplish, but even though some of them have moved on, the group is still strong.

"I'm no longer directly involved, but the basic relationships continue," Kellison says. "I think at the highest levels that this transcends any specific personalities. I've seen

management change in the police department and the sheriff's [department]. Part of
the personality issue, it was important to
start. What you have to strive for is to insti-
tutionalize. It's changed because the TEW has
become more formalized, and doing that gets
past the stage of personality."

So even if all this has happened in laid-
back Southern California, Sullivan, Kellison
and Diaz agree that other cities and counties
can't afford not to start working together.

"There was a lot of denial [about terror-
ism] prior to 9-11," Sullivan says. "I'm afraid
the recognition is going to become more
acute in the coming years."

CHAPTER 15

EMERGENCY RESPONSE PLANS AND HOMELAND SECURITY

John Ouellette

1. Build and nurture partnerships and relationships based on trust and good communication. Strong working relationships are essential to effective response in any kind of emergency. Those partnerships are particularly important in a small community, which will have to rely on good neighbors to provide support in an emergency. Creating and sustaining those relationships before a crisis event is a work in progress that demands constant attention. While technology is an important component of effective communication, people talking to people is the bottom line.

2. Know your community, its assets and vulnerabilities. Building a picture of every segment of your community, better known as "sectoring," will facilitate rapid response in case of emergency. That means developing a profile of every nook and cranny of the community that is easily understood, easily communicated, and easily shared with others who arrive to help out. Federal tools are available to help build this capacity.

3. Know your citizens, their special needs and concerns. When preparing evacuation and shelter plans, be sure to think about special groups, such as senior citizens,

people with physical limitations, people living alone who may need extra help. People with pets also will want to know what the options are for caring for animals in the event of an emergency. While city leaders can't plan for every contingency and every special need, clear instructions, advice and guidance in advance will help individuals be well prepared and ready to make informed decisions about what to do, where to go, and what to expect in case of emergency.

4. Establish a secure and well-equipped emergency operations center. Even the smallest community needs a central place from which to manage emergency response. That place should be secure, known to all emergency responders, and equipped with the tools needed in case of an emergency. Basics like copies of the emergency plan, mutual aid agreements, telephone numbers of key responders, and fundamental tools like flashlights should be stored in a secure cabinet with specific guidelines for who responds to the center and who opens the cabinet.

5. Leverage local tools and resources to maximize readiness. Take advantage of existing resources — people and places within the community — to enhance response capabil-

Originally published as "Protecting Hometown America: Lessons Learned from and for Small Cities and Towns," *Municipal Advocate*, Vol. 20, No. 3, Fall 2003. Published by the Massachusetts Municipal Association, Boston, MA. Reprinted with permission of the publisher.

ity. Business leaders, civic associations, and neighborhood groups should be included in local planning. Local business facilities can be used to supplement government facilities in your response plan.

6. Invest in employees to broaden local capacity. Encourage your front-line responders to reach out to learn from responders in other communities. That means supporting travel and professional development for police and fire chiefs and emergency personnel — even during tight budget times — to ensure that they are sharing ideas and learning from colleagues in other communities. No one needs to reinvent the wheel.

7. Develop a clear media action plan and be prepared for a potential media onslaught. An emergency in a small community can draw lots of national media, which can be a hindrance to response if local leaders aren't prepared to handle the deluge. Establish clear roles and responsibilities for dealing with the media, including who the primary spokesperson is, how often media briefings will be provided, and primary locations for media briefings and staging.

8. Prepare all the necessary paperwork in advance, including proclamations, signed mutual aid agreements, and boilerplate citizen alerts. Take the time to prepare whatever paperwork is needed in the event of an emergency so that you don't have to be writing it all when an emergency occurs. Store copies of all the signed agreements in the emergency operations center so everything is available on the spot.

9. Plan for continuity of government during and after an emergency. Continuity plans should consider both physical government facilities (what to do if city hall or the emergency operations center are affected by the emergency) and leadership lines of succession.

10. Be creative and aggressive in finding federal resources to support local efforts. While new homeland security funds being distributed through the states are an important resource for local efforts, there are a variety of other sources of federal funding that can help support local efforts. Federal support can come in the form of small grants for special purposes and training programs for police, fire and emergency personnel. Regional collaboration is particularly desirable for most federal grant programs.

11. Practice, practice, practice. Drills, simulations, and conversations about how to implement the emergency response plan are essential in communities of all sizes. Regular drills and reviews will ensure that the plan is both up to date and responders know how to implement it. Regular drills also build confidence and strengthen working relationships.

CHAPTER 16

ENTREPRENEURIAL RESOURCES AND HOMELAND SECURITY

Philip Leggiere

Despite the best of intentions, government contracting, particularly in the areas of defense and security, has traditionally remained a rather insular domain of "old buddy" networks consisting of large, established firms that know how to game the system. Not surprisingly, entrepreneurs, though given lots of accolades by government bureaucrats and politicians, often end up on the outside looking in.

"There's always been a problem in communication between government agencies and small firms," Al Martinez-Fonts told *HSToday*. Martinez-Fonts is the special assistant to the private sector for the Department of Homeland Security (DHS).

"Though we want and desperately need the innovation young and small firms bring, we have to learn to get our perceptions more in sync," he said. "Too often, government managers have looked at their strategic needs from the vantage point of 50,000 feet up. They see the big picture, but they've restricted the view of small entrepreneurs to ground level, where they can't see what the market's needs are and where and how they and their products and services could fit in."

Some CEOs look at DHS's rhetoric with a jaundiced eye.

"We've heard before about closing the procurement gap between the big primary contractors and smaller firms, but I'm still skeptical," said Stephen Forte, CEO of Ascendant Telecommunications, a San Jose, Calif.–based seller of servers integrating mobile voice with wide local area network coverage. "But there's so much inertia in the system and somehow change never really happens."

From its beginnings, DHS has been emphatic about its intention to change this situation and truly open up the bidding, procurement and partnership process in a new way to small businesses. While this promise has generated a lot of excitement in both the public and private sector, change — as often happens — has proven more complex and challenging in practice than theory.

"The rhetoric is definitely encouraging," said Tom Goldman, CEO of Netbotz, an Austin, Texas–based firm that has created an Internet-based security solution integrating sensors to detect atmospheric threats in realtime. "DHS is conveying a positive message. However, when you're dealing with a huge bureaucracy, it's still easy to be lost among the big fish. I know of quite a few very innovative firms who've literally spent

Originally published as "Taking the Leap," *HSToday*, Vol. 1, No. 5, September 2004. Published by KMD Media, LLC, McLean, VA. Reprinted with permission of the publisher.

many months trying to figure out how to get the attention of someone in DC."

Matt Walton, CEO of e-Team, a Los Angeles, Calif., designer of collaboration software for crisis management, concurs. "The first two years after 9/11, it seemed to me and most of the small companies in homeland-security-related software applications as if we were in a bad existentialist play called 'Waiting for da dough,'" he recalled. "End users at the state and local levels had real problems they were waiting to solve, and my own and other companies were anxious to provide solutions. But neither of us had any visibility about where or when any money would materialize and how the process would work."

The DHS View

Homeland-security officials charged with reaching out to the small business community acknowledge that getting small businesses more involved means devising new ways of cutting through red tape.

"We've had to realize that the only way entrepreneurs could become real participants in the product and service development process was to give them tools to help navigate the labyrinth of a big government agency," said Kevin Borshears, director of DHS's Office of Small and Disadvantaged Business Utilization. "We're dealing with a huge gamut of possibilities and the challenge is to make that more user-friendly."

One key way to accomplish this, according to Martinez-Fonts, is through more effective information dissemination about contract and funding opportunities. "By publishing regular BAAs (broad agency announcements), we've tried to give entrepreneurial companies a road map of where we hope to be going in terms of technology development," he explained, "so they get a 30,000-foot overview of the agency and can figure out where they might fit in."

Since May 2003, DHS and the Tech-nology Support Working Group have solicited ideas, concepts and technology for more than 50 requirement areas. In September 2003, the Homeland Security Advanced Research Projects Agency (HSARPA), for instance, issued an announcement soliciting next-generation ideas for biological and chemical detectors and systems. More than 40 technologies were selected for testing and 12 contracts were awarded by spring 2004. In November 2003, HSARPA issued its first call for Small Business Innovation Research proposals, inviting small businesses to submit proposals in a variety of high-priority areas. About one-third of the 318 proposals submitted were selected. A second phase of solicitations was launched in early 2004, with contracts due to be awarded during the summer.

Borshears pointed out that in FY 2003 DHS awarded 40.6 percent of its prime contracts to small businesses, far exceeding the federal standard goal of 23 percent.

Still, some entrepreneurs remain skeptical.

"We're encouraged by the commitment to increasing targets for small-business contracts, but to work in the long run they need to have teeth in enforcing compliance," cautioned Forte. "It's still too easy for a prime contractor and big-system integrator to say, 'We've tried to find small companies to partner with but there weren't any.' But if a Titan, for example, knew they wouldn't get paid unless they complied, you'd bet they'd find more new companies, and there'd be far more innovation."

Chip Hazard, managing partner of IDG Ventures, a Boston, Mass., investment fund, believes the BAAs are a crucial tool for empowering smart entrepreneurial companies. "The best DHS can do for small firms is to help avoid the chaos of having everybody knocking on the same door offering solutions that aren't needed," he said. "From there, it's really up to entrepreneurs to figure out where they fit in."

The DHS office of Small and Disadvantaged Business Utilization has also developed a website, Open For Business.com, designed to link small businesses to information on upcoming contracts, grants, research and events, as well as points of contact inside the government and in the private sector who are looking for new products and services.

In addition to clarifying funding and contracting opportunities, the office's other key initiative, Borshears explained, involves making it easier for small firms to get in the loop by fostering contacts and networking opportunities between large contractors and small firms. They have also begun a program in which prime contractors can act as partnering "mentors" for young companies. "Protégé-Mentor isn't a phrase you've probably ever heard before in a government context," Borshears said, "but we see it as fundamental to really getting small businesses involved."

Indeed, some observers see DHS' role as a cultural catalyst involving private capital in the public arena as potentially more important than its role as a funder.

"We're in the first inning of a nine-inning game," explained Mark Thaller, formerly director of the Patriot Venture Fund of Boston, Mass. "The main thing DHS is already on the road to accomplishing, and I find this highly encouraging, is to create a new kind of forum for bringing together groups no one's ever really brought together before. Never before has a space existed where you'll find start-up firms, inventors, private investors, government managers and military officers in a dialogue. A venture capitalist couldn't bring this kind of brainpower, money and talent together. On its own, corporate America couldn't do it either, nor could traditional government agencies. But DHS is making this happen. Where even three years ago you were lucky if you could find maybe one gathering of this type in a year, now there are literally five to 10 a day across the country, formal and informal, and DHS has been the catalyst. It's in these kinds of get-togethers that the magic occurs and deals get made. The days of the golf course schmooze are over.

"A few years ago," Thaller continued, "there was an assumption that DHS was going to be just another funding spigot, a place companies could go for handouts. That was always a dumb idea. The way to creatively respond to the threats of a new era is not to have another soup kitchen for corporations hungry for government money."

How to Succeed in HS

Succeeding in this new market, according to Chip Hazard, requires developing the right skill set and focus. "Homeland security is not an area for every entrepreneurial firm," he pointed out. "Getting involved in this market requires a dedicated, focused effort on identifying critical problems and an intense hands-on direct-sales effort. A company that views this as just a sideline channel to move existing product is not going to be successful."

Hazard's venture portfolio includes such homeland-security-focused firms as Reveal Imaging of Bedford, Mass., which has developed a new technology designed to analyze not just an object's density but also its chemical makeup using both high- and low-energy X-rays.

Michael Stead, director of homeland security investments at Paladin Capital Group, a Washington, DC, venture fund, agrees. "The intellectual shift a young company looking at the homeland-security sector needs to make," he said, "is to get out of thinking, 'This is my product,' to, 'We know your problem and here's how we can help you solve it.' We're in a cycle now where government agencies want not so much to buy new products as to get problems solved, without having to junk tools they already have. So a service orientation is a must." Paladin's portfolio includes two Atlanta, Ga.–based companies: Nexidia, a developer of tools for data mining audio and video materials, and VistaScape, which develops video-surveillance software for at-risk facilities such as harbors and airports.

The ability to adapt one's technology to varied contexts is also crucial, according to Mark Thaller. "The way smart new companies should begin seeing opportunity is in terms of four legs: Technology, government, private capital and the military. They need to be thinking not single-use or even dual-use anymore, but multiple-use adaptability for their solutions."

Kevin Borshears cited four recurring themes he has continually heard from successful businesses in dealing with government contracts: Take the time to study as much background as possible on the needs of your end users; understand the different opportunities for prime and subcontracting; participate in business networking events in your area; and consider all types of contract avenues.

Sometimes newer firms will find that, rather than going first to Washington, a more grass-roots approach is suitable.

"The strategy that works for us is to scout around on the city and state level to find unmet needs and then cultivate relationships with decision-makers on that level," explained Bryan Ware, CEO of Digital Sandbox, a Reston, Va., company developing software to automate risk-management analysis for government agencies and private enterprises. "Rather than just be one of the countless startups trying to get noticed in the Beltway where the noise level is so high, what a firm with a good niche solution needs to do is find one or two places to show how its solution really works in the field. Nothing will attract further funding like a demonstrated success in a pilot project."

Based on early successes in a Port Authority of New York and New Jersey pilot test of their automated risk-assessment and management tool, Digital Sandbox attracted expanded funding for deployment of their services by the city of Tampa, Fla., and the state of New Jersey, sponsored by DHS' Office of Domestic Preparedness.

The e-Team company has also found success through cultivation of adaptability. "Our approach," said Matt, "is to work actively on the periphery with end users, as well as on the federal level. As a technology company, you naturally want to try to have central sales channels, but with the homeland-security market, you have to be willing to customize your sales and service to individual user needs on the city and state level."

This approach paid off recently when e-Team's crisis management solution was chosen by Michigan State Emergency Management Division (EMD), in cooperation with the Department of Information Technology (DIT), for the first ever state-wide deployment of a common emergency-response information-sharing network. The company's software will be part of a wider state network implemented by San Diego, Calif.–based Science Applications International Corp. (SAIC), the state's prime contractor.

Analysis

There's a dawning realization that mobilizing effectively to meet the challenges of 21st-century threats will require public security and defense institutions to develop new skills, perhaps foremost among them speed, flexibility and innovation. These have not, to say the least, been traditional strong points of either public bureaucracies or large private government contractors, at which the bywords have been massive scale, top-down coordination and incremental change.

To truly foster innovation, national, state and local homeland-security agencies need to find ways to creatively shake up traditional processes to promote and encourage a more entrepreneurial culture and more participation and contributions. This is easier said than done. Bridging the traditional gaps between government bureaucracies and smaller ventures is a challenge for which no ready-made template exists.

While the brief experience of DHS so far demonstrates that achieving a "best of both worlds" synthesis of the two cultures will likely involve a slow and painstaking process of adjustment and learning on both sides, it also demonstrates that progress can be made in overcoming the confusion, miscommunication and misunderstanding that has for decades prevented government from tapping the crucial talent resource represented by the nation's entrepreneurs.

CHAPTER 17

EVACUATION PROCEDURES FOR BUILDINGS

David R. Blossom

"Life affords no higher pleasure than that of surmounting difficulties, passing from one step of success to another, forming new wishes, and seeing them gratified. He that labors in any great or laudable undertaking has his fatigues first supported by hope and afterwards rewarded by joy."— Samuel Johnson

It is indeed difficult at this time to think of words such as "success," "gratification," or "joy" in the aftermath of the tragedy of September 11. If we look at our history, we would see that woven in our very fabric is the thread of overcoming adversity and becoming stronger and better for it. We have been handed just such an opportunity. Those people whose lives were taken from this earth will cry out that we learn and become better through their sacrifice. This we must do and do well.

In the aftermath of the attack on our country, the only way to put the pieces together is to look for the opportunity created by such destruction.

Two glaring facts have stood out as a result of this incident: (1) We have expected too much of our firefighters in asking them to fight fires in buildings that are too tall, and (2) we have woefully underestimated the high-rise evacuation issue.

Nothing in this chapter is intended to presume facts about the events at the World Trade Center (WTC) on September 11. The observations included here are based on known facts and initial reports of those who experienced this tragedy. It is also beyond the scope of this article to explore in detail issues related to training and preparation requirements for high-rise safety. One thing that must be kept in mind is that the collapse of the two towers [or any high-rise], as occurred on September 11, was beyond what our collective minds could comprehend as a possibility, although Chief Donald Anthony of the Los Angeles City (CA) First Department had predicted such a possibility after the First Interstate Bank fire more than 10 years ago. We will never again look at a raging fire in such a building in the same way.

What Is a High-Rise?

Over the past 100 years, we have wrestled with the high-rise issue. We finally settled on the definition of a high-rise contained in National Fire Protection Association Standard 101, *Life Safety Code*®: "a building greater than 75 feet in height." This defini-

Originally published as "High-Rise Safety: Have We Missed the Obvious?" Reprinted from *Fire Engineering*, Vol. 155, No. 1, January 2002. Published by Fire Engineering, Fair Lawn, New Jersey. Reprinted with permission of the publisher.

tion beat out "100 feet" and "highest aerial apparatus available." I have a friend who has his own definition: "any building that is too high to jump from and survive." I have no quarrel with the definition that has been applied. However, I have identified a serious flaw of not carrying the *Life Safety Code®* definition to the next step.

Just how far above 75 feet? has made little difference in our thinking. Yet, I believe we will all agree there is a big difference between 100 feet higher and 1,300 feet higher. How did we not recognize this glaring gap in our approach to high-rise safety? I believe it is because, until September 11, a high-rise collapse was not possible — at least, in our thinking. The result of our not addressing this issue to the fullest is that we have built buildings that cannot be evacuated easily and quickly. We have also demanded that our firefighters fix the problem when it occurs, even if it is 1,000 feet in the air and the only way up is by stairs.

Excessive Evacuation Time

Many studies have been done and formulas have been developed to help us determine a reasonable projection of the time for evacuating a high-rise structure. (I will not explain or defend here any particular method of calculation.) It has been estimated that it would take in excess of two to under four hours — not considering special needs — to evacuate occupants from a 110-story structure. One evacuee of One World Trade Center indicated that it had taken him 50 minutes to egress from the 71st floor. Yet, in the 1993 bombing incident at the WTC, we know that it took up to six hours to evacuate the entire building. We also do not calculate the reduction of egress capacity for the portion of the stairways and exits firefighters are using to enter the building, thus reducing exit capacity.

There is no indication of the time lapse between the start of the incident and the decision to evacuate. It is also difficult to take into consideration the nature of a particular incident. Indeed, it would be difficult for building and life safety codes to address such a massive assault of two structures such as occurred in the WTC on September 11. It is highly likely that the protected means of egress for floors above the impact points were compromised and unavailable to those occupants on the highest floors. There is no possible way to predict or prepare for the alternative evacuation routes needed in such situations.

Our high-rise history has dictated that the building will protect us while we evacuate and mount firefighting activity. It is more important that we address the practicality of evacuation for points below the impact areas, which we assume were intact and available for egress. The sheer height of such a building would, without consideration of the emergency situation, affect the occupants' ability to egress in time to be removed to a safe area outside the building. This raises the question: Can we justify such tall structures from which there is no reasonable expectation that we can evacuate occupants within the time available to maintain structural integrity?

In the case of the WTC towers, some articles reported the fire rating to be two hours. Under "normal" conditions, this may even be increased to three hours or longer. Certainly, this level of protection did not take into consideration such a massive fire load introduced from outside the building, nor should it have. Without any doubt, it is almost impossible to believe that towers of such strength could have succumbed so quickly. I tend to agree with one commentator who stated that we should not be so amazed that the buildings failed so soon but that they stood for so long.

The question of how high we should build will haunt us after this tragedy and no doubt will be factored into the planning of new high-rise buildings.

Occupant Response and Evacuation

In my opinion, there are three essential components to evacuation issues: occupant preparedness, permission to evacuate, and capability. In some parts of the country, people have become quite accustomed to working and living in high-rise buildings. However, the conveniences of elevators have caused them to ignore the stairways. Keeping the fact that the stairways exist in the back of their minds does not make them familiar with the process of using the stairs to evacuate the building.

Stair enclosures often are not air-conditioned, are poorly illuminated, are filled with dust and dirt, are all too often used for storage, and are poorly maintained. The stairway is not an area occupants would normally think about. Nor would they think about using the stairway to practice evacuation from time to time.

Most of us subscribe to the theory that catastrophic events happen to someone else, not us, which adds to the indifference concerning the "system" of egressing from a high-rise. Over the life span of a building, the stairs may be needed only a few times for evacuation purposes.

An often overlooked factor pertaining to evacuation is that while the occupants are using the stairs to evacuate, a stream of diligent warriors will be rushing into the building using the same protected passage occupants are using to escape, making it more difficult to exit. This is an aspect of high-rise design with which we must cope.

Permission to Evacuate

Permission to evacuate is of great concern. Almost from the beginning of the WTC incident, building occupants related their initial response was based on an initial feeling that they were in some danger — that "something" had just happened. They didn't rely on notification from alarms or some other mechanical means. One occupant stated that he felt the impact and then decided to go to another floor, where his wife worked. They met and decided to return to their offices. He later reported that he had made it out but did not know where his wife was.

Another occupant said he was aware that something was wrong and went around checking windows before finally going to his superior to ask if they should evacuate because something may be wrong. It was further reported that, after the first attack, one supervisor asked his employees in the unaffected tower to return to their workstations, obviously unaware of the danger that would befall them in less than 20 minutes.

One Fire Department of New York chief reported finding 50 employees huddled near the 70th floor just before the second collapse and ordered them to get out just a few minutes before the second collapse. Clearly, we have not done enough to educate high-rise occupants so that they can make the right decision, or we have taught them too well to rely on the building fire alarm sound and/or automatic directions from the fire alarm voice communication system.

In this situation, the occupants did not appear to be able to or want to make a decision to evacuate the building. People often look for leadership in emergencies.

Have we considered the importance of panic? Yes, panic! It would be difficult for anyone to believe that such tall and strong structures could ever collapse; it seems reasonable to believe that we would be safe as long as we are away from the fire area. The standard operating procedure has been to evacuate the fire floor, the floors above, and two floors below. The question remains, Why have we not given permission to high-rise occupants (or occupants of any other buildings for that matter) to seek safety in the face of possible danger?

Neil Townsend, divisional officer, London Fire Brigade, puts it this way: "I think that when people die in fires, it's not because of panic — it's more likely to be the lack of panic."

I know that this statement flies in the face of what we have told ourselves.

Professor David Canter, of Liverpool University, may have put it in a more acceptable way: "You must think about people's reactions to a fire in terms of the three basic stages of making sense of what's going on, preparing to act, and then acting." There seems to be some breakdown in these areas.

The capability to effectively exit a high-rise depends on many factors: physical capability is only one of the important considerations. Capability hinges greatly on the two issues: Have the occupants made an attempt to become familiar with the protected means of egress from the building? If so, do they understand what to do if they feel a need to use that means of egress? Are they capable of making the right decisions and acting on those decisions when faced with such threats?

Capability also relies on the ability to understand what is going on around you. Initially, many of the occupants in this situation had very little information to process to make the decisions they needed to make. This situation changed as they received calls from the outside with new information.

Types of Evacuation

The most common theories on egress have held that high-rise situations call for two basic types of evacuation: self-evacuation of the total building and controlled selective evacuation.

Self-evacuation, which takes on a life of its own, is essentially a haphazard process. It is based entirely on the decisions and actions carried out by large segments of building occupants. Controlled selective evacuation requires that the building's management have

input in decision-making process and execution of the actions needed to evacuate and that those responsible for evacuating occupants are adequately trained to make the right decisions and provide the leadership to achieve a successful outcome. A controlled selective evacuation should also be coordinated with the local fire department.

Elements in Perceiving an Emergency

Essentially six elements are involved in the perception of a fire incident or other emergency: recognition, validation, definition, evaluation, commitment, and reassessment.

- Recognition occurs when the individual perceives that there is a threat. This perception is achieved through multiple inputs, including visual and audible alarms, the smell of smoke, and a loud noise.
- The above signs lead to validation of the input and raise questions such as the following: What is the source of the sign I recognized? Is the input validated according to my perception?
- The process of definition is more complicated. This is the point at which the individual begins to relate to the validated recognition and moves into action. This is also the point at which anxiety can surface, dependent on the ability to process the information. There is a very narrow timeframe between this stage and the point at which the individual makes an evaluation.
- During the evaluation phase, cognitive and psychological activities motivate the individual to respond to the threat. This is the point at which the initial decision pertaining to course of action is made. If the right decisions have been made, taking planned action can quell anxiety.
- During the commitment stage, the individual decides the course of action based on the initial input. Individuals will com-

plete, partially complete, or abandon their strategy. If they could not make the right decisions, they will return to the initial stages of their reaction and begin the process all over again until they are successful or fail completely.

• Anxiety and defeat can become overpowering in the reassessment stage. If the initial attempts fail, the individuals will become more frustrated, and anxiety will build. To achieve the desired results, the individual must process the relevant information correctly and take the right action. Individuals meeting with success will continue with their plans.

Some considerations here include the following: Have we done all that we can to educate the general public and occupants of high-rise buildings? Do occupants know what to expect in an emergency? Have we given them permission to act in their best interest and the interests of their fellow occupants by moving to a safe area? Have we provided the training that will help them to make the right choices and act accordingly? Have we failed to recognize that the height of the buildings we construct should be limited to a height below that which the great engineering minds can design to stand?

These questions will become more important as we consider the tragic events in New York City and evaluate the potential for occupants in similar situations to respond properly. While we pray that we never again will have to face another such horrific incident that will afford us only one chance to respond correctly, it would be a dishonor to those who perished if we do not take the lessons learned and develop answers that will help others in the future.

Evacuation Training and Firefighting Operations

The *Life Safety Code®* and Department of Labor [Occupational Safety and Health Administration (OSHA)] regulations dictate minimum requirements for occupant training and drills for the workplace. The major difference between the two is that the *Life Safety Code®* is concerned with building occupants, whereas OSHA requirements are directed toward the desired actions employers should take to protect their employees' safety. The main concerns outlined in the OSHA requirements are directed toward the nature of the hazard, recognition of hazards, controls or protective measures, engineering controls, administrative controls, and personal protection controls.

Both the *Life Safety Code®* and OSHA requirements are driven by the concept of the owner/management as the source of responsibility for compliance. Enforcement of these requirements often is sporadic and varies greatly from region to region. High-rise management typically is not aware of what it is required to do and often will resist when "forced" to do something through enforcement procedures alone. Management is much more receptive when it is educated about the requirements and how to comply. Because of this lack of understanding, it is not uncommon for high-rise occupants to be left on their own to respond when an emergency occurs.

Another area in which we have seen little change is firefighting operations. We have demanded that fire department personnel carry tremendous loads of equipment up an excessive number of flights of stairs and then expect them to be capable of initiating firefighting activity — higher and higher into the sky without appreciating the physical demands of just arriving at the fire floor, let alone being able to initiate the strenuous physical activity of rescue, fire attack, extinguishment, and overhaul.

Previous attempts to develop methods of exterior access on upper floors of high-rise buildings have not been practical or successful. Platforms suspended from helicopters have had limited ability to carry personnel and equipment. Landing firefighters on building roofs has also been largely impractical, as this places lives above the fire floor in the direction in which the fire is traveling. There has been some limited success with this approach; however, for large-scale operations, this usually is not an option.

Where does that leave us? Do we stick with what we have, or do we look for other solutions?

Occupant Training Requirements

One of the challenges we encounter when attempting to decide the training and drill requirements applicable to high-rise occupancies involves making a determination as to the type of occupancy with which we are dealing. On the surface, a high-rise such as the WTC would appear to be nothing more than a high-rise business occupancy, defined in the *Life Safety Code®* as "an occupancy used for account and record keeping or the transaction of business other than mercantile." One of the examples given is "General Offices." This seems to fit our needs fairly well. However, on reviewing the requirements in the "Operating Features Section for Business Occupancies," we discover that the only distinction for these requirements is that there be an employee population of either 500 total or more than 100 persons above or below the street level. There, again, is no distinction between one level or 100 levels above street level and anything in between.

We then must determine our occupant load for the building in question. If we use the square footage in Table 7.3.1.2 of the *Life Safety Code®*, we would divide our building area by 100. Thus for one level of the WTC, we would determine the occupancy to be 300 per floor, with some consideration for areas such as elevators, storage, service, and so on. This would result in a total occupant load of approximately 33,000 per tower building.

This may be too few based on some reports of the actual building population. In this situation, we may be expecting far fewer occupants than there really are.

A review of the "Operating Features" section for New and Existing Business Occupancies reveals that occupants must be trained in accordance with Section 4.7 Fire Drills. The training requirements include knowledge of the following:

- the purpose of emergency egress and relocation drills,
- the building's fire safety features,
- the egress facilities available, and
- evacuation procedures.

In addition, occupants must be given the opportunity for instruction, and practice drills should be provided.

There is also a requirement for employee training in the use of the fire extinguisher, although this is not supported in many areas where the fire department preference is for evacuation only.

Clearly, specific training objectives must be achieved. It should be noted that there are no additional requirements based on the business being located in a high-rise.

Requirement under the Department of Labor are found in OSHA 29 CFR 1910.38, *Employee Emergency Plans and Fire Prevention Plans*. OSHA offers guidelines to assist employers with identifying training needs. Section 1910.1200 outlines some basics of worker fire- and life-safety practices. OSHA offers in section 1910.157 the following choices concerning employees and portable fire extinguisher training:

- Option 1: Total evacuation of all employees once an alarm has sounded. The employer in selecting this option must establish an emergency action plan and fire prevention plan.
- Option 2: Designated employees who have been trained to use portable fire extinguishers may use them to fight fires. Employees not selected and trained to do so must evacuate the area immediately once

an alarm has sounded. The employer must create the prevention and emergency plan and comply with requirements for the inspection, testing, and maintenance of the fire extinguishers in addition to providing the training and education.

• Option 3: Applies the above requirements to all employees of the business.

It should be noted that the training must include the elements of hands-on practice under simulated emergency conditions. At a minimum, the fire extinguisher training must include the discharging of fire extinguishers.

In many areas of the country, the fire service disapproves of Options 2 and 3. The preference is for employees to evacuate the building, leaving any and all firefighting activity to trained firefighters. On the surface, this approach appears to be the most rational solution. It contains the element of having the building partially or completely evacuated by the time the fire department arrives. However, there are some situations that must be considered. First, in many situations, it would be far better to have an occupant of the building take action with an extinguisher during the incipient stage of a fire. This may extinguish the fire, thus reducing damage and threat to life. At least, the fire would be held in check until trained firefighters could take over.

The selection of Option 2 creates a situation where only selected employees are trained to use extinguishers and authorized to fight a fire. Although this option provides for both the evacuation of the majority of employees and some level of incipient fire attack, there is always the potential that an untrained occupant may be the first to confront or be trapped by a fire and may lack the skills to take appropriate action. Certainly, many factors must be taken into consideration before determining which option to select. The choice should be made after examining the hazards of the workplace involved, the response and capability of the local fire department, and the capability of the employees/occupants. Note that the employer must select one of the options. Failing to do so often will result in a citation and fines from OSHA for failing to meet its minimum requirements. OSHA has taken these actions many times and has even imprisoned employers who failed to train their employees and develop fire safety and evacuation procedures.

Although some in the fire service may oppose these requirements, the employer has no option under federal law. Both the *Life Safety Code*® and OSHA requirements are driven by the owner/management as the source of responsibility for compliance. Some areas have additional requirements, such as New York City Law 5 for high-rise buildings. However, in many areas there is a lack of understanding of these requirements. High-rise occupants are left on their own to respond when an emergency occurs.

Building Occupancy Considerations

For this discussion, I have avoided the obvious question of occupancy classification. The majority of high-rise buildings may encompass multiple occupancy concerns including those of assembly, mercantile, and residential/lodging issues.

In the weeks following the events of September 11, I encountered two very different attitudes related to high-rise safety. Owners and managers of high-rise buildings in places like New York and other major cities have had increased concerns about high-rise safety and evacuation training. In many other parts of the country, however, little has changed. By contrast, terrorism, a far less likely potential in most metropolitan areas, is receiving far more attention than necessary. High-rise occupants are more likely to encounter fires and other "nonterrorist" events that would present safety concerns.

Mail handling is being given excessive

attention in many situations. Many more deaths will be caused by fire, and even the flu this year, than will be caused by contracting anthrax through the mail system. Yet, there is greater concern in the anthrax area, and the business sector is capitalizing on this.

Add the notion that "it couldn't happen here" to the general lack of understanding the requirements for evacuation training, and it becomes clear that these issues will not be properly addressed on their own. The fact remains that the majority of occupants in high-rise buildings may not have received any training in fire safety and evacuation or may have chosen not to participate when training was given, despite the fact that such training has been a requirement for more than 30 years. From the perspective of the occupants, there is great concern for personal safety. They want to be trained on what to do in an emergency. There is also greater apprehension about working in high-rise buildings.

The main reason for the lack of training is that the "Operating Features" section(s) of the *Life Safety Code®* is not being enforced in many areas. High-rise building owners and management are not being required to comply by providing this training. The legal issues and fines for not doing so bring some accountability for not meeting these requirements, but the fact remains that these actions are taken after lives have been lost.

The Proposed Solution

In the majority of fire departments across our nation, there are insufficient personnel and resources to provide training assistance to meet these requirements. The only viable solution is private sector resources that can assist in the training. In addition to the basic requirements in the occupancy-specific chapters of the *Life Safety Code®*, there is the need to use performance-based options. One such tool well suited for addressing life safety concerns is the "Life Safety Evaluation." A detailed review of this process would require an entire article, but the existence of this evaluation method should be recognized here. The Life Safety Evaluation is intended mainly for assembly occupancies; however, it can be applied to any situation. The code also permits the evaluation to be performed by persons "acceptable to the Authority Having Jurisdiction," minimizing the potential additional demand on public fire and life safety services.

The only way that the required evaluation and training will be completed is through enforcement of these requirements. In some jurisdictions, enforcement has not been pursued because of a lack of resources. It is interesting that these requirements are set aside or simply ignored because of a lack of resources to implement them when this is not the case for other "building"-related requirements.

Management-related issues are of equal or greater concern. Building owners and managers must be held accountable for meeting the safety training requirements for assembly, business, residential, correctional, mercantile, industrial, and health-care occupancies.

Firefighting Demands

Finally, there is the issue of fire personnel waging battle against high-rise fires. No examination of these issues would be complete without addressing the fact that all our prevention and training will not ensure that fires and other emergencies will not occur. As noted, our tradition has been to load individual firefighters with hoses, air packs, hand tools, and other equipment; send them up 20, 30, 50, or 100 flights of stairs; and then have them initiate fire attack and assist with evacuation. It is almost unimaginable that we would expect firefighters to traverse such a great height, let alone with lots of equipment.

If we are to continue to occupy and have fires in "mega high-rises," then we must rethink our expectations pertaining to firefighting personnel and how they access these buildings. Clearly, it is impractical to expect firefighters to carry such heavy loads of equipment. But beyond this, at what height is it impractical to expect firefighters to take themselves higher and higher by stairs alone?

We must examine better methods for getting firefighters to the upper floors more quickly and safely. We should expect building owners to provide for the storage of firefighting tools and equipment on upper floors of high-rise buildings — equipment storage and maintenance under the control of the fire department with the cost defrayed by the high-rise building owner. In some places in California, upper floors of high-rise buildings have been equipped with air bottle filling stations. This is a start, but more must be done. The only practical approach is to ensure that firefighters can access upper floors and be properly equipped in the process without undue demands. Elevators have been off limits during building fires. Is there a solution in bringing back the "dumbwaiter" and having an equipment-only lift in high-rise buildings? Or would it be more practical to construct hardened elevator shafts and equipment that could be used reliably in emergency situations?

Perhaps this chapter has raised more issues than it has solved, but the hope is that you at least have been challenged to rethink high-rise safety. We must reexamine our definition of high-rise. We must look at additional requirements for "mega high-rise" buildings. Collectively, through our code-making process, we can develop changes that will improve high-rise safety. Until then, we must ensure that existing requirements are properly enforced. I am reminded here of one definition of insanity: "doing the same things over and over again, but expecting different results." Let's do things differently, and better. Through better enforcement, education, preparation, and response, we can expect to achieve the goal of greater safety for high-rise building occupants and those sent to fight fires in them.

Notes

1. *The SFPE Handbook of Fire Protection Engineering.* 1995. National Fire Protection Association and Society of Fire Protection Engineers. Philip J. DiNenno, Craig L. Beyler, Richard L.P. Custer, et al., eds.

2. *Blaze: The Forensics of Fire.* Nicholas Faith. (Channel 4 Books: London, 1999).

3. *High Rise Fire & Life Safety.* John T. O'Hagen. (Fire Engineering, 1977).

4. *Building Construction for the Fire Service.* Francis L. Brannigan, SFPE (Fellow), National Fire Protection Association, 1971.

5. *Introduction to Employee Fire & Life Safety.* Gyr R. Colonna, PE, ed. National Fire Protection Association, 2001.

CHAPTER 18

FAMILY PLANNING RECOMMENDATIONS BY THE DEPARTMENT OF HOMELAND SECURITY

Thomas Ridge

Preparing Makes Sense

The likelihood that you and your family will survive a house fire depends as much on having a working smoke detector and an exit strategy, as on a well-trained fire department. The same is true for surviving a terrorist attack. We must have the tools and plans in place to make it on our own, at least for a period of time, no matter where we are when disaster strikes. Just like having a working smoke detector, preparing for the unexpected makes sense. Get ready now.

The Department of Homeland Security, in partnership with the U.S. Postal Service, The Salvation Army, and the U.S. Citizen Corps, recommends that four components be contained in a family's emergency preparedness plan. The four sections of a typical family plan are highlighted below.

Section One: Make an Emergency Supply Kit

Be prepared to improvise and use what you have on hand to make it on your own for at least three days, or longer.

While there are many things that might make you more comfortable, think first about fresh water, food, and clean air.

Consider putting together two kits. In one, put everything needed to stay where you are and make it on your own.

The other should be a lightweight, smaller version that you can take with you if you have to get away.

You'll need a gallon of **water** per person per day. Include in the kits canned and dried **foods** that are easy to store and prepare. If you live in a cold weather climate, include **warm clothes** and a sleeping bag for each member of the family.

Start now by gathering basic **emergency supplies** and setting them aside — a flashlight, a battery-powered radio, extra batter-

Originally published as "Preparing Makes Sense. Get Ready Now," *Brochure*, Department of Homeland Security, Washington, D.C., undated.

ies, a first-aid kit, toilet articles and other special things your family may need.

Many potential terrorist attacks could send tiny microscopic "junk" into the air. Many of these materials can only hurt you if they get into your body, so think about creating a barrier between yourself and any contamination. It's smart to have something for each member of the family that **covers their mouth and nose.**

Plan to use two to three layers of a cotton t-shirt, handkerchief or towel. Or, consider **filter masks,** readily available in hardware stores, which are rated based on how small a particle they filter. It is very important that the mask or other material fit your face snugly so that most of the air you breathe comes through the mask, not around it. Do whatever you can to make the best fit possible for children.

Also, include **duct tape and heavy-weight garbage bags or plastic sheeting** that can be used to seal windows and doors if you need to create a barrier between yourself and any potential contamination outside.

Section Two: Make a Family Communications Plan

Plan in advance what you will do in an emergency.

Be prepared to assess the situation. Use common sense and whatever you have on hand to take care of yourself and your loved ones.

Depending on your circumstances and the nature of the attack, the first important decision is whether you stay put or to get away.

You should understand and plan for both possibilities.

Develop a Family Communications Plan: Your family may not be together when disaster strikes, so **plan how you will contact one another and review what you will do in different situations.** Consider a plan where each family member calls, or e-mails, the same friend or relative in the event of an emergency. It may be easier to make a long-distance phone call than to call across town, so an out-of-state contact may be in a better position to communicate among separated family members. You may have trouble getting through, or the phone system may be down altogether, but be patient.

Create a Plan to "Shelter-in-Place": There are circumstances when staying put and creating a barrier between yourself and potentially contaminated air outside, a process known as "shelter-in-place," can be a matter of survival. **Choose an interior room or one with as few windows and doors as possible. Consider precutting plastic sheeting to seal windows, doors and air vents.** Each piece should be several inches larger than the space you want to cover so that you can duct tape it flat against the wall. Label each piece with the location of where it fits.

If you see large amounts of debris in the air, or if local authorities say the air is badly contaminated, you may want to "shelter-in-place." Quickly bring your family and pets inside, lock doors, and close windows, air vents and fireplace dampers. Immediately turn off air conditioning, forced air heating systems, exhaust fans and clothes dryers. Take your emergency supplies and go into the room you have designated. Seal all windows, doors and vents. Watch TV, listen to radio or check the internet for instructions.

Create a Plan to Get Away: Plan in advance how you will assemble your family and anticipate where you will go. **Choose several destinations in different directions so you have options in an emergency.** If you have a car, keep a half tank of gas in it at all times. **Become familiar with alternate routes as well as other means of transportation out of your area.** If you do not have a car, plan how you will leave if you have to. **Take your emergency supply kit** and lock the door behind you. If you believe the air may be contaminated, drive with your windows and vents closed and keep the air conditioning and heater turned off. Listen to the radio for instructions.

Plans at School and Work: Think about the places where your family spends time: school, work and other places your family frequents. **Talk to your children's schools and your employer about emergency plans.** Find out how they will communicate with families during an emergency. If you are an employer, be sure you have an emergency preparedness plan. Review and practice it with your employees. A community working together during an emergency also makes sense. **Talk to your neighbors about how you can work together.**

Section Three: Be Informed

Some of the things you can do to prepare for the unexpected, such as assembling a supply kit and developing a family communications plan, are the same for both a natural or man-made emergency. However there are important differences among potential terrorist threats, such as biological, chemical, explosive, nuclear and radiological, that will impact the decisions you make and the actions you take.

The Department of Homeland Security recommends that citizens call their toll free telephone number (1-800-237-3239) for a free brochure on these different types of responses, or go on-line (http://www.ready.gov)

to learn about possible potential terrorist threats in your particular geographic area.

Section Four: Remain Calm

Be prepared to adapt this information to your personal circumstances and make every effort to follow instructions received from authorities on the scene. Above all, stay calm, be patient and think before you act. With these simple preparations, you can be ready for the unexpected. If you have a working smoke detector, you understand that preparing makes sense.

Get ready now!

Conclusion

This common sense framework is designed to launch a process of learning about citizen preparedness. The Department of Homeland Security, as well as the U.S. Postal Service, The Salvation Army, and the U.S. Citizen Corps, ask that citizens seeking additional information about family planning, or potential terrorist threats call the Department of Homeland Security's toll-free telephone number or visit their website.

Citizens are also encouraged to contact the U.S. Citizen Corps to find out about how to help prepare their community against a possible terrorist attack. The website for the U.S. Citizens Corps is available on-line 24-hours a day (http://www.citizenscorps.gov).

CHAPTER 19

FATALITIES MANAGEMENT AND HOMELAND SECURITY

Chris DeChant

Most fire departments never will experience firefighter fatalities on the same scale that FDNY did following the terrorist attack on the World Trade Center. Nonetheless, death is an inherent risk surrounding any local, state or federal public safety organization.

The U.S. armed forces are well aware of this reality and have a long history of providing line-of-duty death benefits ranging from legal advice to life insurance benefits for surviving family members. In contrast, many fire departments throughout the United States currently don't have any management system for firefighter deaths and won't be prepared when one occurs.

Line-of-Duty Death Facts

Firefighters risk their lives to protect the public. It isn't a question of whether a firefighter may be killed in the line of duty, the question is how many and when. Of course, fire departments are often caught off-guard by the death of one of their own and may be ill-prepared to deal with the emotional issues surrounding such a personal trauma. Although a fire agency should help handle the

difficulties encountered by the survivors, this task can become overwhelming when performed alongside an investigation and other necessary tragedy-prompted tasks.

A line-of-duty death (LODD) involves many different aspects of urgent responsibility. In addition to an investigation, the most important task becomes handling the needs of a grief-stricken family. The potential to neglect a family's needs would be the greatest injustice that a fire department could perpetrate. The family will remember not only the devastating tragedy of the death, but also all of the events, both positive and negative, following the catastrophe.

How prepared is your fire department to handle an LODD? In 1999 I completed a study involving 18 Arizona fire departments with memberships of 17 to 1,103 firefighters each. They served populations from 3,800 to 405,000 and responded to between 2,300 and 71,000 calls per year. The study also included five departments from throughout the country that had experienced an LODD. These ranged from 28 to 1,200 sworn personnel who served populations from 4,500 to 1.2 million and responded to between 60 and 120,000 calls per year. Both populations included fire chiefs and firefighters, and the

Originally published as "Protocol for the Fallen," *Fire Chief,* Vol. 45, No. 12, December 2001. Published by Primedia Business Magazines & Media, Inc., Overland Park, Kansas. Reprinted with permission of the publisher.

LODD department studies also included surviving family members.

Comparative methodology was used to evaluate fire department LODD preparedness from the perspectives of those who had been or may be affected by an LODD. The results found that 61% of Arizona fire departments and 50% of those that had experienced a firefighter death did not have any line-of-duty death policy or procedure implemented. Clearly, more departments need to prepare for the devastating possibility of such an event.

Strategic Plan Development

A strategic plan should be in place when addressing an LODD. A fire department can become overwhelmed by the immediate needs surrounding the crisis and lose track of all objectives that need to be accomplished. If this happens, the operational needs may prevent a strategic and organizational approach from being developed.

The management of an LODD should be conducted with the same thoroughness and professionalism with which the department combats fire. A death requires myriad tasks and objectives which may take days, weeks or months to accomplish, necessitating that they're approached in a systematic manner, much like a complicated campaign fire.

For this reason, a fire department should implement a command system to allow increased span of control. An effective system is designed to provide a thorough systematic approach that is easy to recognize and follow. For example, The Phoenix Regional Standard Operating Procedure 201.01 states:

"Command procedures are designed to: Fix the responsibility for command on a certain individual through a standard identification system... Ensure that a strong command will be established from the onset of the incident... Establish an effective incident organization defining the incident commander's responsibilities... Provide a system to process information to support incident management, planning, and decision making."

The fireground command system can be applied in the same manner with line-of-duty deaths to ensure that operations do not fail in the areas of:

- Action,
- Planning,
- Command and control,
- Coordination,
- Organization,
- Safety, and
- Communications.

The fireground command system can be applied best for conducting an LODD event through the development and use of standard operating procedures and written representations of a department's philosophy or strategy.

The Fallen FF ICS

A fire department can apply the command model as a way to develop and revamp their procedures as needed. The model explains the necessary functions and applications of a standard operating procedure. It can be divided into five main areas:

- Establishment of a standard procedure,
- Training,
- Application,
- Review and critique, and
- Revision.

If a fire department implements this model, it will give them a structured plan that can be applied, reviewed and revised as necessary.

Fire departments should construct and implement an LODD standard operating procedure and then use the model to further develop, evaluate and revise the procedure as necessary. An infrastructure also must be developed for coordination of all necessary tasks. Departments can use the LODD action plan — Logistic, Empathy, and Nurturing for Fire Department Families (fallen FF) — as an infrastructure to organize their department in such a way.

CISM and advocacy. CISM surrounding an LODD may be neither quick nor easy for a department to deal with. Continued support for firefighters and families may last as long as a year or longer. Although CISM is a structured mechanism for the department to assist the firefighters and family, it can begin at a more basic level through the use of advocacy, which can provide an adjunct to family and friends unwilling or unable to participate with CISM.

Investigation. An investigation of an LODD is a painful but necessary function that must be conducted to ensure that the same situation doesn't happen in the future. The investigation involves many different objectives, requiring the branch to be multifaceted and adaptive as the situation requires.

Funeral. The funeral branch can be the most important branch concerning the family, fire personnel and the public, because it affords a time and place to remember the victim and face the loss. This branch must be in place prior to an incident to provide an honorable service for the victim.

Notification. This branch will attempt to make contact with the family in a caring manner while also being honest and direct. Several main principles must be followed: notification in person, in time and with certainty; in pairs; in plain language; and with compassion.

Public information. LODDS generate widespread media coverage locally as well as nationally. Proper relationships with the media should help to prevent negative results that can occur when the media is inaccurately briefed or not briefed at all. This branch should be initiated at multiple stages, including: at the scene, the hospital, the funeral, the family's home and for an after-action report.

Hospital. This branch will coordinate with hospital officials for the allocation of waiting areas for family, co-workers, and the media. Another function is securing a firefighter as a hospital liaison between the medical staff and the family.

Financial. An individual should be designated to handle monetary donations to the family and ensure proper accountability for the funds.

Family liaison. This branch will provide general support for the family, including screening calls and visits, providing transportation, and assisting in coordination with other branches and their functions.

It's recommended that this system and infrastructure use a cooperative effort of labor and management to accomplish the intended goals. The importance of labor-management cooperation is an integral part of the success of this system. The cooperative effort will pair an IAFF union member with each chief officer assigned as branch commander. This design will facilitate accomplishment of tasks and avoid duplication of effort, while also providing a secondary plan to ensure that at least one qualified person will be present to manage each branch. The IAFF is an invaluable source of LODD investigation protocol.

An integral aspect of fire department preparation and initial stage of implementation is the completion of an emergency notification information data sheet by each employee. A sample can be found in the National Fallen Firefighters Foundation Remembering Our Own instruction manual. The foundation can be contacted via e-mail at <firehero@erols.com>.

Coordinating the Response

After implementing a standard operating procedure and the fallen FF command system, a department must gather the necessary resources to conduct all tasks involved with a LODD. They include:

■ **Local resources, such as**

- Mortuaries and cemeteries,
- Police,
- Local benefits,
- Medical examiner and
- Media.
- **State resources, such as**
  - State benefits and
  - The department of transportation.
- **National resources, such as**
  - The National Fallen Firefighters Foundation
  - The FBI and ATF,
  - The National Transportation Safety Board,
  - Federal benefits,
  - Public Safety Officers Benefits Program,
  - National Institute for Occupational Safety and Health,
  - U.S. Fire Administration,
  - National Fire Protection Agency,
  - Equipment manufacturers, and
  - the IAFF and ICHIEFS.

The fire department also must have a designated system to activate the fallen FF command system once an event occurs. The suggested method would be through the dispatch agency with a text-messaging pager system that could alert all infrastructure members at any time. If a department were to use such a system, the on-duty commander could alert the dispatch center after a line-of-duty event occurs, resulting in activation of the infrastructure and assembly of the fallen FF branch officers.

After activation, the incident commander of the fallen FF system would receive all necessary information and reports to ensure that all tasks were being completed in a timely manner. The incident commander would then be able to acknowledge completed tasks through the use of tactical worksheets.

The incident commander should be the operations chief of the fire department to facilitate operation of the system unless this same chief was the incident commander of the event involving the death. Although the recommendations are for branch officers to be fire department chief officers, the fallen FF should be utilized using any rank of fire department member. This incident command structure is similar to any other command structure and can be expanded or reduced as necessary for the department or event.

Other Aspects

A fire department member also must become familiar with the benefits surrounding local, state and federal governments to assist the family during their time of need. The fire department member assigned this task will assist with benefit coordination under the financial branch officer. This function will be a great asset to ensure that all awarded benefits are distributed to the family not only during the time surrounding the event, but in the future as well. The support will allow the family to concentrate on grieving rather than on financial concerns.

A fire department also should be prepared to provide funeral services for their members. The most effective way to accomplish this goal is through the development of a fire department honor guard. The events surrounding a LODD will not be forgotten by those that it affects, and some events may be developed into traditions and memorials to those that have passed. If a fire department is unsure of how to develop and maintain an honor guard, the National Fallen Firefighters Foundation in Emmitsburg can provide information.

I cannot emphasize enough the importance of developing and instituting a LODD standard operating procedure. Due to fire service culture, fire department members have blind faith in their leaders when unsure of their department's preparedness. The fallen FF ICS should be the beginning of fire department preparedness that must continue to evolve and progress for successful internal customer service.

Although this system provides a "hard" customer service format for fire departments to follow, the "soft" aspect of this system will become the difficult process to implement. Affected families only will be concerned with the end product, not the labor by which it was achieved. It's recommended that fire chiefs and their organizations become better prepared for LODD to ensure that they don't fail their department family members when it counts the most.

CHAPTER 20

FEDERAL EMERGENCY MANAGEMENT AGENCY'S ROLE IN TERRORISM PREPAREDNESS AND RESPONSE

Joe M. Allbaugh

FEMA's Mission

To reduce loss of life and property and protect our institutions from all hazards by leading and supporting the Nation in a comprehensive, risk-based emergency management program of mitigation, preparedness, response, and recovery.

FEMA's Terrorism Mission

FEMA supports local, State, and Federal governments in preparing for and responding to terrorism using unique consequence management authorities, responsibilities, and capabilities.

FEMA's Role in Terrorism Preparedness and Response

PRESIDENTIAL DECISION DIRECTIVE (PDD)-39 AND PDD-62: U.S. POLICY ON COUNTER-TERRORISM

These two PDDs state that the United States will have the ability to respond rapidly and decisively to terrorism and are the basis for FEMA's domestic preparedness and response activities for consequence management in response to terrorist incidents involving Weapons of Mass Destruction (WMD).

FEDERAL RESPONSE PLAN (FRP)

The FRP establishes a process and structure for the systematic, coordinated, and effective delivery of Federal assistance to address the consequences of any major disaster or emergency declared under the Robert T. Stafford Disaster Relief and Emergency Assistance Act.

TERRORISM INCIDENT ANNEX

The FRP Terrorism Incident Annex, created in 1999, defines the structures to coordinate crisis management with consequence management. The Annex:
- Supplements the FRP with special considerations for terrorism response.
- Supports PDDs to establish policy to respond to terrorism.

Originally published as "Terrorism Preparedness and Response," *Brochure L255*, Federal Emergency Management Agency, Washington, D.C., March 2001.

- Describes linkages between crisis management and consequence management activities before, during, and after an event.
- Describes responsibilities of Federal agencies to provide support for technical response operations.

STATE AND LOCAL GUIDE (SLG)—101

Chapter 6, Hazard — Unique Planning Considerations, Attachment G — Terrorism, was developed to aid State and local emergency managers in development and maintaining a consequence management plan for preparing for and responding to a terrorist incident.

FEMA Sponsored Training

EMERGENCY MANAGEMENT INSTITUTE

FEMA provides training at the Emergency Management Institute for State and local emergency management officials. Some of the terrorism related training includes:

- Emergency Response to Criminal and Terrorist Incidents.
- Integrated Emergency Management Course — Consequences of Terrorism.
- Mass Facilities Incident Course.
- Senior Officials Workshop.

NATIONAL FIRE ACADEMY

FEMA also provides on-site and off-site training via the National Fire Academy for first responders. Training includes:

- Tactical Considerations — Company Officer/Emergency Medical Services/Hazardous Materials.
- Strategic Considerations for Command Officers.
- Emergency Response to Terrorism: Basic Concepts/Incident Management.
- Emergency Response to Terrorism: Self Study.

Rapid Response Information System (RRIS)

The RRIS is a Federal interagency program established and maintained by FEMA. The RRIS provides immediate access to information for response to a WMD terrorism incident. Information available on the RRIS includes:

- Federal capabilities that could be made available to State and local communities in response to an incident involving WMD.
- Information on selected WMD equipment and General Service Administration (GSA) excess/surplus property.
- Database on chemical and biological warfare agents with information characteristics and safety precautions.
- Database of radiological materials with information on physical characteristics and safety precautions.
- A listing of reference documents available on the Internet.
- A listing of Federal WMD training courses.

FEMA Grants to State and Local Entities

Funding is provided to State and local entities through the Terrorism Consequence Management Preparedness Assistance (TCMPA) Program via the Emergency Management Performance Grant (EMPG) Program. Funding may be used to enhance terrorism preparedness through planning, training, and exercises.

Federal Assistant and Resources

WHAT FEDERAL ASSISTANCE CAN BE PROVIDED?

- Immediate response for lifesaving and life-protecting needs.

- Planning, training, and exercises.
- Support of disaster operations.
- Restoration, repair, or replacement of public services and facilities.
- Mitigate or lessen the effects of a disaster in the future.

WHAT FEDERAL RESOURCES CAN BE PROVIDED?

- Emergency Response Teams.
- Emergency Support Teams.

- Specialized teams for:
  * Rapid assessment
  * Agent detection
  * Decontamination
  * Emergency communications
  * Medical assistance and support
  * Urban search and rescue activities
  * Emergency power restoration
  * Incident management
  * Community management

FIGURE 1
Key Definitions and Terms

Terrorism

The unlawful use of force or violence against persons or property to intimidate or coerce a government, the civilian population, or any segment thereof, in furtherance of political or social objectives.

Weapons of Mass Destruction (WMD)

Any weapon or device that is intended, or has the capability, to cause death or serious bodily injury to a significant number of people through the release, dissemination, or impact of toxic poisonous chemicals or their precursors; a disease organism, or radiation or radioactivity.

Crisis Management

The law enforcement phase of the incident that involves measures to identify, acquire, and plan the resources needed to anticipate, prevent, and/or resolve a threat of terrorism. The FBI is the lead Federal agency during the crisis management phase.

Consequence Management

Measures to protect public health and safety, restore essential government services, and provide emergency relief to governments, businesses, and individuals affected by the consequences of terrorism. FEMA has the lead Federal response during the consequence management phase.

FIGURE 2
Federal Disaster Declaration Process

(1) Disaster event, either man-made or natural, occurs.
(2) Local/state officials assess damage.
(3) Governor reviews damage reports and decides to seek federal help.
(4) Governor asks FEMA Regional Office to participate in federal/state preliminary damage assessments (PDAs).
(5) Joint FEMA/state PDAs conducted.
(6) Governor requests a federal disaster declaration through its FEMA Regional Office.
(7) Regional Office reviews request and sends its recommendation to FEMA Headquarters.
(8) FEMA officials in Washington, D.C., prepare a declaration packet, review information and recommend approving or denying the request.
(9) FEMA Director reviews the declaration packet and sends a recommendation for approval or denial to the President.
(10) President makes final determination on federal disaster declaration.

CHAPTER 21

GIS IMPROVES EMERGENCY COORDINATION AND RESPONSE

Russ Johnson

Prior to Sept. 11, geographic information systems were typically thought of simply as mapping tools, useful for plotting out utility systems, watersheds, population densities, vegetation and the other systems that make up a geographic area. That has all changed.

From the first moments of the attacks on the World Trade Center and the Pentagon, and through the days, weeks and months afterwards, GIS played a vital role in emergency coordination and operations. Combined with data integration and people and resource organization, GIS has helped numerous agencies assisting in the response efforts. Now, as the emergency response community prepares for potential future attacks, GIS will continue to play a vital role, not only in responding to events, but in planning and preparation.

Mapping the Response

Almost immediately after the attacks on New York, a mapping center was established within Mayor Rudy Giuliani's Office of Emergency Management. The center was equipped with 20 GIS workstations and five mapmaking plotters.

Because New York had long used GIS, the city already had a rich geographic database that included maps and digital imagery of its critical infrastructure. That database provided a foundation for the OEM's GIS efforts, which, in turn, provided a foundation for a number of recovery activities.

What emerged from the OEM's efforts was a database enterprise for storing, managing and editing spatial and related tabular information, which allowed for disparate information pools created independently by private and public utilities, fire, public works, water, sewer, police and other agencies to be integrated and stored in one location. The centralized environment provided dynamic mapping capabilities that spurred optimized emergency field operations.

The OEM created a storehouse of geographic data, including maps that charted:
- transportation and public access;
- major river crossings;
- subway service;
- telephone usage;
- pedestrian and vehicular traffic restrictions;
- power grids;
- operational areas;
- damage assessments;

Orginally published as "GIS at the WTC," *Homeland Protection Professional*, Vol. 1, No. 1, July/August 2002. Published by A. J. Parrino & Associates, Western Springs, Illinois. Reprinted with permission of the publisher.

- fire, emergency services and police emergency response assets;
- staging areas;
- water outages; and
- personnel services, such as food and water stations.

The office also created three-dimensional maps of affected buildings. All told, the mapping services team produced thousands of maps.

Maps and Operations

Those maps were used during daily briefings and for mapping incident action plans that involved breaking sections of Ground Zero into functional units using maps and grids. Using the maps, Urban Search and Rescue teams were assigned to grid sectors each day.

Once a grid sector was searched, information resulting from the search was entered into the database. Recorded information was linked to grid cells.

After a grid cell was thoroughly examined, crane operators carefully removed a layer of debris, which was loaded into trucks and taken to an examination area. The debris was spread out to allow for precise inspection and then marked and recorded so that anything found could be mapped and linked to its grid cell location at the WTC.

As floors were examined and surveyed, voids, or open pockets among debris wreckage, were mapped using GIS. Color-coded maps of building levels revealed the status of the search operations for the floor. For example, color maps revealed whether sections had been searched and cleared, had collapsed, or were flooded or exposed to a hazard such as fire or potentially toxic pollutants.

Aerial photos were overlaid with square grids and mapped to provide a continuous time-stamp monitor for operations. Maps could then be examined to evaluate operations progress. In addition, detailed ground-level photos were hot-linked to the GIS database map so users could select a building or grid cell on the base map and quickly access it.

Asset and infrastructure maps generated before the attacks allowed users to more quickly locate items after the attack by providing reference points in areas where rubble and debris were disorienting for response workers. Maps of floor plans and other assets allowed workers to find items such as downed electric lines, gas mains that needed to be examined for leaks, or other critical infrastructure assets.

Emergency responders also used light-intensity detection and ranging images to create three-dimensional maps illustrating smoldering hotspots, voids and pile movement. LIDAR images were produced daily to provide information on activities such as debris shift and fire progression.

Networked Maps

Beyond mapping, emergency responders used an online intranet application called E-Team, which allowed different agencies to share and update information via the Web and to keep each other apprised of their activities. The application was designed to provide GIS functionality to people without GIS experience.

While the GIS map professionals generated back-end computer mapping capabilities and high-quality maps, E-Team allowed emergency response workers to work with information from their desktops and view an overall map of the incident that was updated as events evolved. An E-Team user simply called up a map with color-coded icons and symbols and then clicked on an icon to get information concerning fieldwork status, background, resources, agencies involved and other relevant activity information.

Emergency Decision Support

Additionally, GIS helped crews locating power lines, telephone and water service; utility infrastructure generators; bridges that would support heavy load removal; and fuel tanks, and it provided them with building ownership information. Deploying emergency personnel, routing crews, identifying larger open areas in lower Manhattan for staging equipment (cranes, for example) and assigning areas of work were made easier with digital maps. As more information was collected and stored in the GIS, advanced modeling features helped staff model the collapse of buildings and how the debris was scattered.

Health officials also used GIS to map air plumes in order to track asbestos, PCBs and other toxic materials.

In addition, GIS helped the city get information to the public. Maps enhanced news stories by providing visual information related to recovery efforts, giving readers a view of the events as they transpired.

Mapping the Future

Obviously, GIS is useful in rescue and recovery efforts. However, GIS could be even more critical in surveillance, preparation, planning and mitigation. Surveillance and detection of potential terrorist activity is crucial in preventing future attacks.

Like any criminal activity, terrorism requires funding, people, materials and logistics, and the connections between those involve patterns in time and space. GIS techniques can be used to correlate apparently disconnected events, letting the big picture emerge from huge volumes of data.

The key is the fusion of data from disparate sources into a common spatial framework. As a growing range of sensors is deployed to gather information concerning suspicious activities, GIS can be used to integrate the resulting information into a meaningful picture.

Assessing and analyzing the locations and vulnerabilities of water supplies, roads, bridges, distribution pipelines, public transportation, populations, schools, hazardous materials, public assemblies, national monuments and other assets can be performed efficiently using GIS. When vulnerabilities are identified, GIS can help identify mitigation strategies and can model various alternatives, including setbacks around buildings, closing certain access points, fencing exposed areas and relocating hazardous materials.

GIS supports other critical homeland security planning requirements, including determining evacuation routes, locations and capacities of evacuation shelters, and potential locations of staging areas, incident management facilities and public safety response assets.

The chaos and confusion created during major emergencies can be more effectively managed when responders and workers have a clear picture of what needs to be done and where it needs to be done. In complex emergency events, many people from different agencies must respond and take coordinated actions, which are usually communicated through the medium of a map.

GIS not only provides maps; it also provides great amounts of additional information about each feature on the map. And though it's a powerful asset in the response and recovery toolbox, its greatest promise may be in helping to prevent future 9-11s.

CHAPTER 22

HEALTH-CARE SYSTEMS AND HOMELAND SECURITY

Trudi Matthews

The events of Sept. 11 present a tale of two cities — New York and Washington, D.C. The terrorist attacks on the World Trade Center and the Pentagon illustrate how unforeseen events can highlight the best and the worst in planning and preparedness for disaster — even when they occur in places that are better prepared than most cities for these kinds of incidents. Disasters present specific challenges to the healthcare system, but states can and should plan for these events.

Experience shows all disasters are local, at least in the beginning. Local police, fire-fighters, paramedics and other emergency personnel are usually first on the scene of a disaster. Local hospitals and health-care workers are responsible for dealing with the injured and the dead as well as with concerned family members and the community.

A well-planned and implemented local emergency response is critical after a terrorist incident, yet local systems can quickly become overwhelmed. It is imperative that community action plans, particularly health plans, coordinate with state and federal leadership and resources to respond effectively and manage the consequences of disasters.

Mass-casualty events present special challenges to health-care systems and professionals. State leaders must ask tough questions about how their cities, districts and state would deal with deaths and injuries ranging from just a few people to hundreds or even thousands.

Challenges to Health Care

Whether they are terrorist attacks, natural disasters such as hurricanes and tornadoes, or man-made disasters such as an airplane or train accident, mass-casualty events demonstrate the need for effective coordination of health-care resources. With hundreds of dead and wounded to deal with, emergency responders must be able to effectively triage patients and transport them to health-care facilities. Those with serious injuries must be transferred to hospitals and clinics that are best-equipped to deal with trauma and closest to the scene. Those with less serious injuries must be moved to facilities farther away.

Communication and transportation logistics are crucial to this task. Multiple, redundant communications systems must be available to health-care workers in the event phone lines are jammed or transmitters de-

Originally published as "Disasters Present Health Challenges," *State Government News*, October 2001. Published by The Council of State Governments, Lexington, KY. Reprinted with permission of the publisher.

stroyed. Ambulances and other methods for transporting the injured to health-care facilities must be coordinated so that no facility is swamped and none is underutilized in a time of need.

Timely identification of the deceased and notification of family members present additional challenges. Emergency personnel, health-care workers, medical examiners and administrative staff must be able to operate quickly with clear procedures for maintaining evidence, tracking the deceased, notifying family members and public officials, and issuing death certificates.

An effective health-system response to a mass-casualty event has become more complicated over the past two decades. Managed care has squeezed the excess capacity out of the health-care system. There are fewer hospital beds available, and few stockpiles of equipment and medical supplies at the disposal of local authorities in times of need. Emergency rooms are already overloaded with patients, and equipment and facilities are tightly scheduled.

Because there is little overflow capacity in most health-care systems in the United States, officials must plan and coordinate how all parties in the system will respond during a mass-casualty event. A designated trauma system can help paramedics and other emergency personnel know where to send the most serious cases. Noncritical patients must be discharged or transferred to other hospitals. Health-care workers must be mobilized to handle the additional patients. Hospitals and facilities in surrounding regions must be on alert to receive any overflow cases.

Levels of Coordination

During the 1996 Olympic Park bombing, Georgia emergency management officials quickly responded to the threat using advanced planning and coordinated efforts among a variety of agencies and systems.

Sixty-thousand people were evacuated, and a medical triage area was established. "Within 32 minutes, medical personnel and equipment were set up in the Olympic Ring area so they could respond instantly, and 118 of the injured were transported to area hospitals," said Trina Hembree, executive director of the National Emergency Management Association, an affiliate of CSG. During that time, 73 victims also received crisis counseling.

Effective planning and coordination must involve all levels of government as well as a number of public and private systems. Horizontal coordination is needed between emergency managers, first-responders such as firefighters and paramedics, and law enforcement, public-health and mental-health personnel. Horizontal coordination is needed between cities and suburbs, within a region, and between states. Vertical coordination is needed between local, state, federal and international agencies and officials, and between government officials, the media and the public.

How Can States Prepare?

Emergency-management experts recommend that states and localities should not focus only on terrorism, but should take an all-hazards approach to disaster preparation and planning. All disasters and emergencies, whether natural or man-made, call upon similar resources and personnel.

The all-hazards approach has the added advantage of spurring more flexible responses to disaster. Officials prepared for multiple kinds of disasters are more likely to have a variety of options available and to think creatively in times of crisis.

In addition, experts urge state leaders to examine whether their state's health-care system is prepared for a terrorist attack or other mass-casualty incident through the following:
• Perform a risk assessment. Risk assessment is critical for the effective use of limited resources. Officials need to think about

what the possible targets of a terrorist attack might be in their state, including certain cities, government buildings, military installations, transportation facilities, power plants, entertainment venues and public events. Those facilities and events vulnerable to a terrorist attack need special attention, resources and readiness.

• Perform an analysis of health-systems capacity. In those areas where the risk is greatest, public officials need to assess the existing capacity in that area. If an attack overwhelms the area's health-care system, where would officials locate additional facilities, personnel, supplies and equipment? Also, officials need to examine whether health-care personnel are adequately trained to deal with various kinds of mass-casualty events, ranging from accidents to chemical or hazardous-materials incidents to bioterrorism. If specialized expertise is needed, such as for a bioterrorist attack, officials need to know how to report suspicious incidents and access the necessary experts.

• Plan. Once an assessment of risk and capacity is performed, a plan must be developed that involves and integrates the vertical and horizontal entities described above. Planning must take into account existing responsibilities, expertise and lines of authority, and must build upon them. "People do best what they do every day, then they improvise in an emergency," said Dr. Georges Benjamin, secretary of the Maryland Department of Health and Mental Hygiene. "States need to build on their existing systems and then continue to learn and develop capacity beyond the everyday occurrence."

• Practice. It is not enough that states and localities have planned for a terrorist attack or other mass casualty event. They also must put the plan into practice through exercises and drills. "When you practice your response to a disaster, you shorten your response time, and innovative

options appear sooner," said Benjamin. "If something goes wrong or doesn't work, a menu of options will be available from past experiences." Putting a response plan into practice also highlights gaps in procedures and identifies outdated protocols and information, such as phone numbers, lists of employees and the like. Exercises and drills also bring together personnel from various departments and agencies that normally do not interact with one another but who will need to do so in the event of a disaster.

• Provide resources. States must allocate the time, attention, personnel, equipment and funding necessary to prepare adequately for a mass-casualty event. Current funding sources are disjointed, coming from variety of agencies at the state and federal levels including law enforcement, emergency management, health care and environmental protection. In addition, because emergency resources are used infrequently, they are subject to fluctuating funding streams. "An all-hazards approach is more likely than a 'terrorism-only' system to get sufficient financing for personnel, equipment, training and exercises, and to effectively sustain the readiness of the resources over time," said Arnold Howitt of the Taubman Center for State & Local Government at Harvard University's John F. Kennedy School of Government in a recent editorial in *The Boston Globe*.

• Respond. Once they have done all of the planning and preparation, state and local leaders must respond to events according to established plans and procedures, but with the flexibility to improvise when needed.

Everyone hopes that events in New York and Washington, D.C., never occur again. However, policy-makers can learn from what has happened and pursue sound policies that can help ensure that the preparedness plans that served these two cities best are repeated in their own state.

FIGURE 1
Bioterrorism:
A Special Kind of Threat

As terrible and horrifying as the Sept. 11 attacks on the Pentagon and the World Trade Center were, terrorism experts agree that if the United States ever experienced a well-planned bioterrorist attack, the effects could be much worse. As states examine their emergency management and anti-terrorism response systems, policy-makers need to consider certain unique characteristics of bioterrorism and prepare their health-care systems to respond to it.

Very different systems and challenges come into play during a bioterrorist attack. Containers carrying biological agents could easily escape detection at most security checkpoints. Unlike conventional terrorist attacks, a biological attack could be done in secret, with no one noticing the release of a biological agent.

The first sign of a bioterrorist attack could be an increase in the number of patients in emergency rooms with flulike symptoms. Before most health-care workers could recognize what happened, hundreds of people could potentially be infected. Furthermore, while most emergency and law-enforcement personnel receive periodic training to recognize and handle a conventional terrorist attack, few health-care personnel are trained to recognize the symptoms caused by a biological agent and respond appropriately.

These unique characteristics mean that the United States is less prepared for a bioterrorist attack than it was for the attacks on Sept. 11. The U.S. Department of Health and Human Services and the national Centers for Disease Control and Prevention have worked with state and community leaders over the past few years to enhance local, state and federal bioterrorism preparedness and response systems.

For more information, look at the following resources online:
- HHS fact sheet on bioterrorism
  http://www.hhs.gov/news/press/2001pres/01fsbioterrorism.html
- National Disaster Medical System and anti-terrorism information
  http://ndms.dhhs.gov
- Centers for Disease Control and Prevention bioterrorism preparedness and response Web site http://www.bt.cdc.gov

---

Note: For additional information on terrorism and bioterrorism, please refer to "Combating Terrorism: Observations on Biological Terrorism and Public Health Initiatives," published by the U.S. General Accounting Office, Washington, D.C., March 1999. Refer to The Council of State Governments' website (www.csg.org).

CHAPTER 23

HIGH-RISE STRUCTURES, DISASTERS, AND PUBLIC SAFETY

John Nicholson

For nearly an hour on September 11, the World Trade Center's twin towers still soared high above Manhattan, even after two hijacked jetliners had ripped into them, spewing thousands of gallons of burning jet fuel over several floors. The 244 closely spaced steel columns of the 110-story towers, the tallest buildings in New York City, held their own as smoke billowed from shattered walls and an inferno raged inside. On most floors, the steel columns still formed the towers' exteriors.

At 9:50 a.m., however, the 1,362-foot (415-meter) south tower collapsed in a tragic display of terror. About a half-hour later, the 1,368-foot (417-meter) north tower went down.

What had finally reduced the well-constructed towers, which had survived a terrorist bombing in a basement parking garage in 1993, to a pile of concrete and steel about 12 stories high?

A number of engineers, including NFPA's building experts, believe each tower could've withstood the impact of a single large airplane, as they were designed to. Once the 24,000 gallons (91,000 liters) of aviation fuel in each Boeing 767 exploded into flames,

however, it was just a matter of time before the towers collapsed, they say.

"A determination will have to be made as to the combinations of the loss of structural support from the initial impact of the aircraft, coupled with the heat from the resulting fires that ultimately resulted in the collapse," says Robert E. Solomon, NFPA's chief building fire protection engineer. "The heat from the jet fuel fires, which are estimated to have reached temperatures of 2,000°F (1,098°C) are well above temperatures that can reduce the structural strength of steel trusses used to hold up the concrete slab floors."

"As an engineer," says Bonnie Manley, NFPA's structural engineer, "I was thankful to see the buildings still standing, but I knew it wasn't beyond the realm of possibility that they'd collapse. One floor collapsed and then the other in what's called a 'pancake failure'— one floor falling down on the other."

To maximize the space inside the buildings, the towers were designed with a column-free interior supported by an inner core of steel columns and the tubular steel that ringed the structures. The aircrafts' impact, the explosion, and the heat from the result-

Originally published as "Collapse: World Trade Center Aftermath," *NFPA Journal*, Vol. 95, No. 6, November/December 2001. Published by the National Fire Protection Association (NFPA), Quincy, Massachusetts. Reprinted with permission of the publisher.

ing fires may have weakened the steel girders until they could no longer support the weight above them. As one floor collapsed into another, the structures collapsed inwardly, minimizing damage to the surrounding area. The tower collapsed downward. The design helped prevent extensive damage to neighboring buildings, says Manley.

Sprinkler System Overwhelmed

In a conventional fire, the towers' sprinkler systems would've been sufficient to control the blaze, but these unconventional fires overwhelmed the suppression systems.

"In a normal office setting, there's quite a bit of material that can feed a fire, but adding the aviation fuel created a fire that was far larger and hotter than a normal system could handle," Manley notes.

As a result, there was never enough water to stop the fires.

According to David Hague, NFPA's senior fire protection engineer, the initial impacts probably rendered the sprinkler and standpipe systems inoperative on the fire floors and displaced any fire-resistance coatings on the structural steel. This exposed the steel to temperatures in the range of 1,600°F (871°C) and higher.

Even if the fire protection systems had remained operative, it's unlikely they'd have discharged enough water to protect the structural steel, he says.

"We can design systems to cope with the fire loading presented by such quantities of jet fuel — it's done constantly in aircraft hangars," Hague notes. "But the system would be a foam-water system, and a foam-water system isn't practical for buildings of this type. Water has some effect on jet fuel, but it's not as effective as a foam-water system."

Hague adds that he can't advocate a foam-water sprinkler system for this type of occupancy simply to prepare for the possibility of impact from an aircraft.

"The money would be better spent on security," he says.

Safety by Design

Dedicated in 1973 after five years of construction, the towers had 10 million square feet (929,003 square meters) of office space. They were owned by the Port Authority of New York and New Jersey, and were designed by Michigan-based Minoru Yamasaki Associates Inc., and Emery Roth and Sons of New York.

When engineers design a building, they calculate the loads and forces to which the building will be subjected over its lifetime. Typically, these include the effects of hurricanes, impact, winds, floods, earthquakes, and, in taller buildings, plane strikes.

The World Trade Center was designed to withstand a lot of stress, even a direct hit from a Boeing 707, which was the state-of-the-art jetliner at the time it was designed. The impact of a large plane and resulting jet fuel fire were factored into the towers' design as a result of lessons learned 56 years ago, when an Army Air Force B-25 crashed into the Empire State building in heavy fog. Fourteen people died, and damage to the building, which was hit between the 79th and 80th floors, came to $1 million. The building's structural integrity wasn't affected.

According to Manley, the towers' designers took into account all types of extremes when they drew up the plans for the World Trade Center more than 30 years ago. However, "there was no way to imagine that this collapse would ever happen when the buildings were designed," she says.

The towers' design has been described by the American Society of Civil Engineers as a "series of load-bearing exterior columns spaced 3 feet (91 centimeters) apart and tied together at every floor by a deep horizontal beam, creating a strong lattice of square tubing around each tower." Special plates were placed among the buildings' trusses to reduce stress caused by winds up to 200 miles (322 kilometers) per hour.

The twin towers also had the world's highest load-bearing walls, designed by Seattle-based structural engineer Worthington, Skilling, Helle, and Robertson as vertical, cantilevered steel tubes. Exterior columns were hollow box sections 14 inches (35 centimeters) square spaced 39 inches (99 centimeters) on center. Spandrels welded to the columns at each floor created huge trusses. This gave the towers, each of which measured 208 by 208 feet (63 by 63 meters), a column-free interior between the outer walls and the 79-by-139-foot (24-by-42-meter) core.

The core surrounding each building's 99 elevators also consisted of a lattice of steel covered by concrete that connected the interior columns to the exterior. Staircases in the buildings were designed to be evacuated in an hour, according to published reports. Each tower also had five underground parking levels.

Redundancy was also a part of the design. Redundancy in a building provides multiple load patterns for dissipating gravity and environmental loads.

"If one link breaks in that chain, the chain no longer functions; however, redundancy means that there are several more chains available to pick up a share of the load that was once carried by the chain," says Manley.

Such safeguards slowed the buildings' eventual collapse and provided occupants more time to evacuate, saving many lives. Eventually, however, the redundant systems were, like the fire suppression system, overwhelmed.

"What happened was completely unexpected, and this extreme situation overwhelmed the systems," say Manley.

What Now?

Will future design standards and building codes take into account events such as the attack on the World Trade Center? NFPA experts working on NFPA 5000, *Building Code*™, don't believe the new code will reference the incident, but there will be a greater sense of awareness within the building community that things such as this can happen.

Following the 1995 bombing of the Alfred P. Murrah Federal Building in Oklahoma City, there was a great deal of discussion about what it would take to destroy a building, but that stopped when experts realized that terrorists could quickly override any standards proposed. When it comes to terrorist attacks, what a building can withstand won't be defined, Manley says.

"Standards, such as those in blast engineering, aren't specific. You can't define the loading because once you do, someone will come up with a way to overcome it," says Manley.

Can engineers design terrorist-resistant buildings? Maybe, but they'd probably resemble fortresses, and people might not use them or be able to afford them.

Which leaves the option of increased security. Among the methods engineers use to enhance building security are reinforced structural frames and perimeters, Kevlar curtains or bullet-proof glass, fewer windows, and more secure entrances. Designs can also eliminate or restrict vehicle access and parking. All of these options will doubtless come into play in the future design and construction of public buildings, particularly high rises. It's too early to know how the lessons learned at such a cost in the attack on the World Trade Center will change the way things are done on many levels; some we can't yet envision.

CHAPTER 24

HOMELAND SECURITY ADVISORY SYSTEM AND NATIONAL THREAT CONDITIONS

Thomas Ridge

The Homeland Security Advisory System provides a comprehensive and effective means to disseminate information regarding the risk of terrorist attacks to Federal, State, and local authorities and to the American people.

As part of a series of initiatives to improve coordination and communication among all levels of government and the American public in the fight against terrorism, President Bush signed Homeland Security Presidential Directive 3, creating the Homeland Security Advisory System (HSAS). The advisory system will be the foundation for building a comprehensive and effective communications structure for the dissemination of information regarding the risk of terrorist attacks to all levels of government and the American people.

About the Homeland Security Advisory System

The Homeland Security Advisory System is designed to target our protective measures when specific information to a specific sector or geographic region is received. It combines threat information with vulnerability assessments and provides communications to public safety officials and the public.

- **Homeland Security Threat Advisories** contain actionable information about an incident involving, or a threat targeting, critical national networks or infrastructures or key assets. They could, for example, relay newly developed procedures that, when implemented, would significantly improve security or protection. They could also suggest a change in readiness posture, protective actions, or response. This category includes products formerly named alerts, advisories, and sector notifications. Advisories are targeted to Federal, State, and local governments, private sector organizations, and international partners.

- **Homeland Security Information Bulletins** communicate information of interest to the nation's critical infrastructures that do not meet the timeliness, specificity,

Originally published as *Governor Ridge Announces Homeland Security Advisory System*, Office of Homeland Security, Executive Office of the President, White House, Washington, D.C., March 12, 2002. On January 24, 2003, Governor Ridge was sworn in as Secretary of Homeland Security.

or significance thresholds of warning messages. Such information may include statistical reports, periodic summaries, incident response or reporting guidelines, common vulnerabilities and patches, and configuration standards or tools. It also may include preliminary requests for information. Bulletins are targeted to Federal, State, and local governments, private sector organizations, and international partners.

- **Color-coded Threat Level System** is used to communicate with public safety officials and the public at-large through a threat-based, color-coded system so that protective measures can be implemented to reduce the likelihood or impact of an attack. Raising the threat condition has economic, physical, and psychological effects on the nation; so, the Homeland Security Advisory System can place specific geographic regions or industry sectors on a higher alert status than other regions or industries, based on specific threat information.

National Framework

There are many federal alert systems in our country — each tailored and unique to different sectors of our society: transportation, defense, agriculture, and weather, for example. These alert systems fill vital and specific requirements for a variety of situations in both the commercial and government sectors. The Homeland Security Advisory System provides a national framework for these systems, allowing government officials and citizens to communicate the nature and degree of terrorist threats. This advisory system characterizes appropriate levels of vigilance, preparedness and readiness in a series of graduated Threat Conditions. The Protective Measures that correspond to each Threat Condition will help the government and citizens decide what action they take to help counter and respond to terrorist activ-

ity. Based on the threat level, Federal agencies will implement appropriate Protective Measures. States and localities will be encouraged to adopt compatible systems.

Factors for Assignment of Threat Conditions

The Homeland Security Advisory System provides a framework for the Attorney General, in consultation with the Director of the Office of Homeland Security, to assign Threat Conditions, which can apply nationally, regionally, by sector or to a potential target. Cabinet Secretaries and other members of the Homeland Security Council will be consulted as appropriate. A variety of factors may be used to assess the threat. Among these:

- Is the threat credible?
- Is the threat corroborated?
- Is the threat specific and/or imminent?
- How grave is the threat?

Unified System for Public Announcements

Public announcements of threat advisories and alerts help deter terrorist activity, notify law enforcement and State and local government officials of threats, inform the public about government preparations, and provide them with the information necessary to respond to the threat. State and local officials will be informed in advance of national threat advisories when possible. The Attorney General will develop a system for conveying relevant information to Federal, State, and local officials, and the private sector expeditiously. Heightened Threat Conditions can be declared for the entire nation, or for a specific geographic area, functional or industrial sector. Changes in assigned Threat Conditions will be made when necessary.

A Tool to Combat Terrorism

Threat Conditions characterize the risk of terrorist attack. Protective Measures are the steps that will be taken by government and the private sector to reduce vulnerabilities. The HSAS establishes five Threat Conditions with associated suggested Protective Measures:

Low Condition: Green

Low risk of terrorist attacks. The following Protective Measures may be applied:
- Refining and exercising preplanned Protective Measures
- Ensuring personnel receive training on HSAS, departmental, or agency-specific Protective Measures
- Regularly assessing facilities for vulnerabilities and taking measures to reduce them.

Guarded Condition: Blue

General risk of terrorist attack. In addition to the previously outlined Protective Measures, the following may be applied:
- Checking communications with designated emergency response or command locations
- Reviewing and updating emergency response procedures
- Providing the public with necessary information.

Elevated Condition: Yellow

Significant risk of terrorist attacks. In addition to the previously outlined Protective Measures, the following may be applied:
- Increasing surveillance of critical locations
- Coordinating emergency plans with nearby jurisdictions
- Assessing further refinement of Protective Measures within the context of the current threat information
- Implementing, as appropriate, contingency and emergency response plans.

High Condition: Orange

High risk of terrorist attacks. In addition to the previously outlined Protective Measures, the following may be applied:
- Coordinating necessary security efforts with armed forces or law enforcement agencies
- Taking additional precaution at public events
- Preparing to work at an alternate site or with a dispersed workforce
- Restricting access to essential personnel only.

Severe Condition: Red

Severe risk of terrorist attacks. In addition to the previously outlined Protective Measures, the following may be applied:
- Assigning emergency response personnel and pre-positioning specially trained teams
- Monitoring, redirecting or constraining transportation systems
- Closing public and government facilities
- Increasing or redirecting personnel to address critical emergency needs.

The United States Government will continue on a daily basis to monitor and analyze threat information and share that information, together with appropriate protective measures, with state, local and private sector authorities as well as the general public as part of the ongoing national effort to prevent terrorist attacks and protect the country.

All Americans should continue to be vigilant, take notice of their surroundings, and report suspicious items or activities to local authorities immediately. Everybody should establish an emergency preparedness kit as well as a communications plan for themselves and their family, and stay informed about what to do during an emergency situation.

FIGURE 1
Citizen Guidance on the Homeland Security Advisory System

Risk Level and Recommended Actions

GREEN: LOW RISK

- Develop a family emergency plan. Share it with family and friends, and practice the plan. Visit www.Ready.gov for help creating a plan.
- Create an "Emergency Supply Kit" for your household.
- Be informed. Visit or obtain a copy of "Preparing Makes Sense, Get Ready Now" by calling 1-800-BE-READY.
- Know how to shelter-in-place and how to turn off utilities (power, gas, and water) to your home.
- Examine volunteer opportunities in your community, such as Citizen Corps, Volunteers in Police Service, Neighborhood Watch or others, and donate your time.
- Consider completing an American Red Cross first aid or CPR course, or Community Emergency Response Team (CERT) course.

BLUE: GUARDED RISK

- *Complete recommended steps at level green.*
- Review stored disaster supplies and replace items that are outdated.
- Be alert to suspicious activity and report it to proper authorities.

YELLOW: ELEVATED RISK

- *Complete recommended steps at levels green and blue.*
- Ensure disaster supply kit is stocked and ready.
- Check telephone numbers in family emergency plan and update as necessary.
- Develop alternate routes to/from work or school and practice them.
- Continue to be alert for suspicious activity and report it to authorities.

ORANGE: HIGH RISK

- *Complete recommended steps at lower levels.*
- Exercise caution when traveling, pay attention to travel advisories.
- Review your family emergency plan and make sure all family members know what to do.
- Be patient. Expect some delays, baggage searches and restrictions at public buildings.
- Check on neighbors or others that might need assistance in an emergency.

RED: SEVERE RISK

- *Complete all recommended actions at lower levels.*
- Listen to local emergency management officials.
- Stay tuned to TV or radio for current information/instructions.
- Be prepared to shelter-in-place or evacuate, as instructed.
- Expect traffic delays and restrictions.
- Provide volunteer services only as requested.
- Contact your school/business to determine status of work day.

Note: Developed with input from the *American Red Cross.*

Note

Additional information was added to this chapter, such as the chart on *Citizen Guidance on the* *Homeland Security Advisory System*, from the Department of Homeland Security's website (http://www.dhs.gov/).

CHAPTER 25

HOSPITALS MUST PREPARE FOR POSSIBLE BIOTERRORISM ATTACK

Russell Bennett

A review of the literature indicates that our hospitals and communities are ill-prepared for bioterrorist attacks involving nuclear, biological, and/or chemical (NBC) contaminants of weapons of mass destruction (WMD). Further, disasters and incidents with hundreds, thousands, or tens of thousands of casualties are not generally addressed in hospital disaster preparedness plans. Nevertheless, they may occur, and recent terrorist actions around the globe suggest that it would be prudent for hospitals and other healthcare providers to improve their preparedness for such contingencies. Hospitals and other public/private healthcare agencies must have organized plans and contingencies in place, which address their organization, community and the public health response. Each facility should determine the extent of their bioterrorism readiness, which may range from notification of local emergency networks and transfer of casualties to a more appropriate facility, to activation of a large, comprehensive communication and event management network.

According to a Bioterrorism Coordinator of the L. A. County Department of Health Service, if the United States had a huge, massive biochemical exposure in a terrorism attack, it would have difficulty responding to it. Healthcare agencies need more money, more resources and more people. A survey of 186 hospitals last year in four Northwestern States found that only 20 percent of the participating hospitals had plans for biological or chemical weapons incidents. Fewer than half had a decontamination unit with ventilation and showers, and only six percent had the recommended minimum materials to handle a nerve gas attack of the type conducted by Aum Shinrikyo in Japan where terrorists released sarin gas in a busy subway station that resulted in mass casualties. The casualties included the public and emergency medical technicians who were secondarily exposed to the casualties and in turn became victims. More importantly, the volume of self-referring patients who may not have been exposed overwhelmed the healthcare system. Because hospitals and healthcare providers were not aware and lacked the appropriate education and train-

Originally published as "Are U.S. Hospitals Prepared for Bioterrorism?" *PA Times*, Vol. 25, No. 6, June 2002. Published by the American Society for Public Administration, Washington, D.C. Reprinted with permission of the publisher.

ing to handle this act of mass terror and the huge volume of casualties, the hospitals had to be shut down because this event paralyzed hospital operations.

No one knows when an incident of terrorism will occur, where it will occur, or what will be its cause. Of course, most hospital leaders hope their communities never experience a mass casualty incident. In an invitational forum convened by the American Hospital Association to address hospital preparedness for mass casualties, a large number of issues were discussed in which preparedness needs were grouped into four broad categories: community-wide preparedness, staffing, communication, and public policy. Selecting from the many individual observations and recommendations on preparedness, the primary conclusions were:

Community-Wide Preparedness

- By definition, mass casualty incidents overwhelm the resources of individual hospitals. Equally important, a mass casualty incident is likely to impose a sustained demand for health services rather than the short, intense peak customary with many smaller scale disasters.
- The public will see hospitals, because of their emergency services and 24 hour a day operation, as a vital resource for diagnosis, treatment, and follow-up for both physical and psychological care.
- To increase their preparedness for mass casualties, hospitals have to expand their focus to include both internal and community-level planning.
- Hospital planners should consider the possibility that a hospital might need to evacuate, quarantine, or divert incoming patients.
- In multi-hospital communities and regions, there is a need to develop a real-time database, including an unduplicated count of potential staff.

Staffing

- Preparedness would benefit from development of a community-wide concept of "reserve staff" identifying physicians, nurses and hospital workers who are (1) retired, (2) have changed careers to work outside of healthcare services, or (3) now work in areas other than direct patient care.
- Hospital preparedness can be increased if state licensure bodies, working through the Federation of State Medical Boards, develop procedures allowing physicians licensed in one jurisdiction to practice in another under defined emergency conditions.
- Hospital preparedness can be increased if medical staffs' Credentials Committees develop a policy on the recognition of temporary privileges in emergency or disaster situations and if hospitals in a community regularly share lists of the medical staffs and their privileges.

Communications

- Everyday communications systems used in the community are likely to be overwhelmed in a mass casualty incident. Backup and redundant systems need to be developed, tested and drilled.
- A single community spokesperson for the mass casualty incident needs to be identified in advance, press and media briefings need to be regularly scheduled away from the hospital(s) but with supporting medical expertise.
- Community-wide systems for locating patients need to be planned with a single point of contact.

Public Policy

- In the present financial environment, where each payer wishes to pay only for the immediate costs of its patients, there is a need for a means to pay for the planning, education, standby supplies, and training costs of preparedness.

• The Emergency Medical Treatment and Labor Act (EMTALA) needs to be refined to establish "safe harbor" provisions so that a hospital assigned a role of caring for unexposed patients does not have to violate either its status as a "clean" facility or its EMTALA obligation.

A new federal approach is needed which expresses the congressional commitment to assist hospitals in disaster recovery. The federal government needs to provide necessary catastrophic financial relief to assist hospitals in caring for disaster victims and in disaster recovery.

Implemented together, these recommendations can increase hospital preparedness for mass casualty incidents.

America will never forget the events of September 11, 2001. Our nation learned a terrible lesson, that America has evil, cold-blooded enemies capable of unprecedented acts of mass murder and terror. The characteristics of American society that we cherish, our freedom, our openness, our great transportation systems, make us vulnerable to terrorism of catastrophic proportions. This vulnerability will exist even after our nation brings justice to those responsible for the events of September 11. With courage, unity, and purpose, America met the challenges of 2001 and must be prepared to meet even greater challenges in the future, one being the preparation of our hospitals for terrorist contingencies.

CHAPTER 26

INFRASTRUCTURE PROTECTION IS ENHANCED THROUGH TECHNOLOGY AND COOPERATION

David Wagman

Think about the gadgets you own; consider it a personal technology inventory. Do you have both a landline and a cell phone? How about a pager? Personal data assistant? Computer? Broadband Internet connection? Big-screen TV?

Now inventory the technology around you. Do closed-circuit tv cameras overlook a busy corner or highway in your area? Does your region have smog detectors or other environmental sensors? Does your agency have a geographic information system or a supervisory control and data acquisition system, or access to either?

Viewed individually, each piece of technology represents a nifty gadget that can make your life more enjoyable or your job a little easier. Taken together, technologies such as these form the basis of the "intelligent city."

The concept refers to a locality wired with sensors and other technology capable of sending a constant data stream to a central point for analysis. Once there, the data can be culled by still more technology programmed to watch for anomalies, which may trigger alerts and proactive responses.

Christian Stalberg, a consultant who has worked with both FEMA and California emergency management agencies, wrote in 1994 that the emergence of the intelligent city in the 21st century would radically transform emergency management. Rather than operating as a separate and distinct function called on only during times of crisis, emergency management, he predicted, would become "integrated into every facet of municipal planning and operations."

The intelligent city, Stalberg wrote, "will incorporate each of the elements of emergency management (preparedness, response, recovery and mitigation) into its overall planning and operational matrix."

Technology in an intelligent city could alert authorities, for example, that the same car has circled a sensitive building five times in the last several minutes, says Dr. James Lewis, senior fellow at the Center for Strategic and International Studies in Washington, D.C.

Hardware is one thing. But you'll also need human imagination, brainpower and cooperation to implement an intelligent city.

Originally published as "Building Intelligent Cities," *Homeland Protection Professional*, Vol. 3, No. 4, May 2004. Published by A. J. Parrino & Associates, Western Springs, Illinois. Reprinted with permission of the publisher.

To be effective, the intelligent city depends on breaking down barriers between agencies and levels of government that have historically hampered information sharing.

In New York City, for example, the fire and police departments have their own 911 dispatchers and computers in separate buildings miles apart. According to the *New York Times*, dispatchers sometimes have to dial 911 themselves to communicate across agency lines.

Private-sector Allies

And you'll need to think expansively, because today's notion of an intelligent city reaches into the realms of economic development and business continuity. What's more, large amounts of data about urban systems are maintained by the private sector, not by government.

"The private sector owns and retains the primary knowledge of our vulnerabilities and consequences for 80% of our critical infrastructure," David Hayman, a director of the Center for Strategic and International Studies told a homeland security conference last December. "They understand the threat better than we do," which means "we need to view the public as an asset, not a liability."

Building an intelligent city means ensuring that information can flow between the public and the private sector and not just within government, agrees Jim Montagnino, general manager of NC4, the National Center for Crisis and Continuity Coordination. <www.nc4.us> The El Segundo, Calif.–based company uses off-the-shelf technologies to improve information exchanges between the public and private sectors.

Achieving the intelligent city doesn't depend on developing new technology so much as it hinges on convincing people to share information across departments and jurisdictions, says Russ Johnson, manager of public safety at ESRI, a Redlands, Calif.–based tech-

nology company. <www.esri.com> City agencies may function separately, but they also operate in a "shared geography with shared risks" and are equally affected by a disaster. "Disasters don't respect boundary lines, institutional or cultural," he says. Recognizing this reality is crucial when it comes to building an intelligent city.

Technology and Credibility

"Technology is not an inhibitor," says Ellis Stanley, general manager of the Los Angeles Emergency Preparedness Department, who adds that most cities have enough technology deployed today to be considered intelligent. He notes the almost ubiquitous nature of cell phones, pagers and environmental sensors that are installed in and around most major urban centers.

"If we have monitors sniffing to tell us what smog levels are, they can also sniff for other things," such as chemical releases, he says.

After all, a city has thousands of pieces of technology in place, from smog monitors to traffic cameras to personal data assistants, and thousands of information gatherers in the field, from postal workers delivering mail to sanitation workers collecting trash.

"We have the capabilities, but we don't always take advantage to use the capability," he says. The challenge for emergency and disaster planners is to take the lead in pulling together all this potentially available data and making use of it locally, regionally and nationally.

The idea of the intelligent city has existed for decades, first as fodder for 1950s science fiction and more recently as a credible public-policy concept. Futurist Alvin Toffler discussed ideas related to intelligent cities in his 1981 book "The Third Wave."

A decade ago, Christian Stalberg wrote that vulnerability to disaster results from the lack of effective communication and control systems. He called catastrophes "the ultimate expression of a natural hazard acting upon a system made vulnerable" by the very lack of such systems. But as technology raises the intelligence of urban systems, emergencies will occur with less frequency as "unexpected situations" or "sudden occurrences" become less likely, he wrote. Stalberg also believed that "virtually all of the technologies necessary to construct the intelligent city have already been introduced." And this was 1994.

Citywide Situational Awareness

Randall Larsen, a retired Air Force colonel and president of Alexandria, Va.–based Homeland Security Associates, says a key goal in developing intelligent cities is to help emergency managers gain "situational awareness," a military concept that suggests a leader's basic ability to know what's going on. In the context of homeland security, situational awareness means gathering information from a variety of sources and getting it out in a timely manner, either to prevent an incident or to help achieve an effective response.

Larsen advocates using simple, cost-effective technology to achieve intelligence. He points to a proposed "922" system being developed by AT&T and Daedalus Medical Systems of Alexandria, Va., <www.daedalusproject.com> which would use tv, radio, telephones and a centralized computer to help health officials and emergency management professionals nationwide gather and analyze information as well as communicate with the public during a disaster.

922 may be particularly effective in communicating information related to chemical or biological attacks, he says. Consider the scenario in which a Los Angeles hospital begins seeing emergency room cases involving an unknown pathogen. The victims all come from the same geographic area. Implementing the 922 system, public health officials use tv and radio to ask residents living in the same area to dial 922 on their telephones. Once connected, callers are quizzed about possible symptoms or exposures.

Depending on the circumstances, callers may be advised to shelter in place, evacuate to a secure location or seek medical attention. And because 922 uses a centralized computer, data collected from around the country would be available for comparison and trend analysis. Officials would know, for example, that illnesses similar to those in Los Angeles were reported a week earlier in San Antonio.

Conceptually, 922 allows emergency officials to rapidly achieve situational awareness, Larsen says, a goal behind building an intelligent city. The proposed system has the added benefit of using existing, widely available technology, making it cost effective. Larsen says a pilot 922 project is slated to start this October.

Fusion, Not Stovepipes

922 is an example of "data fusion," an important intelligent city idea. Data fusion refers to the ability of multiple systems to collect a wide array of data and assemble a picture of what is going on, says George Park, managing scientist at Exponent Inc., a California-based engineering and scientific consulting firm <www.exponent.com>.

For example, even as local hospitals are reporting an outbreak of a flu-like illness, water quality sensors are detecting a problem at the local water treatment plant and law enforcement personnel are reporting an unsolved break-in at the reservoir. Fusing three entirely independent streams of information, officials may be able to identify not only the health threat but also determine who caused it and why.

Park says an example illustrating the lack of data fusion occurred in the 1984 outbreak of salmonella poisoning at restaurants in The Dalles, Ore. Authorities knew something was wrong, but didn't realize for some time that the city was under attack by cult followers of Bhagwan Shree Rajneesh, who were trying to sway a local election. Around 750 people became ill as a result of this biological attack.

Another step in moving toward an intelligent city is to have data stored in such a way that it can be retrieved and acted on quickly. Most government agencies traditionally have data "silos" or "stovepipes," which isolate data and make sharing difficult.

Even in a post–Sept. 11 world, "agencies still stovepipe information," says CSIS's Lewis. "We need a commitment to transform cities to a network" of information sources.

One approach involves geographic information systems, computer-based systems that can store large amounts of data and retrieve them to build maps and other geography-based analysis tools. A basic GIS of an urban neighborhood might contain data locating roads, buildings, electric lines, water lines, natural gas lines, communications facilities and public buildings. Other data files could archive police, fire and EMS activity; hazardous material locations; and even census and demographic information.

During last October's California wildfires, 18 public and private agencies used a shared GIS to gain information on the fires and on endangered residential neighborhoods and facilities. Satellite photos taken by Space Imaging of Thornton, Colo., augmented the GIS data. The California Department of Forestry and Fire Protection and several incident command teams used the satellite pictures to create firefighting maps.

After the fires were extinguished, agencies continued to use GIS to identify areas vulnerable to mudslides. When rain gauges reported heavy rain in late December, emergency personnel alerted residents in those vulnerable areas, says ESRI's Russ Johnson.

Achieving this sort of mitigation ability is based on three elements, Johnson says:

building a foundation of basic geographic data, collecting real-time data during an event and then fusing both sets of data to deliver useful information to the people best able to act on it.

"In almost real time, everyone is getting information they can act on," he says.

Building Urban Viability

The need for fast, actionable data in the intelligent city extends beyond first responders. Kevin "Kip" Thomas, associate director of research programs in George Mason University's Critical Infrastructure Protection Program in Arlington, Va., says homeland security contains four elements: national security, public health and safety, public confidence and economic security.

"Where we need to think about investing in intelligent cities is not just what is the 'gee-whiz' thing," he says. "It's more a question of how to develop a rational investment to make a city more viable."

Of growing importance is the need to deploy systems and foster a culture in which businesses can be part of the official information loop. One tragedy of the World Trade Center attack was the announcement advising tenants in the second tower not to evacuate the building. Many office workers returned to their desks and were killed, but one Deutsche Bank executive ignored the advisory and has been credited with saving many lives by continuing the evacuation.

NC4 is now working with Deutsche Bank and other companies in New York to deploy a system to help bring businesses into the emergency communications loop, both to receive and provide information. The system is being implemented in Los Angeles as well as in New York.

New York has had a watch command in place for years to monitor incidents on a round-the-clock basis. The command formerly tracked incidents with sticky notes and white boards. As part of the new approach being deployed by NC4, a GIS has been installed to locate incidents and track them using off-the-shelf software.

Incident managers can decide when an event is serious enough to warrant alerting local businesses. In one recent exercise, New York incident managers responded to a hypothetical plume of toxic chemicals. Using the NC4 system, businesses likely to be affected by the toxic plume were notified electronically and given instructions to pass along to employees. The system also lets businesses respond back to incident managers at the city's emergency management center.

The alert system helps emergency managers automate their incident response processes. It also creates a structure for businesses to receive and report information, says Montagnino.

Filters allow businesses to limit information they receive to specific types of incidents within a certain distance from their location. Incident reports are transmitted regularly and include reports about traffic tie-ups and water main breaks. Montagnino says this helps users at both ends get comfortable with using the system daily, making them better prepared to use it in a larger emergency.

Leading Efforts

Emergency managers and disaster planners have a key role to play in moving toward the intelligent city. Montagnino says emergency managers in the past focused on coordinating just the actions of law enforcement, fire and emergency medical responders. "They are experienced in putting plans in place and coordinating groups," he says.

But as homeland security evolves, he says, emergency managers will increasingly be involved both with preventing incidents and in leading recovery efforts that extend beyond these agencies.

Emergency management leaders are well positioned to identify threats to their communities, says Dan Furtado, a Campbell, Calif., city councilman and member of the DHS Special Working Group on Homeland Security. Planners also need to consider what critical pieces of infrastructure could be affected in an attack. The loss of one or more electrical substations or cell phone towers could render even the most intelligent of cities clueless.

Geary Sikich, who heads Indiana-based Logical Systems Management, tells of a financial services company in New York City's World Finance Center that installed not just backup electrical supplies, but five independent electrical feeds. Trouble was, all the feeds came from the same substation, which negated the effort at redundancy.

Sikich says that noting such potential weak links is part of a careful planner's search for unintended consequences. "How do you manage to run the smart, information system–based city if you lose the capability to generate electricity?" he asks.

Equally important is the growing need for emergency managers to work at the county, region and even at the state level, says Karen J. Anderson, mayor of Minnetonka, Minn., and a member of the DHS State and Local Senior Advisory Committee.

One change she has seen in the two and a half years since Sept. 11 is a greater willingness among agencies to work together on a variety of projects. For example, 175 governmental entities in seven counties around Minneapolis–St. Paul are working to install an 800-MHZ emergency communication system. Once installed, the system will give first responders a common communications platform.

Ongoing Process

A technology inventory of most American cities likely would show an adequate supply of "intelligent city" technology already in place. Even so, most places still view the concept as a goal to work toward.

"We're in the information age, but there's a lot of development to be done," says George Park at Exponent Inc. "It's an ongoing process and we're not there yet."

The more intelligent cities become, the better the chances are that "we'll prevent attacks and we'll respond better," says Randy Larsen of Homeland Security Associates. He says fewer Americans will die in incidents and economic hardships will be reduced as a result.

Intelligent cities thrive on more data, not less. Homeland security comes down to searching for a needle in an intelligent haystack, says John MacGraffin, a consultant and former CIA station chief.

He told a homeland security conference last December, "I know it's counterintuitive, but you need to put more hay on the stack to find the needle, not less. Until we get through the fact that there has to be more hay, we are walking in the wrong direction. Less hay hurts. It does not help you find the needle."

CHAPTER 27

LAW ENFORCEMENT'S RESPONSE TO THE WAR ON TERRORISM

W. Ronald Olin

Events since September 11, 2001 have done little to soothe the fear and uncertainty of our citizens and law enforcement executives. While the war efforts in Afghanistan and other countries continue and no attacks have subsequently occurred in the United States, members of the al Qaeda network are believed to have exploded a car bomb on October 12 in a nightclub district on the Indonesian Island of Bali, causing hundreds of casualties. This was just the latest in a string of fatal attacks that include sniper shootings in Kuwait, Afghanistan and the Philippines, and suicide bombings in Pakistan and Tunisia. While most citizens want a return to normalcy and a resumption of "pre–September 11" life, those who are involved in countering the terrorists believe that the threat is here to stay.[1]

September 11 marked a profound and fundamental change in the terrorist conflict. The United States was attacked with resulting mass casualties, destruction of property valued at more than a hundred billion dollars, an economic crisis, and deployment of troops in a war to disrupt future terrorism

against our country. While this conflict is described as a war, it is not war as we have traditionally known it, and it is not war in which the rules are completely understood. There is little doubt that this is war that threatens our existence and a war that the West must win. As noted by former Israeli Prime Minister Benjamin Netanyahu, "[Western democracies] believe in the sanctity of each human life, [are] committed to the ideals of liberty, and champion the values of democracy. But those who practice terrorism do not believe in these things. In fact, they believe in the very opposite."[2]

The September 11 attacks and the West's response have shaken the foundations of law enforcement throughout the world. Traditional law enforcement models are challenged by the nontraditional, asymmetrical attacks. Observers of the terrorist phenomenon have predicted these attacks for decades. But most were still shocked at the complexity of the operation and enormity of the destruction. Now that the attacks have occurred and thousands have died, we know the nature of our enemy and we must shift the way law en-

Originally published as "Why Traditional Law Enforcement Methods Cannot Win the War on Terrorism," *The Police Chief*, Vol. LXIX, Vol. 11, November 2002. Published by the International Association of Chiefs of Police, Alexandria, VA. Reprinted with permission of the publisher.

forcement agencies at all levels — international, federal, state, and local — operate in the future. How tens of thousands of law enforcement officers and thousands of law enforcement agencies evolve in handling the future threats against our countries will, in large part, determine how modern civilization fares against a determined foe.

A recent debate has emerged in attempting to understand and respond to the terrorist threat. This debate is one that confuses citizens, academicians, politicians, and law enforcement officials: Should we treat terrorism as a crime or an act of war? Is terrorism a problem for traditional law enforcement and the courts? Or is it a threat that is so significant and dangerous that it requires a revision in our fundamental beliefs about a variety of issues?

This struggle challenges our resources in locations around the world, and our basic beliefs at home. Significant decisions are being made such as when law enforcement may investigate one's religious beliefs, how to use ethnicity without "profiling," when we may justifiably incarcerate someone, when authorities may deny a suspect due process, and how America and its allies should conduct a series of battles unprecedented in complexity. To understand the unconventional nature of the terrorist war we must contrast the differences between the law enforcement response to traditional violent crime and its response to terrorism. An analysis may then be made and conclusions drawn about the future response that the law enforcement profession will undertake.

Traditional Violent Crime and Law Enforcement's Response

A victim of a violent crime in any country suffers a devastating effect from the event. The secondary effects on family, friends, police officers investigating the incident, and society are impossible to measure. From a street crime to serial killings, a crime and its impact do not normally threaten the integrity of the country where it occurs. While this may be different when the victim is the leader of the nation and the remaining government too weak to continue, it is rarely the case.

A traditional law enforcement response to violent crime follows a rather repetitive path. Officials learn of the crime, investigate it, and then arrest and prosecute the offender(s). Today, a more sophisticated response has evolved to address those more intractable crime problems. These solutions are varied and depend upon a law enforcement agency's historical successes, local and state politics, the factors motivating the violence (gangs, drugs, jealousy, and so on), and other issues.

Most police agencies perform some kind of crime analysis to identify, track, and/or target crime trends and repeat offenders. This is developing intelligence information, albeit in a dramatically limited and restricted way following legal restrictions that were enacted in the 1970s. The sophistication of gathering, analyzing, and disseminating intelligence varies greatly among law enforcement agencies and countries in the world.

Law enforcement agencies have learned to use more aggressive tools in combating such problems as exchanging information with other institutions with which a potential offender would interact. These include schools, courts, correctional facilities, welfare offices, parole and probation officers, and other law enforcement agencies. Multijurisdictional task forces permit agencies to maximize investigations with increased numbers of officers from several agencies. Collaborative information exchanges permit more complete criminal intelligence and a better understanding of the criminal events that are transpiring.

Recent successes in U.S. law enforcement also reflect the importance of community interest and involvement. An informed, engaged community that embraces the goals of law enforcement is an indispensable tool in the battle against violent crime. And a law enforcement agency that adds officer accountability to the community model has been shown to be even more effective in fighting crime. This "ownership" places law enforcement and good citizens together on a path towards enlightened policing practice and success.

The Problems of the Terrorist War

We then enter the terrorist world. A terrorist kills civilians incidentally and attempts to destroy the society of his or her target. In the case of the current threat — Jihadism — we face a formidable foe. There are more than one billion Muslims in the world. Only a very small number of Muslims embrace radical fundamentalist Islam. Nevertheless, the potential for a continuing wave of terrorist attacks is alarming. If only one out of every 10,000 Muslims supports the Jihadist movement we may be facing a determined force of more than 100,000 people. During the time that the training camps in Afghanistan and other countries were in operation an unknown number of people, certainly in the tens of thousands, were educated in terrorist techniques. Members of the Jihadist movement are in at least 60 countries around the world.

The recent history of Jihadism may be traced back to the 1981 assassination of Egyptian President Anwar Sadat during a troop review. Al Qaeda's number two, Ayman al-Zawahiri, served prison time for his involvement in the assassination. He was released from prison and began again to wage the most recent jihad. Various attacks against the West and others deemed to be countries of the nonbelievers have followed.

Why? The concepts of a separation of church and state, women's rights, freedom of speech, democracy, individualism, choices of lifestyles and behaviors, and secular education are among the values that we believe are our strengths. Jihadists, on the other hand, see them as unholy, corrupt, or unimportant. The Jihadist's assumption of the role as an agent of God, a messenger of God's word and will, places the members of their movement, in their minds, on a moral plateau above those nonbelievers in the West. This collision of cultures helped create the current situation.

The stated objective of this movement is to spread jihad through the world. As Abdulla Azzam, a legendary Palestinian mullah and rival of Osama bin Laden, remarked, as the Soviets prepared to depart from Afghanistan in defeat, "Why stop there? The Middle East was full of corrupt secular rulers who had abandoned the true faith.... If the U.S.S.R. could be defeated, Azzam argued, so could the U.S."[3]

Faced with the rise of the Taliban and al Qaeda, the openly declared jihad against the West, and the series of subsequent attacks that tragically culminated in the September events, we must acknowledge the awful truth. The Jihadists are a threat to our existence and have the ideology, money, personnel, and time to change our way of life. Unlike common criminals, they also have an international network, state connections, and developing access to weapons of mass destruction in their war against us.

In a recent newspaper editorial, Bernard Lewis, professor emeritus of Near Eastern Studies at Princeton, quoted some observations Osama bin Laden made before September 11, 2001. Bin Laden opined, "We have seen in the last decade the decline of the American government and weakness of the American soldier, who is ready to wage cold wars and unprepared to fight long wars.... This was proven in Beirut when the Marines fled after two explosions. It also proves they can run in less than 24 hours and this was also repeated in Somalia.... (Our) youth were surprised at the low morale of the American soldiers.... After a few blows, they ran in defeat, ... they forgot about being the new world order. They left, dragging their corpses and their shameful defeat."[4]

The investigations of targets and support networks, and the intelligence gathering necessary to respond to a Jihadist enterprise that spans more than 60 countries, transcend any possible traditional law enforcement response. These facts alone place the investigation of the attacks in the hands of international coalitions, a few federal agencies, the military, and selected local jurisdictions. The magnitude of this endeavor should not be lost on many local and state law enforcement executives who want to help but, in most cases, cannot in the global context of the war.

All dangers, however, are also local. Every law enforcement officer needs basic information on the terrorists' motivation, tactics, and threats. The officer then needs to know how to apply that information during citizen contacts. Every law enforcement executive needs basic information on leading one's agency through these turbulent times. A more seamless merger of knowledge and action will provide an integrated and comprehensive response for local and state contributions in the terrorist war.

The Future

The next steps in our antiterrorist response will continue to be calculated and precise. Our challenges are many and varied. How do we prevent the next terrorist act? What do we do to educate our police officers, law enforcement executives, and our citizens? How do we address our citizens' fear? How do we restore safety and stability in the civilized world? Let us examine each of these questions.

Although a determined terrorist can always perpetrate an incident, some preemptory steps may prove effective. The most important focus is on prevention. This requires

strengthening, to the best of our abilities, our intelligence gathering systems. New investigative procedures have been implemented to obtain criminal evidence and intelligence gathering during military strikes around the world. Considerable information has been obtained from documents, computers, and forensic evidence. Interviews to obtain information from detainees housed from Guantanamo to Karachi also contribute to our understanding of the threat against us. We are moving to identify the individuals who have attacked us and take our fight to them using all of our resources.

Some work has already begun in the United States and other countries with a reordered law enforcement response. In the United States, the Federal Bureau of Investigation established Joint Terrorist Task Forces (JTTF) in each of its field offices throughout the country. This collaboration is a step toward information exchange and investigations using local, state, and federal partners.

The continued cooperation of local, state, and federal partners and members of the international law enforcement community is a welcomed and powerful tool in the fight against terrorism. Only with this dynamic shift towards coordinated law enforcement will we be able to cross the jurisdictions and borders to operate effectively against an elusive foe. Our deep losses in September 2001 demonstrate conclusively that we must prevent terrorism from occurring. And prevention is possible when combinations of intelligence gathering, investigations, and interventions all come together to disrupt the terrorist networks wherever they exist.

The educational component is a critical one. In the law enforcement work, a comprehensive training program is underway to develop the curriculum for all United States officers. The State and Local Anti-terrorism Training (SLATT) program is working to create, test, refine, and deliver a basic presentation on terrorism for all 650,000 American law enforcement personnel.

We must recognize that there is a fundamental shift in the roles and responsibilities of law enforcement officers in our society. While a traditional law enforcement response alone will not impact modern terrorist threats, this new training combined with our knowledge of community, interactions with citizens, and networking with others such as postal workers, street crews, utility, and sanitation employees give the local law enforcement officer access to important information. Integrating these sources into a useful appraisal of the threat improves the security of all of us.

Thousands of law enforcement executives in the United States are asking what they can and should do. The questions are difficult but are not without answers. First and foremost, every law enforcement agency in the United States should continue with its community policing emphasis to strengthen the connections between citizens and the government. This emphasis on community awareness and law enforcement interaction begins at the top levels of any organization. We must complete our community threat assessments to determine our vulnerabilities.[5] We must also develop and refine our efforts to collect, analyze, and submit information concerning activities in our jurisdictions.

We should expect this to mean reorganizations, new legal tools, and altering the responsibilities of law enforcement agencies. These evolving changes in our profession will come with time. In the meantime, executives are faced with trying to put into perspective the totality of the threat, the leadership one may exert at the local level, and the individual agency's place in the response. Many law enforcement executives see only one-way information flow and CNN headlines. The fact is that local law enforcement's need to take care of business is even more critically important today than ever.

The education of our citizens is also a key component and remains a difficult issue. The ways in which we address the ignorance of our citizens concerning the terrorist threat and the enormity of the actual dangers we face will take a concerted effort by the law enforcement profession. Police executives may take the lead in balancing an honest discussion of reality with the expectations of citizens who wish only to live their lives unhampered by the fears of terrorist events. When citizens are informed and maintain a high level of awareness our work is made easier.

A component of our education includes a review and revision of our understanding and response to Jihadism. We are facing an ideology and organization that resembles none of our earlier foes. We are not facing a country that will agree to surrender or a leadership that agrees to appeasement or accommodation. Jihadists are a group of people who if captured and then freed will continue their holy war. We need to think in the long term about battles, inside and outside of the United States, and for processes, procedures, and laws that support the unique nature of the battle against global terrorism. There will be new attacks. We will respond. Preparing for that response and striking a balance between personal rights and our countries' continued existence will be the challenge for all Western nations.

The traditional local law enforcement model cannot address the worldwide Jihadist threat alone. Nonetheless, traditional law enforcement is more important than ever in understanding our communities, guarding critical infrastructure, and contributing to the overall security of each jurisdiction. In this context, every law enforcement executive "owns" a part of the antiterrorist war and can contribute to its success.

Law enforcement's long-term commitment to adapt to the challenges we face is a strength that serves all of our citizens. New ideas, such as changes in intelligence guidelines, training programs, the treatment of incarcerated prisoners, coalitions, strategies, tactics, and law enforcement techniques are necessary. Each of us should be prepared for the seismic shift in the requirements of our profession and be ready to assist in the terrorist war.

Notes

1. *The Wall Street Journal*, April 19, 2002, A12; *Albuquerque Journal*, Sunday Journal, May 5, 2002, A4.

2. Ibid., A18.

3. Steven Emerson, *American Jihad: The Terrorists Living among Us* (New York: Free Press, 2002), 62.

4. *The Wall Street Journal*, April 26, 2002, A10.

5. See Bill Flynt and W. Ronald Olin, "The Red, Gray, and Blue Model: A New Tool to Help Law Enforcement Executives Address the Transformed Security Environment," *The Police Chief* 69 (February 2002): 50–58.

CHAPTER 28

MULTI-AGENCY COOPERATION ENHANCES HOMELAND SECURITY PRACTICES

Kevin Baum

Like every city in America, on Sept. 12, 2001, Austin, Texas, found itself wrestling with a whole new set of challenges. As the capitol city of the president's home state, we knew we could be the next target.

On that day, Toby Hammett Futrell, then the deputy city manager over public safety, called a meeting of all Austin public safety executives. She got right to the point: The public needs us, so it's time to put turf and competition aside and get to the business of public safety. We will do this collaboratively through a unified approach, and anything less is unacceptable.

Thus began Austin's journey to come together as a public safety collective and, in the process, dismantle longstanding barriers to cooperation between local emergency services. While it's arguable that we still have a long way to go in our effort to break down barriers and achieve synergy in service delivery, Austin has achieved a healthy measure of success, one that has been put to the test on several occasions. Given the likelihood of future terrorist attacks on American soil, we believe this story is worth telling.

A History of Silos and Turf

Before 9-11, Austin had been a typical American city riding a healthy economy. Our police, fire and emergency medical services had always been top-notch, but as in so many large cities, our emergency services were frequently in competition, some of it good-natured, some not.

There had been efforts to develop a collaborative approach to public safety prior to 9-11, but generally these were half-hearted and often bogged down in turf battles and semantic debates. There was simply no burning platform to motivate public safety officials to alter long-standing traditions and roles. Each agency was happy to operate within the protective shield of its service silo. Sept. 11 changed all that.

To achieve her goal of collaboration in public safety, Futrell created a Public Safety Task Force with the specific intent of bringing together the multiple roles of Austin's emergency services into a clear homeland security strategy. Directors, assistant directors and key officers from police, fire and EMS,

Originally published as "Austin City: No Limits," *Homeland Protection Professional*," Vol. 3, No. 2, March 2004. Published by A. J. Parrino & Associates, Western Springs, Illinois. Reprinted with permission of the publisher.

plus executives from stakeholder agencies such as the Office of Emergency Management, public health and the city's utilities staffed the task force.

The central directive for the task force was to develop a unified command and control structure for major events. If 9-11 taught us anything, it's that in the absence of a coherent system for managing complex emergency incidents, one that includes provisions for multi-agency communication, information exchange, command and decision-making, emergency responders quickly will become controlled by the incident.

Adopting an incident management system that all public safety agencies could agree on was thus fundamental to an integrated approach to local homeland security. Secondary to this was the need to develop tools and processes to foster open and ongoing discourse among Austin's emergency services. Given their history of competition, this was a tall order.

Breaking Down Barriers

Not too surprisingly, perhaps, as the Public Safety Task Force began to meet, members began to discover that many of the preconceptions they'd held about each other were in error. Indeed, it's well documented in the academic literature that increasing contact and interaction between groups in conflict can significantly mitigate conflict. The more often we spend time with those from other groups or factions, the less likely we are to assign stereotypes and false motives to them.

Likewise, as groups begin to interact meaningfully, they begin to recognize that each party brings its own unique set of perspectives, assumptions, values and priorities to the table. Over time and through continued issue-based discussions, fragmented groups will begin to respect the perspectives of those around them.

While all of the task force members were familiar with each other, this was the first time they'd met to make collaborative decisions on major public safety strategies and protocols. Getting together and discussing important issues in the context of national urgency had the effect of slicing through petty prejudices and fostered an environment where each agency could share its perspective without fear of "losing" something. It rapidly became easy to focus on weighty issues that would save lives, rather than petty issues that would save face.

Who's More Important?

Here's what we learned. As we built mutual understanding for the unique roles and goals of each public safety agency in Austin, we began to recognize that each agency's core mission complements the others,' it doesn't compete with them. All emergency incident goals and objectives have equal value, whether they are rescue, triage of multiple casualties or preservation of a major crime scene.

No single mission or agency role necessarily has to be dominant; it depends on the changing circumstances of an event. No single agency, therefore, has to be considered the "lead" on major incidents.

This is a crucial point and the crux of our story. Till now, the war between the emergency services in Austin — and, arguably, between public safety agencies across the country — has been over who retains ultimate authority at major incidents. Of course, embedded within this deep-rooted debate is that ugly question, rife with political consequence: "Which agency is more important?"

No single issue has contributed more to the rift between public safety agencies than the debate over who'll be in charge, whose role is dominant. In fact, it's likely that any effort to achieve collaboration in the interest of homeland security that requires one agency to be the central command of all major incidents is doomed to fail. This approach triggers too many preprogrammed responses of turf protection. And while we all hate to admit it, this very issue contributed to the public safety tragedy of 9-11.

Our experience suggests that it doesn't have to be that way. As Richard Herrington, director of Austin/Travis County EMS, notes, "The key principle that underpins the Austin model of IMS [Incident Management System] is that you have to understand major incidents from the perspectives of each agency, not just your own. Once you are there, you begin to appreciate the multiple concerns of each department and quickly realize that they all have equal value. It is a simple conclusion that no one agency should be in charge, but rather all of them should have a lead role."

Today, the City of Austin manages multi-agency incidents through a flexible unified command framework based on the principles, language and concepts of the National Incident Management System. (Two of our task force members sit on the NIMS Advisory Committee.) This framework allows flexibility for incident command staff to respond to major changes in service demand. On the command team, each member is considered a vital player, and major decisions to direct the incident are agreed to collectively, with respect and deference given to subject-matter experts.

No single commander is "in charge" at all times. Instead the team allows room for command decisions to evolve with the incident. Like the passing of a baton, lead authority transfers from one department commander to another as the demands of the incident change.

The three fundamental elements of command and control (unity of command, chain of command and span of control) aren't compromised within each agency; each commander still retains ultimate authority for his/her department personnel. What's differ-ent, and what constitutes the success of this model, is that multi-agency commanders are together and communicating with each other at the strategic level. Major decisions are made in concert, rather than in chaos.

Command Collegiality

Of central importance to this incident management model is pre-incident planning and coordination: the how-tos, what-ifs and wherefores that need to be asked prior to any major event. In the past, these questions were asked, but they were considered individually, within the protective silos of individual departments, and we've seen the consequences of that approach.

To break through this barrier, the task force members quickly realized that they were going to need to push their philosophy of collaboration and communication down throughout each organization, onto the streets where the officers and rescuers execute the mission.

This was no small challenge. The Austin Fire Department has almost 1,000 firefighters, the Austin Police Department employs more than 1,300 officers, and the Austin/Travis County EMS Department has 390 full-time paramedics. So how do you execute a cross-departmental cultural change when so many players are involved? You start at the top and slowly push it down. If interaction on meaningful issues between agencies can work for department directors, it can work for the front line.

To push this collaborative philosophy to the street, the Public Safety Task Force created the City of Austin Public Safety Command College. This is designed to bring together key officers and members from each department for three days of study and interaction on the Austin incident management model.

By giving participants assigned seats (forcing them to mingle) and then walking them through multiple tabletop exercises, the college compels members from each organization to consider major incidents from new perspectives. Commanders from each agency were given the opportunity to describe incident priorities from their perspective, and then groups were asked to bring them all together into a coherent strategy and plan of action for managing a major event. No individual agency was given a lead role. Rather they were asked to develop a collaborative approach with joint decision-making.

Perhaps the greatest value to come from the college is that over several days of interaction, command-level officers from each organization could build personal relationships with their peers from other agencies. Connecting faces to names and building trust and camaraderie between counterparts greases the gears of interaction when these commanders find themselves at a major incident together.

As Fire Chief Gary Warren notes, "It's common knowledge that people prefer to do business with friends rather than strangers. By bringing our incident commanders together, the very men and women who will be on the street making joint decisions under tremendous pressure, we eliminate the awkwardness that comes from a lack of familiarity."

Police Chief Stan Knee agrees. "Historically, our officers wouldn't even know where to look to find their counterparts on a major incident scene. Today, they not only know who their counterparts are, where to find them and what their missions are, but most importantly, they're all speaking the same language in terms of incident action plans, communication, command and control. When you eliminate confusion, you save lives."

Maintaining Momentum

In addition to the college, which is methodically working its way down through the ranks of each department, the task force created a number of mechanisms to support continued interaction between agencies, some formal, some not.

For example, all members of the initial Public Safety Task Force attend a monthly meeting with Assistant City Manager Laura Huffman. This meeting is designed to reinforce the message that top management supports a collaborative approach to homeland security, and it also provides a forum to address pressing homeland security issues and develop local strategies for response, such as the numerous and often contentious war protests that were staged on the Texas State Capitol grounds.

Additionally, each week command members from each organization have an open invitation to attend a public safety luncheon, an informal gathering to exchange ideas, discuss problems and issues, introduce new players and develop new relationships. What's important here is that all agencies have agreed that the city's success in building a synergistic approach to public safety will continue only if they all maintain an aggressive, ongoing commitment to continuing, meaningful interaction.

Many Benefits

The benefits of cooperation among Austin's emergency services have been numerous and ongoing. One key benefit has been a dramatic reduction in management inefficiency and service redundancy. Through open discourse, department managers are able to make important decisions collectively, through an overarching public safety perspective.

For example, just four months after 9-11, the Public Safety Task Force was able to bring a unified homeland security funding package to the city council. This request was a specific response to local homeland security needs, but it also was the first time in Austin's history that all three public safety agencies came together for funding. The power of a unified political front for funding requests shouldn't be ignored, especially as the federal government prepares to distribute more than $3.5 billion to state and local governments for homeland security.

While it stands to reason that you can do more with less when working collaboratively, it's also true that you can get more to boost your efforts, in terms of funding and support, when you bring a unified team to the discussion, one with a clear understanding of roles and goals.

The greatest benefit to come from integration in public safety has been the effect our approach has had on public confidence. Today, as the public struggles to process the rapid-fire pace of international events, they need to know that their local emergency responders are trained, prepared and talking to each other. In Austin, our citizens hear from us regularly as we communicate our message of homeland security through the media, showcasing our collaborative efforts during major events, such as University of Texas football games, war protests and other high-profile events.

"Our ongoing effort to achieve integration in public safety is all about accountability to the citizens," says City Manager Futrell. "In fact, given what is at stake, collaboration in public safety is the only way to go.... It's the difference between managing for results and hoping for results."

CHAPTER 29

MUNICIPAL ELECTRONIC OPERATIONS AND DISASTER PLANNING

Paul Bockelman and *Robert T. O'Connor*

The word "disaster" conjures images of a fire, flood, hurricane, or even a terrorist attack. But a city or town is much more likely to face disaster from a more common threat — a computer server failure, an electronic virus, a computer hacker, a mundane hardware problem or equipment failure, or human error. Such a disaster can bring a community's entire operation to a standstill.

Every community has an emergency preparedness plan that addresses what to do in case of a public safety emergency. These plans focus on contacting key personnel, maintaining access to fuel and equipment, and keeping communications systems operational.

Few communities, however, have planned for how to access their data if the entire computer network is lost due to fire, water damage, or other natural or man-made disaster. Most communities have daily backup systems for their computer data, including provisions to store data off site. But disaster recovery planning is not just about backing up data; it's about business continuity. Especially during an emergency, city or town government is expected to be operating at or near full capacity. How quickly you have your core activities up and running again — your e-mail system, assessors' records, payroll system, and databases, for example — will be a measure of your success as a municipal leader. Every community needs a strong and thorough disaster management plan for its electronic operations.

A comprehensive survey of your computer operations will help you identify vulnerabilities, though experience may have pointed some of them out already. For example, the town of Reading recently suffered a computer crash and discovered, unfortunately, that its e-mail system was not part of the normal backup procedure.

To protect their electronic operations, some organizations have adopted a new standard requiring future server purchases to have redundant drives in order to increase the availability and reliability of data. A state agency recently increased its backup schedule from twice a week to nightly and upgraded its backup equipment to high-speed tape drives to dramatically reduce the time it

Originally published as "Disaster Planning Must Include Electronic Operations," *Municipal Advocate*, Vol. 20, No. 3, Fall 2003. Published by the Massachusetts Municipal Association, Boston, MA. Reprinted with permission of the publisher.

takes to complete a backup or to restore data. An analysis of power lines revealed the need for power protection for critical servers and network equipment, so uninterruptible power supplies will be recommended.

The Recovery Plan

An electronic operations disaster recovery plan has three goals:
- **Save data**
- **Save hardware, software and facilities**
- **Resume critical processes and restore data**

Such a plan may be developed using the following seven-step system:

1. Identify the risks your community faces — both "worst case" and "most likely" scenarios.
2. Identify the information technology resources (i.e., computer equipment) that are at risk.
3. Prioritize "mission-critical" data (data that is required for your key operations).
4. Identify the systems you need to get back up and running immediately (phones, e-mail systems, payroll systems, etc.).
5. Develop and implement a plan to protect against the threats you've identified.
6. Test procedures to ensure that the plan works.
7. Develop a plan to enable full recovery and resume normal operations.

The Massachusetts Interlocal Insurance Association has a disaster recovery/contingency plan for its property and casualty functions that includes laptop computers and servers set up at a remote location. Each laptop is configured with the operating system and all applications that MIIA staff use. The remote servers are connected to the main system, so data on the backup server is never more than five minutes old. In an emergency, the back-up system can be operating within an hour. The laptops and servers are stored in four movable crates that can be moved quickly to another location if necessary.

Cities and towns may be able to develop a similar plan without spending a fortune. For instance, outdated computer hardware and laptops may serve well as backup equipment after a community undergoes a computer upgrade. Some communities may form a partnership to store data on each other's servers and become each other's disaster recovery location. This can be done cost effectively and securely with adequate log-on IDs, passwords, encryption, and other security features.

CHAPTER 30

MUTUAL AID AGREEMENTS BUILD LOCAL DISASTER-RESPONSE CAPACITY

Thomas E. Poulin

To provide an effective response to the consequences of a terrorist attack, it is vital that local governments work collaboratively. Since the first World Trade Center bombing in 1993, this has been a recurring theme in professional and academic literature. Still, many local agencies have not entered into formal agreements, which could lead to an ineffective and inefficient governmental response during a disaster. Local government has an obligation to aggressively pursue collaborative relationships and state governments have a duty to create an environment where such relationships can flourish, if the public is to be protected to the greatest extent possible.

Collaborative relationships may take many forms, with one of the most common being the mutual aid agreement. The mutual aid agreement is a pact between local governments whereby each pledges to assist the other in time of need. The agreement is voluntary, and should clearly identify the roles and responsibilities of both the requesting party and the organization providing assistance. A mutual aid agreement permits local governments to temporarily combine operations, within a narrowly identified geographic and temporal setting. Although mutual aid agreements differ from situation to situation, there are common elements that should be in each document.

Common Elements of Mutual Aid Agreements

First, there should be some consideration given as to what circumstances justify requesting assistance. In some instances, aid is only to be requested when an event is so large, or when so many events are occurring simultaneously, that local resources are exhausted. This may take the form of one locality sending ambulances into another during a mass casualty incident. In other agreements, mutual aid is given because resources are more readily available from an external source, due to time or distance. Illustrative of this latter model are the automatic aid agreements used by fire departments in metropolitan areas where the closest fire

Originally published as "National Threat — Local Response: Building Local Disaster Capacity with Mutual Aid Agreements," *PA Times*, Vol. 28, No. 3, March 2005. Published by the American Society for Public Administration, Washington, D.C. Reprinted with permission of the publisher.

companies respond to an incident, even if they must cross jurisdictional boundaries to do so. There are many views on how to construct such an agreement. Prior to entering into mutual aid agreements, organizations should insure the final agreement mirrors both their managerial vision and their organizational needs.

Second, financial issues must be addressed. Under normal circumstances, when organizations request assistance from one another, a financial liability is incurred. Most government agencies entering into mutual aid agreements do so with the understanding that reciprocal aid will be offered in return. The arrangement is viewed as a benefit to both, essentially enhancing and expanding local response capacity at no additional cost. Viewed as a quid pro quo arrangement, no financial liability would be incurred by requesting assistance. If this is the case, the mutual aid agreement should clearly indicate that both parties waive claims to compensation. If limited reimbursement is possible for costs incurred above and beyond normal operating costs that too should be clearly identified in the agreement. Once again, the specifics of the arrangement must reflect the relationship desired by the agencies entering into the agreement, but they should be established before an incident to eliminate any misunderstandings, which could lead to disputes that weaken the agreement in the future.

Third, many mutual aid agreements include a stipulation that the agency requested to provide assistance may refuse because of extenuating circumstances. This type of clause was intended for those very unusual circumstances when service demand in both localities is very high at the same time. For example, while a police department might request assistance to provide additional law enforcement resources during a civil disturbance, a neighboring police department may already be taxed because of a hostage situation in their own jurisdiction. Under such circumstances, it would be unreasonable for

them to send any of their scarce resources to another locality. In the post–September 11, 2001, environment, when it is projected that a large-scale terrorist event might simultaneously impact multiple jurisdictions in a metropolitan area, it would be unreasonable to expect a city to send its units into another locality until they were sure that their own citizens were completely protected. Additionally, some local governments have decided that if the national terror alert is raised to orange or red they will not provide any mutual aid, regardless of pre-existing agreements. Understanding the implications of this type of clause is vital. Failing to consider it when designing disaster plans may cause a locality to rely on resources that will not be available when called. If the possibility exists that such conflicting needs will exist, contingency plans should be developed.

Fourth, worker's compensation issues should be addressed. While the ideal basis for collaborative relationships can be viewed as altruistic, they exist in the real world environment. Employees must be paid. If injured, they must be compensated. If killed, their families must be cared for. In times of disaster, there is a higher probability that employees may be injured or killed in the line-of-duty. Consequently, mutual aid agreements should discuss such matters. Typically, the language in mutual aid agreements indicates that the employers of the employees involved will continue to pay their wages and provide any worker's compensation benefits, waiving all claims against the party requesting assistance. Clearly stating this in a mutual aid agreement will insure that employee's rights are protected, while also clearly identifying the responsibilities of the organizations involved. Clarifying this issue prior to an event should insure there is no misunderstanding between the agencies at a later date.

Fifth, the framers of mutual aid agreements should insure all the legal requirements for such agreements are verified and cited. While in some situations mutual aid agreements between agencies may be entered into through an agreement between the agencies' directors, in some instances state or local law may stipulate that only the governing body of a locality may enter into a mutual aid agreement. While the approval of a city council may be pro forma once a department head has reviewed a document, it is necessary to provide the legal foundation for the implementation. The legal implications of a mutual aid agreement can greatly affect the ability of local authorities to act in a lawful and ethical manner.

The Legal Requirements

Legally, government authorities at the local level are vested with powers commensurate to the needs of their day-to-day roles. The basis for formal authority, especially in the case of public safety officials, is grounded in state and local law. Typically, they are empowered only when acting in accordance with the requirements of their position, and only when they have a duty-to-act. As local responders typically have no duty-to-act in other localities, they may effectively have no authorities or legal protections beyond that of the average citizen. While this may have little implication for public works employees clearing debris from a public roadway after a storm, it may be a problem for law enforcement agencies and fire departments. In the course of their duties they are often exempted from traffic laws, may have the authority to arrest, and may be permitted to force entry into property without a warrant. If they engage in such activities in a locality where they have no duty-to-act, there is the potential for opening themselves and their employers to a host of legal problems, including possible criminal charges and civil suits. Additionally, employees injured or killed during the performance of tasks where they have no duty-to-act may not be covered by worker's compensation benefits. A properly executed mutual aid agreement provides a duty-to-act in another locality, and, consequently, it should ameliorate legal problems, should events go awry.

Unfortunately, many public managers are not familiar with the legal requirements of mutual aid agreements. It is not uncommon to find agreements signed by the heads of agencies that are legally invalid. It is not uncommon for mutual aid agreements to include non-governmental organizations, which may unintentionally extend the coverage of sovereign immunity to private groups working in conjunction with local government, but working outside the direct control of local officials. In such circumstances, local government may become liable for the actions of the non-governmental organization. Like any governmental agreement, mutual aid agreements must meet the requirements of the law, while concurrently not creating a relationship in which a locality incurs a heavy fiscal burden, opens itself to legal liability, or reduces its own emergency response capacity to unreasonable levels. It is vital that public managers work closely with their legal advisors in crafting an effective and appropriate mutual aid agreement.

Local Cooperation a Necessity

The threat of WMD includes the possibility of mass casualties, collapsed buildings, the release of toxic substances, and a host of other challenges to be faced after any catastrophe. No local government can be expected to unilaterally prepare for a disaster, including a terrorist. Until state and federal assistance can arrive, local governments must fend for themselves. The most cost-effective and practical means of expanding and enhancing local emergency response capacity is to work collaboratively with other local governments, with the objective of making all communities safer. Mutual aid agreements provide a framework to support that objective.

CHAPTER 31

NATIONAL INCIDENT RESPONSE PLAN: A COMPREHENSIVE INTERAGENCY APPROACH TO EMERGENCY MANAGEMENT

Thomas Ridge

On October 10, 2003, U.S. Homeland Security Secretary Tom Ridge approved the Initial National Response Plan (INRP), an interim plan designed to help develop a unified approach to domestic incident management across the nation.

The INRP represents a significant first step toward the overall goal of integrating the current family of federal domestic prevention, preparedness, response, and recovery plans into a single all-hazards national response plan.

The initial plan was developed in conjunction with state and local governments, law enforcement, and the fire and emergency management communities, tribal associations, the private sector, and other nongovernmental organizations. The objective was for the United States to be better prepared by integrating emergency response plans that cover terrorist attacks, major disasters, and other emergencies.

Presidential Directive 5

In the Homeland Security Presidential Directive 5 (HSPD-5)[1] the purpose of the INRP was to enhance the ability of the United States to manage domestic incidents by establishing a single, comprehensive national incident management system. HSPD-5 outlines the policy as follows:

> To prevent, prepare for, respond to, and recover from terrorist attacks, major disasters, and other emergencies, the United State shall establish a single, comprehensive approach to domestic incident management. The objective of the United States government is to ensure that all levels of government across the nation have the capability to work efficiently and effectively together, using a national approach to domestic incident management. In these efforts, with regard to domestic incidents, the United States government treats crisis management and consequence management as a single, integrated function, rather than as two separate functions.[2]

The presidential directive designates the secretary of homeland security as the princi-

Originally published as "Initial National Response Plan," *The Police Chief,* Vol. LXXI, Vol. 2, February 2004. Published by the International Association of Chiefs of Police, Alexandria, VA. Reprinted with permission of the publisher.

pal federal official for domestic incident management. Pursuant to the Homeland Security Act of 2002, the secretary is responsible for coordinating federal operations in the United States to prepare for and respond to terrorist attacks and to coordinate the use of the federal government's resources during recovery from terrorist attacks, major disasters, and other emergencies. For this action to take place one of four conditions must apply:

- A federal department or agency acting under its own authority has requested the assistance of the secretary of homeland security
- The resources of state and local authorities have been overwhelmed and the appropriate state and local authorities have requested federal assistance
- More than one federal department or agency has become substantially involved in responding to the incident
- The secretary of homeland security has been directed to assume responsibility for managing the domestic incident by the president of the United States

As this effort evolves, the U.S. homeland security effort will be guided by the concept of one plan.

State and Local Authorities

Presidential Directive 5 clearly recognizes the roles and responsibilities of state and local authorities in domestic incident management. The directive recognizes that the initial responsibility for managing domestic incidents generally falls on state and local authorities. The federal government's role is to assist state and local authorities when their resources are overwhelmed, or when federal interests are involved.

The Department of Homeland Security is tasked with coordinating with state and local governments on planning, equipment, training, and exercise activities. The Homeland Security Department provides assistance to state and local governments to develop all-hazards plans and capabilities and ensure compatibility with federal plans.

Elements of INRP

The Initial National Response Plan strengthens the U.S. emergency response process by harmonizing existing federal response plan activities with incident management leadership responsibilities assigned to Homeland Security. As a result, the nation's responders will now be supported with new incident management capability including the following:

National Homeland Security Operations Center: The INRP provides for the establishment of the permanent Homeland Security Operations Center (HSOC) to serve as the primary national-level hub for domestic incident management operational communications and information pertaining to domestic incident management. The HSOC is located at Department of Homeland Security headquarters; the HSOC provides threat monitoring and situational awareness for domestic incident management 24 hours a day, seven days a week.

Interagency Incident Management Group: The Interagency Incident Management Group (IIMG) is to facilitate national-level situation awareness, policy coordination, and incident coordination during domestic incidents. The IIMG is made up of senior representatives from federal departments and agencies, nongovernmental organizations, as well as Department of Homeland Security components to facilitate national-level situation awareness, policy coordination, and incident coordination.

Principal Federal Official: The secretary of homeland security may designate a Principal Federal Official (PFO) during a domestic incident to serve as the personal representative of the Department of Homeland Security locally during an incident. The PFO will oversee and coordinate federal incident activities and work with local authorities to determine requirements and provide timely federal assistance.

Joint Field Office: Federal activities at a local incident site will be integrated during domestic incidents to better facilitate coordination between federal, state, and local authorities through a Joint Field Office (JFO). The JFO is expected to incorporate existing entities such as the Joint Operations Center, the Disaster Field Office, and other federal offices and teams that provide support on the scene.

National Incident Management System

In addition to the new emergency planning measures established by the INRP, the Department of Homeland Security and responders from around the United States continue the development of a National Incident Management System (NIMS) that will create additional standardized coordination procedures for incident managers.

The INRP represents a significant first step toward an overall goal of integrating the current family of federal domestic prevention, preparedness, response, and recovery plans into a single all-disciplines, all-hazards plan. When the INRP is supported by the NIMS, a national system will exist that creates standardized incident management processes, protocols, and procedures.

CHAPTER 32

NEIGHBORHOOD WATCH PROGRAMS AND HOMELAND SECURITY

Deborah J. Daniels

In Stafford County, Va., just south of Washington, D.C., John Scott and his wife are "on watch" against terrorism as part of a new effort led by the National Sheriffs' Association and the Office of Justice Programs under President Bush's Citizen Corps initiative. The Scott's kitchen window overlooks a bridge that carries critical infrastructure for the nation's capital—a fuel pipeline for Dulles and Reagan Washington National airports and telecommunications fiber-optics cables for MCI, Sprint and Quest.

Under Stafford County's Homeland Security Neighborhood Watch program, a brainchild of Stafford County Sheriff Charles Jett, the Scotts and their neighbors have received special training on how to be "on watch" against terrorism. The training provides community volunteers with descriptions of the critical infrastructure areas near their homes, the basics of an effective Neighborhood Watch program and information about possible terrorist and sabotage risks to the community. Each volunteer receives a special homeland security notebook containing information about how to contact the proper authorities to report suspected terrorist activity or call for emergency assistance. In addition, contact information for each Neighborhood Watch member is plugged into the sheriffs office's Reverse-911 computer database so that volunteers can receive terrorism alerts and other homeland security information.

The Stafford County program is just one of thousands of new Neighborhood Watch programs that have been launched in response to the President's call for citizen volunteers to enlist in helping ensure our nation's security. Under the President's Citizen Corps initiative, NSA and the Office of Justice Programs are working to double the number of Neighborhood Watch groups across the nation by January 2004 and to incorporate terrorism prevention into this highly successful program's long-time mission of preventing neighborhood crime.

The Citizen Corps is part of the USA Freedom Corps, which President Bush established following the September 11 attacks to respond to the groundswell of public interest in doing something to help protect our

Originally published as "Citizen Corps: Mobilizing Citizens to Be 'On Watch' Against Terrorism," *Sheriff*, Vol. 55, Vol. 4, July/August 2003. Published by the National Sheriffs' Association, Alexandria, VA. Reprinted with permission of the publisher.

homeland from future terrorism. In establishing the Citizen Corps, the President tapped one of this nation's most valuable resources: its dedicated civilian volunteers. Citizen Corps enlists the talents and energy of citizen volunteers in activities that make communities safer, stronger, and better prepared to respond to any emergency situation. Through a range of programs, Citizen Corps helps local residents take a more active role in crime prevention, risk reduction and emergency preparedness in their communities.

Over the past 18 months, NSA and the Office of Justice Programs have been working under a cooperative agreement to reach Citizen Corps' goal of doubling the number of Neighborhood Watch programs by 2004. To spread the word about the Neighborhood Watch concept and to help local groups incorporate the prevention of terrorism into their mission, NSA launched and maintains the USAonwatch Web site (www.USAonwatch.org). This state-of-the-art Web site includes a searchable database, a national registry of Neighborhood Watch groups and information about how to implement and manage a Watch group. Since the Web site's debut in January 2002, about 500 copies of the Neighborhood Watch implementation manual have been downloaded each week.

As a result of NSA's outstanding leadership, the National Neighborhood Watch Program is well on its way to reaching its goal. There are now more than 10,000 registered Neighborhood Watch programs throughout the country, up from 7,500 just a year ago, all working to increase the safety of their neighborhoods and be "on watch" against terrorism. And NSA has issued a call to law enforcement agencies, citizen organizations and the general public to "Meet the Challenge" of reaching the 15,000-program goal by encouraging local residents to start new Neighborhood Watch groups or revitalize existing ones.

All across America, communities are answering this call to service. In Hillsborough County, Fla., sheriff's deputies have formed a Business Watch, to help local business owners better protect themselves and their property in the case of a terrorist event or other emergency. In Hinds County, Miss., Neighborhood Watch is developing a brochure that describes possible terrorist targets in the area and explains to residents what they should do in case of an emergency. And in Washoe County, Nev., the sheriff's office has helped launch a new Citizen Homeland Security Council consisting of residents who are trained on terrorism issues and emergency response. Council members will assist the sheriff's office when needed and train their neighbors on how to prepare for an emergency.

Volunteers in Police Service

The Neighborhood Watch partnership between NSA and OJP is one of several initiatives making up the President's Citizen Corps. OJP also is working with the International Association of Chiefs of Police (IACP) on the Volunteers in Police Service (VIPS) program. VIPS addresses the increasing demands faced by state and local law enforcement agencies in response to terrorism and other crime by training civilian volunteers to perform certain tasks and free up law enforcement professionals to better perform their frontline duties. VIPS encourages civilians to volunteer to work in their local law enforcement agencies. At the same time, VIPS helps law enforcement agencies to identify ways to expand their use of citizen volunteers, enhance existing VIPS programs or start a new one.

Based on their specific needs, local law enforcement agencies both determine what roles volunteers can play and provide the appropriate training. To assist with this process, the VIPS Web site (www.policevolunteers.org) provides detailed information about existing volunteer programs, as well as helpful documents and forms that can be downloaded for agencies' use.

Civilian volunteers can perform a range of activities — everything from reading parking meters, to servicing police vehicles, to conducting research, to taking police reports. There are also suggestions on the Web site for ways civic organizations, businesses and other groups can assist local law enforcement, such as cleaning up local parks, providing automation and computer services, or funding public service announcements on crime prevention topics.

Law enforcement agencies can also use the VIPS Web site to identify themselves as agencies that welcome volunteers. The Web site allows citizens to search the database for local VIPS programs throughout the country. In VIPS' first year, these programs have grown from just 76 programs in 27 states and the District of Columbia to more than 500 in 49 states and the district. Currently, nearly 22,000 citizens volunteer in law enforcement agencies through VIPS.

Community Emergency Response Team Program

A third Citizen Corps component, the Community Emergency Response Team (CERT) program, is administered by the Federal Emergency Management Agency in the new Department of Homeland Security. Also designed to assist law enforcement in ensuring community safety, CERT trains civilian volunteers to help themselves and their neighbors in emergency situations until professional first-responders arrive. Volunteers receive 20 hours of training in disaster-response skills, including fire suppression, urban search and rescue, and basic medical techniques. The goal is to help citizens take a more active role in emergency preparedness.

CERT is proving to be an important component of Neighborhood Watch in at least one community. Law enforcement officials in Polk County, Mo., have teamed with emergency management officials to incorporate Community Emergency Response Team training into their Neighborhood Watch programs. In the event of an emergency, team members would check on neighbors to make sure everyone was safe and accounted for. They also would try to eliminate any fire hazards, such as shutting off gas mains to prevent an explosion.

Training has been provided to 70 county residents, including a group of teenage Civil Air Patrol cadets. The local Wal-Mart is a partner, and the county has appointed a coordinator to encourage other businesses, daycare centers and schools to participate in this innovative community safety effort.

CERT teams currently are operating in 42 states. More information is available on the CERT Web site (http://training.fema.gov/emiweb/CERT/).

The Medical Reserve Corps

The Medical Reserve Corps (MRC) is another aspect of Citizen Corps administered by the Department of Health and Human Services. The Medical Reserve Corps marshals and trains volunteer health professionals, and others interested in health issues, to provide ongoing support for community public health needs and resources during large-scale emergencies. Volunteers are trained to assist emergency-response teams, provide care to victims with relatively minor injuries and perform other tasks to improve the overall health of their communities. More information is available on the MRC Web site (http://www.medicalreservecorps.gov/).

Through these Citizen Corps initiatives, citizens in communities throughout the country are answering the President's call to national service in defense of our homeland.

However, as Adams County, Miss., Sheriff Tommy Ferrell, past president of NSA, notes on the "USAonwatch" Web site, "Citizens and law enforcement have made great strides in improving the security of our neighborhoods and our nation since September 11, 2001, but we must continue to be vigilant. We face a new day in which we realize that our homeland requires the hard work and diligence of all its people to retain the freedoms we treasure and have fought so hard to enjoy."

The Department of Justice appreciates NSA's leadership in this critical effort, and we encourage all law enforcement and other criminal justice professionals to enlist citizen volunteers in Citizen Corps and in ensuring the security of our homeland.

CHAPTER 33

PERSONAL IDENTIFICATION TECHNOLOGIES, PRACTICES, AND HOMELAND SECURITY

Jennifer Pero

Immigration officials and law enforcement agents arrested 24 people and seized fake documents and counterfeiting equipment near the Adams-Morgan neighborhood of Washington, D.C., in early May. Officials seized 360 bogus green cards, 281 fraudulent social security cards, 70 fake employment authorization cards and 46 counterfeit driver's licenses from California, Utah and Florida.

The incident highlights a national identity crisis. An identity-related crime occurs in America every 63 seconds. Approximately 500,000 identity theft cases are expected in the U.S. in 2002 alone.

But even legally-obtained identification credentials can be problematic. The majority of the 19 hijackers on Sept. 11 had followed steps to obtain identification without raising any red flags.

Proposals are being heard in Washington and elsewhere about the need for a national ID card system, or at least a plan to improve our system of de facto identification cards — the state-level driver's licenses.

Tools exist — from biometrics to smart cards — that are capable of increasing our na-tion's security by ensuring the integrity of our citizens' identification documents. But as proponents clamor for a standardized national ID system, others scramble to oppose it. While admitting that the events of Sept. 11 highlighted gaps in our Homeland's defense, opponents see a national identification system as more knee-jerk reaction than an effective plan. Still, with identification so easily obtainable, a need to tighten existing standards — or create new ones — has evolved.

Nearly 114 countries already have a national identification system in place, and yet a broad-based national system seems somehow un-American. Arguments against this idea raise questions worthy of discussion: Who would an ID card protect? Would the system be mandatory? Who would have access to a cardholder's information? Who would be responsible for logging, updating and maintaining the data?

Whether it be in the form of computer database, biometrics or smart card, technology is available to vastly transform how we identify people and what information we col-

Originally published as "Who Are YOU?" *Government Security*, Vol. 1, No. 4, July 2002. Published by PRIMEDIA Magazines & Media Inc., Overland Park, KS. Reprinted with permission of the publisher.

lect about them — how to use it is the question.

The Root of the Problem

Traditionally, so-called breeder documents — such as birth certificates and passports — are required to obtain state or government-issued identification, such as driver's licenses and social security cards. Additionally, certified naturalization documents, immigration identification cards, passports, resident alien cards or valid employment authorization cards can also pass as breeder documents in obtaining government-issued identification. The nation depends on the validity of such breeder documents to verify identity, but all too often, these documents are compromised.

"The real hole in security systems today is that people are presenting false documents," says Bill Thalheimer, CEO of Imaging Automation, a Bedford, N.H.-based supplier of authentication technologies.

In early June, someone broke into the Tacoma, Wash., Immigration and Naturalization Service (INS) inspection office, stealing four stamps used to allow foreigners to enter the U.S. Although the intent in that case was apparently not to steal INS equipment per se; in the wrong hands, the stamps could have potentially approved visas, visa extensions and temporary green cards — a result, investigators admitted, that could have facilitated forgery. If a false breeder document can pass to legally obtain government-issued identification, then the issue of identity has not been solved. Mike Shlasko, director of business development for Symbol Technologies, Holtsville, N.Y., says one must be protected before the other. "If we can't control visas," for example, Shlasko says, "we're not going to be able to solve the problem of securing [any other government-issued] identification documents stemming from them."

On December 19, 2001, the Document Security Alliance (DSA), an ad hoc group of industry leaders associated with ID-card document processes, met to discuss methods by which document security and security procedures could be improved. The DSA represents more than 60 companies and government agencies and consists of more than 80 members, including card and smart card manufacturers, biometric providers, system integration houses, security laminate/document providers, encryption organizations, data processing companies, proximity card providers and card printer manufacturers.

In its forum, a significant amount of time was spent on fraud associated with breeder documents. The meeting began with presentations by the U.S. Secret Service, where members reviewed cases and samples of document fraud. Accordingly, members agreed, the forensic task of determining document origin has become far more difficult.

Driver's Licenses and Beyond

The identity discussion starts with our current system of state driver's licenses. Driver's licenses are already used to drive a car, buy cigarettes or alcohol, vote, establish a bank account or credit card, or board an airplane. Already required to secure transactions such as getting a job, cashing a check or buying a gun — it seems natural for driver's licenses to be used for other security measures as well. "Federal and state governments have all agreed that driver's licenses serve as an identification document — but it needs to be strengthened," Shlasko says.

How to standardize and add functionality to state licenses is among the plans being discussed. An open question is how far should we go — or more accurately, how far do we need to go?

The American Association of Motor Vehicle Administrators (AAMVA) proposes standardization of our system of state driver's licenses. Several congressmen and government advisory committees — such as the Office of Homeland Security — back this plan. Larry Bowne, chairman of the DSA and senior industry manager, identification systems for Eltron Card Printer Products, Camarillo, Calif., also serves as a representative on AAMVA's Industry Advisory Board (IAB). Bowne represents the card printer unit on the IAB, and several AAMVA members are a part of the DSA.

"In relevance to the question of the rationale behind standardizing driver's licenses," Bowne says, "it relates to two issues"— from homeland security to safer drivers.

But some proponents maintain a distinction between driver's licenses and national ID cards. "If you're trying to put this issue in with the national ID card debate," says Jason King, a representative of the AAMVA, "then you've got it all wrong." While King contends the driver's license is the most widely used form of identification in the U.S. today, it was never intended to be so. The AAMVA is looking to Congress to mandate a more unified look to state's driver's licenses — not turn them into a national ID card. King admits that loopholes in our driver's license framework are one of the biggest threats to our national security system. However, he quickly points out why driver's licenses should not be used as a de facto national ID card — a national ID card is government-issued and mandatory; a driver's license is state-issued and voluntary. "What we're trying to do, while balancing both security and privacy," King says, "is to strengthen the issuance of driver's licenses."

The AAMVA, which is looking to Congress to mandate a more unified look to state's driver's licenses, recommends that driver's licenses should have common identification features, so that departments of motor vehicles (DMVs) will be able to locate fraudulent cards; thus, securing the nation against illegal cardholders and eliminating issuing more than one card to the same person.

State-linked Databases for Triple Validation

To verify that a cardholder has already been entered into the system, eliminating the possibility that a person can obtain more than one license, the AAMVA has also asked that driver's license databases be linked state to state. It's a process already in place by the AAMVA for commercial driver's licenses. The proposed plan would link each state's DMV records to a central database used by local and state law enforcement personnel. Law enforcement officials would be able to access personal identification such as name and address and would also have access to the cardholder's driver history. By providing this information in a central database, the AAMVA intends to create safer highways, reduce license forgery and strengthen the validity of the cardholder's identity. Says Bowne, "There's a tremendous wealth of technology and experience that could be brought to bear in issues such as this"— specifically, he says, the inoperability of available information.

Senator Richard Durbin (D–Ill.), in a hearing outlining the current state of driver's license security, said he would introduce legislation to improve the reliability and security of state-issued driver's licenses as well as state-issued identification cards for nondrivers. Durbin supports the efforts of the AAMVA and favors uniform standards for issuance and administration of state-issued licenses and stricter penalties for the fraudulent use of state IDs. "After Sept. 11, use of fake IDs is no longer just a teenaged trick or merely about drunk drivers trying to hide their bad driving records," Durbin said. "It is about our national security."

It makes sense then that Durbin would propose that the AAMVA set standards of identifying driver's license applicants before issuing them a card. If his bill is passed, Durbin proposes that the same state law enforcement officials who have access to the database also have moderate access to Social Security Administration and INS databases, to "cross-check" a cardholder's identification.

Setting Standards

With the identification system being managed by the states, the Progressive Policy Institute (PPI), Washington, says, "Congress has an important role in setting minimal standards to ensure the system's security and integrity. In a policy report entitled, "Modernizing the State Identification System," PPi recommends that Congress "set minimum standards for documentation that states must require before issuing an ID card."

The Security Industry Association's (SIA) Homeland Security Advisory Council has also recommended that Congress enact legislation to secure such standards. SIA suggests legislation that would secure, standardize and modernize existing technology and practices used to identify and authenticate individual identity (specifically state and federal IDs); and develop a policy to drive standardization designed to keep citizens safe, while not infringing on civil liberties. Among the suggested baseline standards, the SIA suggests:

- uniform appearances such as types of ink, paper, size and shape;
- data to be included on the card's database, including a photograph, address, date of birth, and a digitally-imprinted thumb print;
- incorporated technology such as holograms, microchips, magnetic stripes, barcodes, proximity cards and readers;
- production requirements such as material specifications; and
- protocols and conditions for identification issuance such as background checks, or the establishment of a two-day waiting period.

Biometrics to the Rescue

Driver's licenses use photographs, height, age, weight and address to verify that the cardholder is actually who he claims to be. But biometrics, such as fingerprints and digital signatures, can add additional layers of security that traditional identification documents cannot. The AAMVA proposes to standardize state's biometric identifiers, as well as its means of encoding them, mandating that each state use the same type of biometric identifier on the same type of encoding system. This would help DMVs nationwide recognize each other's identifier.

This summer, the INS plans to use electronic fingerprinting in airports across the U.S., scanning foreign visitors to ensure their identities. So-called smart cards — cards containing computer chips — are also a possibility. With chips that store biometric data, such as a fingerprint or eyescan, government officials view them as a solution to securing identification in unauthorized areas. So agrees the Smart Card Alliance, Princeton Junction, N.J., which views smart cards with biometric features as "capable of meeting the requirements of a wide range of policy and legal mandates" and suitable for "providing the technical solution for secure identification."

Security technology providers propose magnetic stripes, barcodes or electronic "smart" chips be integrated in driver's licenses to hold identification information. Symbol Technologies is focusing on card technology, promoting standardizing biometrics and digital signatures through the use of a 2D barcode. Companies such as Datastrip Inc., Exton, Pa., also propose a 2D barcode be printed on identification cards to store personal and demographic information, as well as one, or multiple, biometric identifiers. Says Charles Lynch, vice president of marketing and sales for Datastrip: "Because all the information is stored on the card, and not the computer, there's virtually no chance of identity theft. We believe that there should be a universally accepted way to identify individuals."

As the need for security increases, so does the need for technology. But there must also be a means of authenticating that technology. "So often, the person who's in charge of authenticating [whether a document is real] doesn't always know what factors should be included in the process," Thalheimer says. Imaging Automation offers technology that detects whether identification documents are real — perhaps a less-invasive approach than adding an additional identifier to the card itself. Imaging Automation's BorderGuard product claims to view plain text, encoded machine-readable text, ID photos and logos on identity cards. But it also claims to view IR ink, UV patterns, secure laminate, tamper marks and facial biometrics to the cardholder's identification. Additionally, Border-Guard uses five different kinds of light, high-resolution cameras and an embedded PC in its application to focus on biometric analysis, pattern matching and character recognition.

Whether attached to a driver's license or a separate ID card, Symbol suggests the building of a solid infrastructure, enhanced security of documents both visibly and invisibly, and more standardized use of machine-readable documents. Adds Shlasko: "You can't take a simplistic view in this, the issue has grown with technology."

Magnetic stripes, barcodes and electronic chips are able to store many bytes of information, thus leaving additional room, after required information is stored, to be used by the cardholder for convenience transactions. Incorporating a cardholder's banking or healthcare information, for example, would provide a single platform for transactions.

Expanding functionality to a national identification system could ease the public's initial resistance to adopting a national ID card. Cardholders could choose what type of information they would like to have on their cards, and ultimately, get a sense of control of the amount of information others could access. Not being able to access this information without a physical biometric, such as a fingerprint or retinal scan, actually further secures the information stored on the card. "The user controls the database because they provide the biometric," says Lunch. "[When] all the information is stored on the card, there's virtually no [chance of] identity theft."

Arguments Against

Studies show that, generally, Americans are willing to give up some civil liberties in exchange for a more secure environment. In a Pew Research Center poll taken just eight days after Sept. 11, more than half of total respondents (55 percent) agreed that to curb terrorism in this country, it would be necessary for the average person to give up some civil liberties. Other surveys have gathered similar responses. A Gallup poll taken between January 28 and March 22 concluded that four of five Americans are willing to trade some freedoms for security, and seven in 10 favor a national ID.

But privacy advocates and civil liberties groups, those like Privacy International and the American Civil Liberties Union (ACLU), stand in steadfast opposition. Supporters of a national ID card wonder, "What's to fear if you've got nothing to hide?" Privacy International contends that the debate is not so much about privacy, but more about losing control of such private information. The group notes the debate can be seen in a three-stage process:

Stage one. At first, a popular view is expressed that identification is not an issue related to individual rights — when an identity card is proposed, public discussion is initially focused on the possession of the card itself— who will mandate it, who will control it, who is responsible for it.

Stage two. The second stage is marked by a growing awareness of the hidden threats an identity card holds — function creep, potential abuse by authorities and problems arising in losing the card.

Stage three. Eventually, the last stage of discussion involves more complex questions about rights and responsibilities — the significance of the computer backup and the numbering system.

At each level, ownership seems to be re-routed — from having great control to having no control at all — and opponents feel as if their civil liberties are being taken away.

Benjamin Miller, founder and chairman of the CardTech/SecurTech Conference, has worked with such companies as American Express, IBM, MasterCard, and the U.S. Departments of Energy and Defense in consulting on card and biometric strategies. "When the national ID card issue is raised, it's not necessarily good for the industry, because it elicits such extreme reactions," he says. Miller points out that, all too often, technology is misrepresented, and opponents are stuck with the idea of a national ID card turning into an "Orwellian nightmare."

National ID Cards vs. Driver's Licenses

Despite being armed with tools capable of increasing our nation's security, fundamental problems are keeping such technologies at bay. Standardizing driver's licenses raises the eyebrows of privacy and civil liberties advocates who already view driver's licenses as de facto national ID cards. The possibility of the card — and, most importantly, the information it would hold — being used for sinister purposes is of monumental concern to its adversaries. In an article outlining reasons national ID cards should be rejected,

the ACLU states: "Once put in place, it is exceedingly unlikely that such a system would be restricted to its original purpose" — a statement that applies to the fear of linking state DMV databases with those of federal agencies. What starts out solely as a safer driver's license, opponents fear, may turn into something else.

Should national ID cards be tied into government databases for security reasons, electronic trails of other information might be accessible as well. "We're increasingly facing the likelihood of the government trying to dupe the American public by bringing forth a national ID scheme through a legislative back door," says Katie Corrigan, an ACLU legislative counsel.

What's Next

The creation of a modernized identification system — whether through a separate national ID card, or an existing driver's license — will rely on more than new hardware and legislation. It will also take money and time. Just how long would it take to implement a national ID card system? Both sides agree: Security is needed now, not eight to 10 years down the road.

While a complete plan has yet to surface, several quick-fixes are emerging to stave off future identity-crisis issues such as those of Sept. 11. Legislation has been passed to allow some states to coordinate driver's licenses with immigration visas — so that when one expires, the other will too. Additionally, some states have raised the bar on acceptable forms of identification and proof of residency.

What's next in identification? Biometrics will likely have a role, so will smart cards. But at what price to privacy?

CHAPTER 34

POLICE SERVICES AND HOMELAND SECURITY PRACTICES

Roger L. Kemp

Federal and state officials have made substantial progress in the field of homeland security since September 2001. City and county managers and their elected officials, however, are at the forefront of this movement. After all, local governments were the first responders to the terrorist acts of September 11. While national and state leadership are essential, the future of homeland security will depend on preparedness initiatives at the local level. Law enforcement officials have developed new emergency management practices, applied new computer software to this field, and have begun to initiate new security measures and safeguards to protect citizens. All of these new measures fall into one or more of the four phases of emergency management: *mitigation, preparedness, response,* and *recovery.*

In less than two years, state law enforcement agencies have standardized many of their practices in emergency management for those cities and counties within their respective boundaries. The national government has responded with a new agency, the Department of Homeland Security. As this department evolves, coordination among federal agencies in the area of homeland security will improve. Equally important, federal departments are initiating training programs to educate police personnel in the area of homeland security. Many of these state-of-the-art practices are examined below, listed under the four phases of emergency management. Police officials throughout the nation should learn these evolving practices, since the public expects that they take the necessary steps to safeguard their life and property during times of disaster.

Mitigation

Federal Assistance Programs. There are numerous federal programs available to educate law enforcement officials in the various aspects of homeland security. The Federal Emergency Management Agency (FEMA), the Federal Bureau of Investigation (FBI) and the Department of Justice (DOJ) provide many of these training programs. Many of these programs are provided free of charge, or for a limited cost, to police personnel. In many cases, these training programs are listed on the Internet websites of these federal agencies.

U. S. Homeland Security Advisory System. In 2002, Thomas Ridge, the Secretary of the new Department of Homeland Security, set forth a national warning system for advising all levels of government, as well as the American public, of the possible risk from a terrorist attack. Under this five-level color-coded warning system, several levels of possible terrorist threats confronting the nation are specified. They are: low (green), guarded (blue), elevated (yellow), high (orange), and severe (red). This national warning system spells out various "protective measures" suited for each warning category. Police personnel are involved in many of these activities. So far, the highest level of alert the nation has witnessed under this code model is "orange."

Threat Analysis and Assessment. To properly analyze and assess the threat level of possible terrorist acts local police officials should work with the appropriate state and federal law enforcement agencies. Possible terrorist targets, both public and private, must be examined, analyzed, and ranked by their level of possible risk. Appropriate safeguards and security measures should then be taken according to this ranking process. This comprehensive approach to dealing with emergencies fits well with FEMA's National Incident Management System (NIMS), which provides the necessary framework for an all-hazards approach to emergency preparedness.

Measures to Improve Building Safety. The use of police officers, metal detectors, and surveillance cameras can help protect citizens by identifying possible threats in advance. Police officers can inspect the personal belongings of people as they enter public buildings. Property owners, both public and private, owe this level of security to those citizens that work in and visit their buildings.

Pedestrian and Vehicular Evacuation Routes. To ensure that the public can properly evacuate from buildings in a timely manner, local public safety officials should prepare building evacuation plans and procedures. The safest and most expeditious exit routes from all buildings, especially high-rise ones, should be clearly explained. Buildings most vulnerable to a terrorist attack may need spe-

cial instructions for the public in case they must be evacuated. Vehicular evacuation routes leading out of town from urban centers should also be identified and made available to the public.

Preparedness

Emergency Plans and Possible Hazards. The emergency plans for cities and towns should include preparedness procedures for all types of likely disasters. These plans should detail the technical expertise that might be needed in the event of a terrorist attack, the required resources, and the proper procedures for requesting assistance from neighboring jurisdictions as well as higher levels of government. Increasing emphasis must be placed on the interactions of local, state, and federal law enforcement officials. Police personnel in areas with sites that might be the prime target of terrorists, such as nuclear power plants and busy ports, should include these sites in their local emergency response plans.

Mutual Aid Agreements. Police departments typically have mutual aid agreements with neighboring communities. These agreements ensure a prompt response to an emergency from a police department in an adjacent municipality. The goal is to provide a seamless response to an emergency once local resources have been exhausted. Since a terrorist attack might affect more than one community, these agreements should be made with all contiguous cities, as well as the county in which a city is located. County governments should have similar mutual aid agreements for the same reasons.

Simulated Disaster Exercises. When police officials revise their emergency plans, they should periodically test them against reality by conducting simulated disaster response exercises. These exercises should also include law enforcement officials from appropriate state and federal agencies. These exercises give police officials a chance to work the "bugs" out of their local plan, and prepares them when they must respond to an actual emergency. These exercises help police officials to limit the loss of life and property during a real disaster.

Training for Police Personnel. Since the September 11th terrorist incidents, specialized training programs have become available for public safety personnel in several areas relating to man-made disasters. Training programs are emerging in the areas of stress management for public safety employees, the management of fatalities, proper responses to weapons of mass destruction, enhanced intelligence and information networking, medical services readiness, and the provision of necessary services to the victims of a disaster. Many of these training programs are provided free of charge by state and federal law enforcement agencies.

Use of the National Incident Management System (NIMS). FEMA recommends the use of the NIMS when police and fire officials respond to a significant emergency. This response system works best when multiple agencies respond, including local, state, and federal. The NIMS process allows for the immediate coordination of police services from numerous sources, including other levels of government. Local police officials can use NIMS to enhance their effectiveness, streamline their chain-of-command, and eliminate the possible duplication of services. State and federal agencies provide valuable training to law enforcement personnel in the use of this state-of-the-art emergency response practice.

Response

Early-Warning Public Notification Systems. A key feature of a local government's response to an emergency is prompt notification of the public. In case of a flood, for example, public officials may have several hours lead-time in which to warn citizens. In

the case of a terrorist act, however, the warning to the public must be immediate. Reverse 911 notification systems are prompt and flexible enough to issue a warning to citizens on a block-by-block, or neighborhood-by-neighborhood, basis. The traditional means of notifying citizens, such as the media, may not be readily available because of the time of the day or night that an incident takes place. Citywide sirens (some have voice-over capability) can also be used to inform the public. Police officials are closely involved with decisions on how, and when, to make public announcements.

Evacuation Procedures and Practices. In the case of a terrorist act, such as an arson fire or bombing, citizens must be evacuated immediately from all impacted buildings and surrounding areas. Procedures should exist to facilitate the smooth evacuation of large numbers of people in the shortest possible time. In the case of fire or the imminent collapse of a building, a prompt police response could save many lives. Vehicles owned by the local government, such as buses and vans, can also be used to facilitate an evacuation. The number of vehicles available, as well as issued relating to their accessibility, should be known in advance of an emergency. The availability of safety equipment and medical services should also be known in advance.

Geographic Information Systems. Computerized mapping using Geographic Information Systems (GIS) can provide immediate assistance to police officials when responding to an emergency. Law enforcement officials should know the location of power grids, public utilities, public telephones, hospitals, and other vital information, in advance. The location of these items should be on a police department's computer database. Staging areas, incident command posts, emergency shelters, designated medical facilities, and approved evacuation routes should all be plotted on GIS. The use of GIS was critical in New York City's response to the September 2001 terrorist attack, and helped public safety personnel limit the loss of life and property.

Public Information and the News Media. In the case of a man-made disaster, such as an act of terrorism, news media (both print and broadcast) at all levels (local, state, and national) will likely have a keen interest in a local government's response for some time. It is essential that Public Safety Directors designate someone at the Emergency Operations Center (EOC) knowledgeable about the event and the ongoing response to deal with the media. The media provides an excellent way for public safety officials to issue warnings and evacuation notices to the public. The media, for safety reasons, should be kept away from the epicenter of a disaster.

Recovery

Crime Scene Security. Man-made disasters such as terrorist acts are crimes, and the location of such an incident should be treated like a crime scene. Evidence at the site must be secured, collected, and properly protected for future use in legal proceedings. This evidence may be used to prosecute the perpetrator(s) at a later date. This means that public access to the site must be limited. First-responders must be trained in the proper law enforcement procedures to both identify and protect evidence at a disaster site. For this reason, debris removal must be undertaken under special, controlled, circumstances.

Crisis Counseling. Following a disaster, public safety employees often suffer from a variety of stress-related symptoms, including anger, depression, headaches, and insomnia. Debriefing and counseling sessions for police employees by experienced counselors should take place as soon as possible. Psychologists, chaplains, family counselors, and mental health professionals typically provide these valuable services. Many Employee Assistance Programs (EAP) also offer such counseling

services. Ideally, these services should be provided quickly, usually within 24 to 48 hours after an emergency takes place.

Management of Fatalities. The limited scope of most local disasters does not require extensive planning for the management of on-site fatalities. In the case of a terrorist incident, however, public safety officials may need to make arrangements for temporary morgues, depending upon the size of the incident. Local mortuaries should be put on alert in advance to handle the additional deaths created by these types of emergencies. Procedures for properly notifying the victims' next-of-kin must be worked out in advance. Homeland Security Plans must include a section pertaining to the management of on-site fatalities. Resources for this function are an integral part of the recovery phase of a police department's response.

Restoration of Public Infrastructure and Open Spaces. After a disaster, citizens expect their local government officials to restore the public infrastructure (for example, sewer and water lines, electricity, roadways, sidewalks, and public transit) and public open spaces (parks, playgrounds, walkways, bikeways, beach access, and waterways, to name a few) in a timely manner. While the public sector must hold citizens accountable for the restoration of their private property, citizens should hold their local government officials accountable for the timely restoration of all public property. Local public safety officials must work closely with public works and legal employees to gain the trust of citizens in this regard. Improvements in and around a disaster area, particularly public amenities, should be restored as soon as possible after a terrorist incident.

Conclusion

After the terrorist attacks on September 11, 2001, the federal government coined the phrase "homeland security" to describe the actions of all levels of government to protect citizens from future actions of this type. While the emergency management practices that evolve during the coming years will be different from those of the past, the goal of these initiatives will still be the same. That is, to minimize the loss of life and property when such acts occur. FEMA's NIMS approach to emergency management enables public safety officials to prepare plans that encompass all potential hazards, including man-made ones such as terrorist acts. For the time being, external threats have focused the attention of law enforcement officials on man-made disasters.

Law enforcement officials are taking the dangers posed by the threat of a possible terrorist attack seriously, and have implemented many state-of-the-art homeland security practices over the past few years. New homeland security practices will be developed and tested by public safety officials at all levels of government during the coming years. The trends examined above are at the promising forefront of this new field. Police and fire personnel, along with health and public works officials, are now working together to prepare homeland security plans to safeguard our nation from a future terrorist attack.

FIGURE 1

Homeland Security and Police Services Trends

(listed under the four phases of emergency management)

Mitigation:
Federal Assistance Programs
U. S. Homeland Security Advisory System
Threat Analysis and Assessment
Measures to Improve Building Safety
Pedestrian and Vehicular Evacuation Routes

Preparedness:
Emergency Plans and Possible Hazards
Mutual Aid Agreements
Simulated Disaster Exercises
Training for Police Personnel
Use of the National Incident Management System

Response:
Early-Warning Public Notification Systems
Evacuation Procedures and Practices
Geographic Information Systems
Public Information and the News Media

Recovery:
Crime Scene Security
Crisis Counseling
Management of Fatalities
Restoration of Public Infrastructure and Open Spaces

FIGURE 2
Acronyms for Homeland Security and Police Services

ARC   American Red Cross

ATAC   Anti-Terrorism Advisory Council

ATF   Bureau of Alcohol, Tobacco, and Firearms

CBRN   Chemical, Biological, Radiological, Nuclear Response Team

CB-RRT   Chemical and Biological Rapid Response Team

CBW   Chemical and Biological Weapons

CCP   Civilian Corps Program

CISM   Critical Incident Stress Management

DHS   Department of Homeland Security

DMAT   Disaster Medical Assistance Team

DMORT   Disaster Mortuary Response Team

DOJ   Department of Justice

EOP   Emergency Operations Plan

ERRT   Emergency Rapid Response Team

FEMA   Federal Emergency Management Agency

FRERP   Federal Radiological Emergency Response Plan

IRZ   Immediate Response Zone

LETPP   Law Enforcement Terrorism Prevention Program

NAS   National Advisory System

NDPO   National Disaster Preparedness Office

NECC   National Emergency Coordination Center

NIMS   National Incident Management System

PDA   Preliminary Damage Assessment

PTE   Potential Threat Elements

RAP   Radiation Assistance Program

RERT   Radiological Emergency Response Team

SRT   Search Response Team

WMD   Weapons of Mass Destruction

FIGURE 3
Internet Resources for Homeland Security and Police Services

American Red Cross (*http://www.redcross.org*)

Bureau of Alcohol, Tobacco, and Firearms (*http://www.atf.treas.gov*)

Central Intelligence Agency (*http://www.odci.gov/terrorism*)

Counter-terrorism Office (State Dept.) (*http://www.state.gov/s/ct*)

Department of Homeland Security (*http://www.dhs.gov*)

Domestic Terrorism Research Center (*http://www.ksg.harvard.edu/terrorism*)

Emergency Management Institute (FEMA) (*http://training.fema.gov/emiweb*)

Federal Bureau of Investigation (*http://www.fbi.gov*)

Federal Emergency Management Agency (*http://www.fema.gov*)

International Association of Chiefs of Police (*http://www.iacp.org*)

National Infrastructure Protection Center (*http://www.nipc.gov*)

Office of Domestic Preparedness (Dept. of Justice) (*http://osldps.ncjrs.org*)

U. S. Department of Health and Human Services (*http://www.hhs.gov*)

U. S. Department of Justice (*http://www.usdoj.gov*)

Bibliography

Allbaugh, Joe M., *Terrorism Preparedness and Response*, Brochure L255, Federal Emergency Management Agency. Washington, DC: March 2001.

Howitt, Arnold M., and Robyn L. Pangi, eds. *Countering Terrorism: Dimensions of Preparedness.* Cambridge, MA: The MIT Press, 2003.

Kayyem, Juliette N., and Robyn L. Pangi, eds. *First to Arrive: State and Local Responses to Terrorism.* Cambridge, MA: The MIT Press, 2003.

Kemp, Roger L. ed. *Homeland Security: Best Practices for Local Government.* Washington, DC: International City/County Management Association, 2003.

Mayer, Harry. "Homeland Security: Collaborative Planning in Readiness Enhancement," *Public Management*, Vol. 85, No. 5. Washington, DC: International City/County Management Association, June 2003.

McEntire, David A., Robie Jack Robinson, and Richard T. Weber. "Managing the Threat of Terrorism," *IQ Report*, Vol. 33, No. 12. Washington, DC: International City/County Management Association, December 2001.

Morial, Marc H. *A National Action Plan for Safety and Security in America's Cities.* Washington, DC: The U. S. Conference of Mayors, December 2001.

Murphy, Gerard R., and Martha R. Plotkin. *Protecting Your Community from Terrorism: The Strategies for Law Enforcement Series*, Vol. 1. Washington, DC: Police Research Forum, March 2003.

Nicholson, John, "Collapse: World Trade Center Aftermath," *NFPA Journal*, Vol. 95, No. 6. November/December 2001.

Raymond, Gary, and Rick Wimberly. "Obtaining and Using High-Speed Notification Technology in a Cross-Jurisdictional Setting," *Police Chief*, Vol. LXIX, No. 6. June 2002.

Reimer, Dennis J. "The Private Sector Must Be a Partner in Homeland Security," *Homeland Security*, Vol. 1, No. 4. September 2004.

Rothman, Paul. "Setting Priorities to Protect the Nation's Infrastructure," *Government Security*. April 2002.

CHAPTER 35

PRESIDENTIAL COMMISSION ADVISES ON WAYS TO PROTECT THE INFRASTRUCTURE

John R. Powers

One day in 1995 John Deutch, director of the Central Intelligence Agency, walked into his office and asked to be shown America's emerging information warfare capabilities — the ability to disrupt and destroy enemies using information and computer networks. Officials at the National Security Agency and at the CIA's Langley headquarters briefed him. When it was over, he exclaimed, "Wow! If we can do this today, our adversaries will be able to do it to us in three to five years!"

That exclamation eventually led to formation of the Presidential Commission on Critical Infrastructure Protection (PCCIP). This was a searching look at America's infrastructure — its banking and finance, rails, computer networks, water, electrical and power grids and everything that makes the country work — where it was vulnerable and what needed to be done to protect it.

A working group was formed under the leadership of Jamie Gorelick, then-deputy attorney general, that framed the problem and recommended a presidential commission as the best way to study the problem. In the summer of 1996 the PCCIP was established with a charter to lay a foundation for infrastructure assurance and information security that would keep pace with the threat as it developed. Robert "Tom" Marsh, a retired Air Force general and former chairman of Thiokol Corp., was named chairman and 10 commissioners were selected from key infrastructure sectors and the lead federal agencies. I served as a commissioner and executive director.

The PCCIP turned in its report in the late fall of 1997. Now, six momentous years later, it's worth a look back on what it did and didn't accomplish. Not only have we experienced the attacks on Sept. 11, we've just been through a major electrical blackout and a very disruptive computer virus attack. Never has the focus on infrastructure been greater or more relevant.

Our Adversaries

The capabilities available to our adversaries — hostile nation states, subnational ter-

Originally published as "The Clinton Commission," *Homeland Defense Journal*, Vol. 1, Issue 7, October 2003. Published by *Homeland Defense Journal*, Arlington, VA. Reprinted with permission of the publisher.

rorist organizations and, of particular concern, organized crime — are indeed awesome. What makes this threat all the more serious is that, like a perfect storm, it emerged during the confluence of three potent global forces in the 1990s.

One was diminution of governmental influence on a global scale. During the cold war, the United States and Soviet Union could more or less prevent mischief by their respective satellite states. After the Soviet Union dissolved, those restraints were off.

The second was the ascendancy of commerce as the global organizational principle. Trade and commerce now came to the forefront as the ties binding the world's peoples together.

The third was the spread of information technology as the primary engine of both global and domestic commerce.

Given the dependence on information technology and the willingness of organizations to subordinate security to operational needs and convenience, it's surprising that we haven't been victim to more infrastructure attacks. While terrorism was ruled out as the cause of the most recent blackout, the system remains vulnerable. There are ways that terrorists could have caused this disruption — a classified matter best not exposed here.

One of the major contributions of the PCCIP was to increase dramatically the public awareness of these emerging problems. As a result, infrastructure owners and operators became more vigilant in monitoring their systems and this made intrusion attempts more visible and attempts to exploit system vulnerabilities more difficult.

The ability of individual owners and operators to recognize and counter intrusions, however, cannot be achieved by awareness alone. The Commission recognized, as the president intended, that this threat was going to change and mature and the nation needed a capability that would grow at a pace equal to the threat.

Public-Private Partnerships

Creating such a capability required public-private partnerships for sharing information about system vulnerabilities, attempts at exploiting them and best practices for countering those attempts. Most of the critical infrastructure was in private hands — as was the cutting edge technical and system knowledge to deal with the problem. From this recognition emerged the concept for the Information Sharing and Analysis Committees (ISACs).

Like the spokes of a wheel, a central hub would integrate information from different sector ISACs — for example water, electricity, transportation etc.

The FBI suggested formation of a National Infrastructure Protection Center (NIPC) as the hub and the Commission endorsed that recommendation. However, industry worried that the information being shared might be used to launch criminal investigations rather than to protect the infrastructure. In the years since, the NIPC has worked well with industry but industry remains concerned about the uses of the information it reports and its comfort level rises and falls depending on the circumstances.

Early on, the ISACs did some excellent work, especially in the banking and finance sectors. Additional ISACs were soon formed in other sectors. At the outset, the private sector partners linked their business interests, sector interests and the national interests. Stephen Katz, chief information security officer of Citi-Group and financial services sector coordinator, led the way and encouraged other major banks to become involved — an effect that cascaded over time.

After an auspicious start, however, the private sector partners had increasing difficulty bearing the costs involved in protecting against what were considered national security risks. As a result, some sectors energetically shared information while others became disillusioned and disheartened.

Paying for Protection

One of the major weaknesses of the Commission was its failure to make an effective case for addressing the divergence between the national interest and the corporate interests of the infrastructure owners and operators. One example of this was the difference between the costs to an electric power company from the revenues lost during a period of the disruption and the costs to the primary and secondary users of that infrastructure. The latter costs could be huge.

We take so much of our infrastructure for granted that most businesses and individuals fail to do any contingency planning for a major disruption. It's probably unreasonable to expect the infrastructure owners and operators to shoulder the full financial load since there are simply limits to what they're able and willing to devote to this mission. Those limits are based on what makes good business sense and are inviolate if they're to survive. Until the "who pays" issue is fully explored, the nation will be stuck with extremely creaky infrastructures.

Even the Commission discovered these limits within the federal government when it attempted to provide a modest budget for staffing and operating the sector ISACs. Commission members argued that the United States needed to bridge at least part of the divergence between business risk and the national security risk. When this proposal was taken to the White House, however, a staffer at the Office of Management and Budget took the coins out of his pocket, tossed them on the desk and stated flatly, "This is all of the funds that I can see for CIP."

This clearly was an unacceptable response — yet it would be equally unacceptable to ask the United States to exclusively bear the costs of infrastructure protection. Industries have an obligation to assure service, but there is a yet unresolved dilemma of which portion of this is private versus public good. This is an extremely complex issue that

---

FIGURE 1
The Infrastructures*

In its report, the PCCIP divided the country into five key infrastructure sectors:

- Information and communications
- Banking and finance
- Energy, including electrical power, oil and gas
- Physical distribution
- Vital human services

It then looked at eight key infrastructures supporting the country:

- Telecommunications
- Electrical power systems
- Gas and oil
- Banking and finance
- Transportation
- Water supply systems
- Government services and
- Emergency services

*For a copy of the 1997 report summary in HTML, go to: http://www.ciao.gov/resource/pccip/summary.htm

To obtain the summary in PDF format, go to: http://www.ciao.gov/resource/pccip/summary.pdf

The entire 192-page report can be obtained in PDF format at: http://www.ciao.gov/resource/pccip/PCCIP_Report.pdf

---

must be resolved but, given the vastly different views of risk, it's unlikely that there will ever be an easy resolution.

Standards and Credentials

The Commission struggled over the problem shared by many small organizations, namely, the difficulty of assessing which, if any, of the new technologies will meet their needs and perform as advertised. A small water utility, a small power producer, a small municipal police department all share one thing in common: They have no ability to provide operational test and evaluation on any of the latest whiz-bang products that are constantly being introduced to their offices.

The Commission toyed with the idea of recommending something like an Underwriters Laboratories approval or a *Consumer's Reports* for the benefit of prospective users. There are a number of federally funded research and development centers, national laboratories or DoD components, such as the US Army Research, Development and Engineering Command at Fort Monmouth in New Jersey, that could provide this very necessary function. Even users, such as Bell South, which has a large information security staff, would be hard pressed to subject most of the new offerings to substantive testing. They too could benefit tremendously from an independent assessment.

This problem extends to the area of vulnerability assessments where the federal government might have helped. Industry has wasted a lot of money on security "experts" who provided a poor product in return. If, several years ago, the United States had put together a list of qualified or certified vulnerability assessment vendors, industry would have saved considerable money and produced significantly better results. At a minimum, it should have established a list of acceptable methodologies. This is easier said than done. For 25 years the computer security industry has grappled with criteria to certify security software and the physical security industry has tried, unsuccessfully, to do the same for intrusion alarm system hardware and software.

Interdependencies

Interdependency — the reliance of one system on another to function — emerged as a major theme in the Commission's findings. Most of the members discounted the possibility of a cyber–Pearl Harbor. Today, though, we're having second thoughts about that conclusion — or at least the conclusion that a cyber-aided Pearl Harbor would be possible. The attacks by Al Qaeda in 2001 confounded experts with their technical expertise, intelligence gathering, complex planning, determined action and internal security so a rethink of this possibility is warranted.

One of the major concerns is an infrastructure attack in the midst of a response to a major terrorist event. At best, the response to any major emergency will border on controlled chaos during the early hours after an event and this is when all of the backbone infrastructures are fully functioning. If Al Qaeda were to disrupt key infrastructures immediately prior to an attack that included a major explosive, chemical, radiological or biological weapon, our response apparatus would be seriously hampered.

Analysis

The Commission established a goal of an initial operating capability by 2000 and a fully functioning operating capability by 2003. We know that we're very far from the 2003 goal.

Nonetheless, there's more that can be done.

We need a national awareness campaign. This was proposed but never got off the ground (although awareness did increase and the report is still being read).

We need continued development of our intellectual capabilities to counter terrorism. In the field of cybersecurity, some excellent cyber work has taken place at Purdue University, James Madison University, George Washington University and Carnegie Mellon University.

We need strong national leadership in the White House.

It is vital that we have a partnership for critical infrastructure security between industry and government. To the degree that it exists, it has started to yield benefits.

We need improved information sharing

and resolution of any lingering doubt that information can be shared safely.

We need adequate research and development for critical infrastructure assurance, especially modeling and simulation of the infrastructures and their interdependencies.

We must have comprehensive response planning for an attack that would result in extended physical damage to an infrastructure.

We also need continued sympathetic attention to the tension between national security on the one hand and privacy and civil liberties on the other.

If we can continue to make progress toward these goals, if we put the effort, the will and the resources toward achieving them, the United States will be a far stronger and more protected country than it was on Sept. 11, 2001— or that morning when John Deutch walked into his office with a brainstorm.

CHAPTER 36

PRIVATE SECTOR'S RESPONSE TO THE WAR ON TERRORISM

Jon Fleischman

The devastating attacks against our nation taught us that all Americans, whether in the public or private sector, have roles to play in keeping this country safe. More than 85 percent of the critical infrastructure in the United States is owned and operated by the private sector. According to the U.S. Department of State's *Patterns of Global Terrorism*, businesses suffer the majority of terrorist attacks worldwide. It is critical that we involve the private sector in preparing to respond to a potential act of terrorism.

On April 8, 2002, in Knoxville, Tenn., President George W. Bush delivered a speech emphasizing the importance of community involvement and the growth of Citizen Corps across America. In his remarks, the President singled out about a dozen local communities where "Americans are involved in activities that will make their communities safer and better prepared to respond to emergencies..."

One of the communities the President mentioned in his remarks was Orange County, Calif. A press release from the White House noted the creation of Orange County's new Private Sector Terrorism Response Group.

Located just south of Los Angeles, Orange County is the largely suburban home to more than 3 million residents. The county generates approximately 9.5 percent of the Gross State Product, representing $137 billion a year. It is home to such major attractions as Disneyland, Knott's Berry Farm, Anaheim Stadium, the South Coast Plaza Mall, John Wayne Airport and California's largest recreational yacht harbor in Newport Beach.

Orange County Sheriff Michael Carona knew it was imperative to find a way to integrate the private sector into discussions and activities surrounding emergency preparedness and response. He believed that the pre-9/11 paradigm of public agencies alone preparing for and dealing with the impact of acts of terrorism needed be improved.

"A partnership between public and private sectors is essential in combating terrorism," said Sheriff Carona. "The public sector provides the early-warning mechanism to prevent and defend against terrorist attacks, while the private sector strives to harden their defenses against attack and shares information that is critical if first responders are to accomplish their mission in an emergency."

Starting with organizational meetings in late 2001, the Orange County Private Sector

---

Originally published as "Engaging the Private Sector in Local Homeland Defense: The Orange County Private Sector Terrorism Response Group," *Sheriff*, Vol. 56, Vol. 5, September/October 2004. Published by the National Sheriffs' Association, Alexandria, VA. Reprinted with permission of the publisher.

Terrorism Response Group (OC-PSTRG) was created to involve and integrate the private-sector community into the homeland defense arena in Orange County.

Loosely modeled after a similar program in the neighboring Inland Empire, the OC-PSTRG has established more than 150 points of contact throughout the county with key private-sector business partners. These partners include many of Orange County's largest employers: sporting arenas, tourist destinations, hotels, retail centers, transportation venues and educational institutions.

The mission of the OC-PSTRG is to bring businesses into the first-responder community, with the goals of:

- informing, educating and empowering those private-sector segments of our community impacted by the war on terrorism
- creating a positive plan of action consistent with state and federal objectives that seek to protect citizens, business and our economy
- mitigating the severity and degree of any potential loss to the community, commerce and industry
- contributing to the development of public policy concerning terrorism
- fostering coordination between various community sectors that could be impacted by terrorism, public agencies and the private sector
- increasing the capacity of Community Emergency Response Teams (CERTs)
- adding a terrorism-prevention component to existing Neighborhood Watch programs.

Members of the OC-PSTRG are invited to come together every other month to hear from subject-matter experts, receive updates on relevant current events and they have an opportunity to network with first responders as well as fellow members. At the latest OC-PSTRG meeting, the lead video-surveillance expert in the Los Angeles office of the FBI talked with members about the latest tech-

nology available in fixed video cameras, as well as the importance of working to make sure that first responders have an ability to plug into those systems. He even offered his direct assistance to work with members on an individual basis as they review their systems. Other training topics have included fighting cyber-terrorism and protecting businesses against suicide bombers.

Between meetings, OC-PSTRG members have an opportunity to exchange thoughts and ideas with each other, as well as with the law enforcement community. Timely advisories are disseminated to members, alerting them of threats, changes to the Department of Homeland Security Advisory System and activities potentially impacting the businesses of OC-PSTRG members. Also, members are constantly apprised of training opportunities, conferences and seminars.

On March 10 of this year, the Orange County Sheriff's Department conducted an interactive table-top exercise dubbed "Operation: Mid-Day Shadow." In this simulation, terrorists conducted a series of attacks in waves across the country, starting on the East Coast, moving across the nation, ultimately leading to attacks in California, and in Orange County. More than 200 role-players were involved, representing more than 50 government entities at the federal, state and local level, and more than 20 private-sector members of the OC-PSTRG.

In the simulation, OC-PSTRG member businesses were among the targets attacked by terrorists. Rarely do private-sector security and emergency-management personnel get to practice disaster response together. Yet these businesses participating in the simulation were able to practice their emergency-response plans as they coordinated with our County Emergency Operations Center. Many of the official observers of the exercise were from the private sector as well.

Ron Williams, president of Talon Executive Services, a member of the OC-PSTRG, said, "This exercise provided PSTRG members with a very real understanding of what would take place, operationally, in the case of local acts of terrorism." Williams' company played an integral role in the planning and facilitation of Operation: Mid-Day Shadow.

On September 15, Orange County will conduct a major Weapons of Mass Destruction exercise at the Orange County Fairgrounds. This exercise will involve thousands of players, with involvement from many agencies at every level of government. As with Operation: Mid-Day Shadow, members of the OC-PSTRG will be integrated into this exercise, as both participants and observers.

It is important to note that the OC-PSTRG represents a collaborative effort between law enforcement, fire and health, as well as local governments. As a subcommittee of the county's Terrorism Early Warning Group, all activities are sanctioned by an 11-member Operational Area Executive Board, which includes representatives of the Orange County City Managers Association, the local Police Chief and Sheriff's Association, the Public Works Managers Association, Fire Chiefs Association, Board of Supervisors,

Health Care Agency and Orange County Emergency Manager.

The activities of the OC-PSTRG are coordinated on a full-time basis by Heather Houston, a senior program coordinator with the Orange County Sheriff's Terrorism Early Warning Group.

"With all of the success that we have had so far with this program, the exciting part is that it is just the beginning," commented Houston. "The PSTRG continues to grow at a strong pace, and our members are excited to be playing a meaningful role in assisting the first-responder community in keeping Orange County well prepared."

It is well known that one of the primary aims of a terrorist attack is the disruption of business and commerce as terrorists seek to wreak havoc on the day-to-day lives of Americans. By engaging the private sector, we are better able to prevent a terrorist act, and we stand infinitely better prepared to cope with the effects of a potential terrorist attack should one occur. The Orange County Private Sector Terrorism Response Group is just one such example.

CHAPTER 37

PROFESSIONAL STANDARDS RECOMMENDED BY THE NATIONAL FIRE PROTECTION ASSOCIATION

Robert Yates

Consider this: According to Oxford Metrica, an international strategic advisory firm, in any five-year period, there's a 40% risk that a Global 1000 company will lose 30% or more of its value within one month due to a crisis, whether a fire, hurricane, regional power failure, terrorist attack or other emergency.

Next, consider that there is as yet no single recognized standard for companies or government agencies to use as the basis for preparing for a crisis.

It looks as though that's about to change. On April 29, the American National Standards Institute recommended to the 9-11 Commission that a National Fire Protection Association <www.nfpa.org> standard, NFPA 1600, Disaster/Emergency Management and Business Continuity Programs, be recognized as the national preparedness standard. The commission will consider this recommendation in preparing its final report to Congress and the president.

"This recommendation, if it's adopted by the commission, would be significant, in that there would be strong top-down support for government and the private sector to build upon the same standard for preparedness," says Robert Fletcher of Readiness Consulting, Annapolis, Md. "That's a big deal."

The 9-11 Commission had selected ANSI <www.ansi.org> to canvass existing standards to identify "a single over-arching, high-level standard, a reference point for businesses looking to develop programs and for businesses with programs to do an analysis of the gaps in their programs," says William Raisch, director of the New York Safety Council's Emergency Corps Program and chairman of the Working Group for Private Sector Preparedness <www.workinggroup.us>, who testified before the commission. "The 9-11 Commission is an opportunity to put the spotlight on 1600 as the national preparedness standard."

Originally published as "Standard Practice," *Homeland Protection Professional*, Vol. 3, No. 5, June 2004. Published by A. J. Parrino & Associates, Western Springs, Illinois. Reprinted with permission of the publisher.

What 1600 Is

NFPA 1600 establishes a process for organizations to define and identify risks and vulnerabilities and plan for short-term recovery and long-term continuity of operations. As Dr. Johnson might say, it gives an organization an opportunity to concentrate its mind on disasters.

The standard, which first emerged in 2000 following five years of work by an NFPA committee, has been slightly refined for 2004, and its annexes of emergency management resources have been greatly expanded, but its slow march toward national recognition has been accelerated by the deepening understanding of the Sept. 11 tragedies.

Formally, NFPA 1600 is a process-based standard that "identifies the key functional areas and an overall strategy for disaster preparedness and business continuity for both private and public sector organizations."

It's a set of criteria, laid out in a series of statements ("The entity shall identify hazards, the likelihood of their occurrence, and the vulnerability of people, property, the environment, and the entity itself to those hazards") that let an organization confront, in a step-by-step way, every aspect of planning for the four phases of an emergency or disaster: mitigation, preparedness, response and recovery.

"1600 is the working standard for those who want to know what goes into a program, what companies should address," says Martha Curtis of the NFPA. "It says, 'These are the things that should be in your plan.'"

The process begins with the laws and regulations the organization has to consider, moves to the hazards that have to be addressed, then the preparation needed for each of the hazards and the possible mitigation of the hazards. From there, the organization can consider the best responses to the hazards, training and exercises, and communicating with government agencies during a crisis, all the way through to continuing the organiza-

tion's functions once the crisis is over. It's intended to be a "total program approach" to emergency management.

"Before 1600, there never has been a description of emergency management, how to view emergency management, other than the ability to respond," says Fletcher. "The most valuable aspect of 1600 is that it provides emergency managers with the architecture to look at their own programs. 'Have I thought of everything?'

"Before 1600, there was no way of doing that. And before 1600, management was in a reactive mode; all facets of emergency management were not addressed. The 1600 program guidelines put management into emergency preparedness.

"1600 identifies the component parts of an emergency management program and requires you to identify every hazard with a potential impact and to dispose of that hazard," Fletcher continues. "We have floods, or we have earthquakes, or we have hurricanes. 1600 requires you to prioritize those hazards and to prepare for them. It's a process of analysis and planning to manage hazards."

Additional Resources

Though 1600 itself wasn't changed substantively for the 2004 edition, the NFPA made the annexes an important part of the standard. "The big changes with 1600 are in the updating of the resource lists in the annexes," says Curtis. "The 2004 edition really beefed up the annexes; it gives people a bigger picture."

The annexes list federal agencies involved in disaster management, international organizations connected with emergency and disaster management, universities, non-governmental organizations, publications, and state emergency management agencies.

"Knowing where the resources are helps a company to recover its mainline business, and the better prepared a company is, the more quickly it can recover," says Curtis. "The annexes tell you what the resources are in your area. What is the level of capability? How do you contact agency X or organization Y?"

For example, a company in Denver that wanted to start the 1600 process from scratch could look in the annexes for resources and start with FEMA, which alone has a wealth of emergency management information, the DHS, the EPA and OSHA.

For concerns about chemical terrorism, the U.S. Army Medical Research Institute of Chemical Defense. For earthquake information, the U.S. Geological Survey in Denver. The University of Colorado–Boulder has a Natural Hazards Research/Application Center; the Disaster and Emergency Response Association is in Longmont.

For earthquakes alone, the annexes list 11 sources; 24 resources on chemical and biological emergencies; for disaster planning and emergency preparedness in general, 41, in addition to the emergency management agencies for each state.

The EMAP Connection

Though 1600 can be used as a self-evaluation tool by agencies and businesses, the most stringent, and valuable, application is through the Emergency Management Accreditation Program <www.emaponline.org>, which uses 1600 as a base document, along with the Capability Assessment for Readiness offered by FEMA.

"Who's looking at the program? Who's looking at protection from evolving hazards such as SARS and West Nile virus? Who validates that the program can address these hazards?" asks Fletcher. "Without an accredited program, there is no objective assessment."

An organization has 18 months to conduct a self-assessment against the 54 EMAP standards and then applies for the on-site assessment. An EMAP assessment team comes out to an agency, reviews the proofs of compliance, interviews people in the agency and observes the agency at work. The team then writes its report, and, if the candidate can bring its program into compliance in nine months, issues a conditional accreditation. To be in compliance, the candidates have to meet every standard.

The Accreditation Journey

The first two jurisdictions to achieve EMAP accreditation are the District of Columbia and Florida. Arizona and North Dakota have been granted conditional accreditation.

"Have you ever had a root canal?" asks Craig Fugate, director of Florida's Division of Emergency Management. "It doesn't take as long. A year's process is not a small undertaking. You have to go back, find the standard in writing, implement it, train on it and make sure your staff can articulate the standard. We formed a team to play the EMAP assessors. You take every item, every procedure. If there's a shortfall, you go back.

"1600 is an outline of what you should be doing, what you should accomplish, and EMAP uses 1600 as a baseline about what is measurable," Fugate explains. "But how do you take 1600 and measure those standards? EMAP spells it out. You have to prove, in writing, that you're meeting those standards. The assessment team requires the procedures in writing, and then interviews the staff responsible for the procedures.

"You can look at the standards and say, 'Yeah, we do that, we do that. We have a lot of disasters in Florida, so we have a lot of standards,'" says Fugate. "But, for example, the EMAP process makes you identify in writing who in your organization is responsible for coordinating your emergency management programs. How is the program coordinator designated? By statute? By executive order? By policy? If the program coordinator is appointed by the governor, what is the documentation for the appointment? Your business card and title aren't enough. Show us your position description.

"It made us much more disciplined," he continues. "It gives you the foundation of documentation, so you're not relying on someone's memory of what you did in response to a disaster three years ago. It touched every part of what we do. It made us stronger. It gave us a foundation for documentation, cross-training, examining what we do, and the discipline to know that what we do reflects the procedures."

The District of Columbia began its assessment in 2002, was assessed in July 2003 and was accredited the following September.

Barbara Childs-Pair is the director of the Emergency Management Agency for the District of Columbia, which is the intersection for an astonishing array of federal, state and county agencies, including 49 law enforcement agencies within the district itself.

"Past disasters have put us light years ahead of most places," Childs-Pair says, "but we still had gaps in our interaction with agencies. EMAP made us take a look. It gives you a baseline assessment of what you have and gets you to move forward. We found gaps we didn't know we had. Due partially to EMAP, we now have a better ability to talk to each other. On 9-11, we couldn't talk to each other except by two-way radio."

Twenty-two other states, plus Guam, the Virgin Islands and Puerto Rico, are in the process of conducting their baseline assessments for EMAP. But as the public sector's understanding of the need for preparedness grows, the private sector lags far behind.

Denial and Incentives

In his testimony to the 9-11 Commission, Raisch said: "Businesses and other private-sector organizations own 85% of America's infrastructure and employ the vast majority of our country's employees. Furthermore, these resources of people and property are organized workplace units which can be more efficiently coordinated in an emergency situation than 'the general public.'"

The private sector's resistance to fully engaging emergency preparedness is tied, of course, to the bottom line. Preparedness costs time and money, and businesses, historically, have not given much priority to what probably won't happen.

But the private sector needs to open its eyes to the possibility that businesses can be put at risk by hazards. The Oxford Metrica research quoted above can still be seen by businesses as something that will happen over there, not here, despite evidence from the last three years: Sept. 11 in New York and Washington; Hurricane Isabel in North Carolina, Virginia and Maryland; the northeastern power outage; wildfires in San Diego.

But even if businesses are more interested in emergency preparedness, there's confusion over what to do about it. And, once again, we return to the significance of establishing NFPA 1600 as a national standard as the means to cut through the uncertainty and say, "Here, these are the steps you need to take to prepare your company."

The search is on, then, for incentives that will make it economically worthwhile for the business community to come to grips with implementing emergency preparedness. And they're out there, in recommendations to the 9-11 Commission, and in evolving legal and corporate standards. First, emergency preparedness can be tied to the cost of insurance. Insurers can give preferential benefits and rates to businesses that conform to NFPA 1600.

Second, a recent federal court holding that the airlines could have foreseen the 9-11 highjackings opens the door to legal liability for a company's negligent failure to plan for emergencies, which companies could defend against by demonstrating good-faith efforts to prepare under the guidelines of a nationally recognized standard. Certainly, if a company can be held liable for, say, ignoring fire codes, it could be held liable for failing to adhere to a national standard for preparedness.

And third, under the rubric of corporate governance, a corporation has a fiduciary duty to its shareholders and its employees to prepare for emergencies.

And so, if the president and Congress accept the recommendation to make NFPA 1600 the national standard for emergency preparedness, the nation, both in the public and private sectors, could be much closer to a real state of readiness.

CHAPTER 38

PUBLIC INFORMATION DURING A CRISIS

John Ouellette

In the event of a terrorist attack, one of the most important jobs of local elected officials is to provide the public with reliable information about what happened, what people can do to protect themselves and their families, and how the government is responding.

In *Making the Nation Safer—The Role of Science and Technology in Countering Terrorism*, a special committee appointed by the National Research Council of the National Academies concludes that there is a "human dimension" to every type of terrorist attack. As much as they may want to destroy buildings and infrastructure, the main goal of terrorists is to generate "behavioral, attitudinal, and emotional responses" in the populations they target. One way for local officials to blunt the effects of terrorism is to influence the human response through an effective program of communications. "The human response to terrorism can be influenced by such factors as adequacy of preparedness, effectiveness of warnings, and confidence in agencies designated to deal with the crisis."

While government can't control how people will react to a terror attack on their city or town, officials can help shape attitudes and behavior by providing helpful in-formation. *Making the Nation Safer* asserts, "The more information that is made available about how to behave in the event of different kinds of attacks (including readiness training and drills, for example), the more likely it is that people will have a sense of control over uncertain situations and they will be less anxious."

Most important, of course, are communications in the immediate aftermath of a terror event. *Making the Nation Safer* recommends that governments prepare now to communicate as best they can once an attack occurs. Among the book's recommendations: appropriate and trusted spokespeople should be identified and trained now so that, if a terrorist attack occurs, the government will be prepared to respond not only by supplying emergency services, but also by providing important, accurate, and trustworthy information clearly, quickly and authoritatively.

Cardinal Rules

Emergency communications should be an essential element of any local emergency response plan. In Polk County, Oregon,

Originally published as "Crisis Communications," *Municipal Advocate*, Vol. 20, No. 3, Fall 2003. Published by the Massachusetts Municipal Association, Boston, MA. Reprinted with permission of the publisher.

officials developed an annex to their Emergency Operations Plan outlining the process for disseminating emergency information and instructions to the public during periods of disaster. The assumptions behind the plan can provide guidance to other local officials as they consider how to plan their emergency communications activities. These assumptions are as follows:

- An effective program combining both education and emergency information can significantly reduce disaster-related casualties and property damage.
- Both the media and the public will expect and demand that information about an emergency be provided in a timely manner.
- The local media, particularly radio and television, can perform an essential role in providing emergency instructions and status information to the public, both through news bulletins and Emergency Alert System broadcasts.
- Demand for information during a disaster can be overwhelming if sufficient trained staff are not available.

In 1988, the U.S. Environmental Protection Agency published *Seven Cardinal Rules of Risk Communication*, which provides local officials and others with a concise set of guidelines for keeping the public informed in crisis situations such as terrorist attacks. The rules laid out in the publication are as follows:

1. Accept and involve the public as a partner. Your goal is to produce an informed public, not to defuse public concerns.
2. Plan carefully and evaluate your efforts. Different goals, audiences and media require different actions.
3. Listen to the public's specific concerns. People often care more about trust, credibility, competence, fairness, and empathy than statistics and details.
4. Be honest, frank and open. Trust and credibility are difficult to obtain; once lost, they are almost impossible to regain.

5. Work with other credible sources. Conflicts and disagreements among organizations make communication with the public much more difficult.
6. Meet the needs of the media. The media are usually more interested in politics than risk, simplicity than complexity, danger than safety.
7. Speak clearly and with compassion. Never let your efforts prevent you from acknowledging the tragedy of an illness, injury or death. People can understand risk information, but they still may not agree with you; some people will not be satisfied.

Communications Planning

In an article prepared for the National Conference of State Legislatures, NCSL Public Affairs Officer William Wyatt writes that successful communications depend on several factors, not the least of which is developing a positive communications atmosphere within an organization. That means placing an emphasis on effective communications long before disaster strikes — for example, by making public information officers an integral part of your organization's crisis response planning. That way, everyone involved in the operations will know what to expect from the communications team and vice versa. Similarly, information professionals will know what should be disseminated and what should not.

Also important is the development of a detailed crisis communications plan, according to Wyatt. He suggests that the planning effort entail the following steps:

- Designate a crisis manager who will serve as the chief spokesperson to the media and the public. A crisis manager must be able to communicate the message effectively and must have a level of credibility that is reassuring.
- Establish lines of communication. Determine in advance how information will get

to the crisis manager, and make sure he or she has access to the best information available.

- Determine your resources. Figure out in advance what resources are available to communicate with members of the media, the public, and other key audiences. Which of these resources will reach the most people at once? Do you have capability to provide information in more than one language? Can the Internet and e-mail support and broaden your communications effort, and in what ways?
- Lay it on the table. When a disaster strikes, the crisis management team is responsible for developing the message that is going to be communicated to the public and the media depending on the crisis. This doesn't mean playing fast and loose with the facts. Quite the opposite, good communication involves laying it all on the table. The public wants to know who, what, when, how and where. And they want to know as soon as possible.

Once your city or town has a crisis communications plan in place, it is critical that you test it. A dry run, says Wyatt, will allow the communications team to work out the kinks and mend any breaks in the chain of communication while working to decrease overall response time.

Wyatt says the public expects four things from its elected leaders: openness, accessibility, responsiveness and trust. During a crisis, it is critical that these qualities drive the information that gets to the public.

The International Association of Emergency Managers advises local governments to establish a Joint Information Center to ensure a timely flow of reliable information to all key audiences. The JIC is a coordinated and centralized information repository that can serve as the central location for conducting briefings by relevant officials. Ideally, the JIC should have representation from each component entity (at all levels of government) that is contributing to the response effort.

In the event of a terror attack, your government has a special responsibility to work with school officials to ensure that local children are receiving age-appropriate information about what happened and how to respond. The following advisory issued to New York schools on September 11, 2001, by the state Commissioner of Education provides some guidelines for city and school officials to consider in your crisis communications planning.

- Follow your district and school crisis plan.
- Preference is to keep schools open and to try to keep life as normal as possible for students.
- Stay as calm as possible. Adults need to be role models for children.
- Encourage communication opportunities in classrooms. Let students/adults talk about their feelings.

Note

This article was adapted from the National League of Cities guide "Practical Tools for Local Government." The complete guide is available from the NLC website (www.nlc.org/nlc_org/site/files/reports/terrorism-pdf).

CHAPTER 39

PUBLIC WORKS DEPARTMENTS AS EMERGENCY RESPONDERS

Janet Ward

Certain events — Pearl Harbor, the Kennedy Assassination, the Challenger disaster — become the defining points for a generation, the one event for which everyone in that generation will say, "This is where I was when I heard."

The Sept. 11 attacks on the World Trade Center and the Pentagon were such a defining point. But for Peter King, they had a double significance. King, executive director of the Kansas City, Mo.–based American Public Works Association (APWA), was in Philadelphia at that organization's annual conference when the planes hit.

He and the 26,000 members of APWA immediately grasped that neither the country nor the public works community would ever be the same. "There was talk of shutting down the conference," King says. "The decision was to continue. We immediately convened the board of directors and the emergency management committee. It couldn't have been a better group of people to have together at that time. All of them were public works directors trained in emergency response."

APWA moved quickly to address the Sept. 11 attacks. By the time Philadelphia's hotels began rolling out the tv screens to allow their visitors to follow the events, the APWA leadership was calling together its forces. The group met with convention center security personnel and began putting together a communications center to allow its members to contact their communities. The board of directors and the emergency management committee agreed to meet hourly to assess the situation and discuss strategy.

Blue-collar First Responders

But what was fortunate for King presented problems for cities and counties across the country. Once the reality of the attacks settled in, communities began to panic. For many of them, the heart and soul of their public works departments were in Philadelphia, with no way to get home once the nation's air transportation system had shut down.

A number of those cities and counties actually footed the bill for their public works directors to purchase vans and cars so they could drive home. Many communities began to doubt the wisdom of having so many of

---

Originally published as "Public Works: The Nation's Forgotten First Responders," *Homeland Protection Professional,*" Vol. 1, No. 1, July/August 2002. Published by A. J. Parrino & Associates, Western Springs, Illinois. Reprinted with permission of the publisher.

their critical personnel away from home at one time. It was a time of validation for the public works community, though that validation has worn thin in the subsequent months.

Some 20 years before the Sept. 11 attacks, the Federal Emergency Management Agency had developed the policies and procedures that would form the basis of its terrorism response guidelines. In developing those policies, FEMA targeted what it defined as "first responders," police and law enforcement, public health, fire and public works personnel.

Since Sept. 11, the term "first responder" has gained a cachet that no one could have predicted. New York's fire and police departments have become the nation's new heroes, and, as a result of the anthrax scares later that fall, reams of paper have been devoted to the critical importance of the country's public health system. And public works? Well, public works has become the forgotten first responders.

It's a role that, while not exactly relished, is accepted by public works professionals around the country. "They're the ones who handle the rescues," says Paul Brum. "We serve in a support role. We're the ones who set up the barricades and make sure the Porta-Potties work."

As Oklahoma City's longtime public works director, Brum has some experience with the issue. His office was a critical component in recovery efforts after the 1995 bombing of the Alfred P. Murrah Federal Building. "They're the people in the white hats," he says of the police and fire personnel. "We're the blue-collar workers. We accept that."

National Emergency Response and Rescue Training Center

However, while most public works employees have no problem accepting their sup-

port role, many think that role is rarely fully appreciated. First-response training programs abound, but they are often geared to public safety and health professionals, despite the fact that much of the information imparted is critical to the operation of public works in the wake of an emergency. The one program specifically designed to train public works professionals to respond to Sept. 11–like crises is relatively new.

The National Emergency Response and Rescue Training Center (NERRTC), operated out of Texas A&M University's Texas Engineering Extension Service, offers counterterrorism training at its College Station headquarters directed at public works departments throughout the country.[1] Additionally, the center funds on-site training free to any city or county public works department that requests it. Since Sept. 11, calls to the center have mushroomed. "We used to do one course a week, now we're doing three to four," says Mark McCain, principal consultant with St. Helena Island, S.C.–based Public Works Emergency Management Services and an NERRTC instructor.

The center's three-day courses are based on eight modules, which vary in length. The first module covers an introduction to weapons of mass destruction and encompasses the motives for their use and the types of actions that might be expected. Modules on legal issues, vulnerability assessment, incident command, resource management, incident response, recovery and plan development follow.

By the summer of 2002, the center has trained between 1,600 and 1,700 people in some 55 communities. Its integrated approach — it is designed for public works personnel, but all first responders are welcomed — is what sets the program apart.

"We did a training exercise in St. Croix," says Roy Robinson, an NERRTC course manager. "Ron Hatcher, the training officer for the Virgin Islands Police Department, said it was the first time everyone had been at the same table. That's pretty much the message we hear. We try to engage the other folks—fire, law enforcement, hazmat, emergency medical, public health—because we want an integrated response. It can seem strange for some people, because they're not used to having public works people involved."

"I recommend it very, very strongly," says Phil Chin, assistant to the public works director for the City and County of San Francisco, which just completed the training. "It helped us focus on the effects of terrorism. We have a fairly good handle on natural disasters, but we weren't too knowledgeable about the specifics of terrorism or WMD. An earthquake is fairly non-discriminating. Terrorism is focused. We learned what to look for and what to look at."

Other Training Opportunities

Besides the NERRTC, three of the best training programs, the Center for National Response in Kanawha County, W.Va.; the Center for Domestic Preparedness in Anniston, Ala.; and FEMA's Emergency Management Institute in Emmitsburg, Md., offer a number of tracks that cover functions generally considered part of the public works bailiwick: hazmat response, mass transit episodes and multi-hazard building design.

The Center for National Response

The Center for National Response operates out of Memorial Tunnel, an abandoned turnpike tunnel in southern West Virginia.[2] Operated by Titan Systems Corp.'s Defense Programs Division and financed by the National Guard Bureau of the Department of Defense, the center provides training to federal, state and local emergency teams.

Intriguingly, the center has no defined curriculum; the staff creates response situations designed for whatever kind of group is currently taking its training. The center has designed scenarios ranging from production of biological toxins to subway derailments to accidents involving over-the-road toxic cargo. Cameras record response actions from start to finish, giving participants a take-home record of the training.

The Center for Domestic Preparedness

Located at the former Fort McClellan (Ala.) army base, the Center for Domestic Preparedness is the product of a congressional directive to create a site that would "serve as a training facility for all relevant federally supported training efforts that target state and local law enforcement, firefighters, emergency medical personnel and other key agencies such as public works."[3] It has offered courses in dealing with WMD response, with concentrations in technical and hazmat response and incident command.

The Emergency Management Institute

FEMA's Emergency Management Institute has been popular with a number of public works departments, including Oklahoma City's.[4] Its Integrated Emergency Management course is a four-and-a-half day "exercise-based training activity" primarily aimed at elected and appointed local government officials. Some versions of the course involve events in generic communities, and some target specific communities.

Training at all three centers is free; transportation and lodging are picked up by the participants. "If you're not going through a training process at least every two years, you will miss something," says Oklahoma City's Brum.

"The Mop-up Guys"

Getting public works professionals to these centers has not been easy. People who run the country's water and wastewater plants — who fill its potholes, repair its bridges and wear overalls to work — tend not to see themselves as occupying the rarefied strata that include traditional first responders.

That surprises some people, like Paula Gordon, director of special projects of the research program in social and organizational learning at George Washington University. Gordon, who wrote "Infrastructure Threats and Challenges: Before and After September 11, 2001" for the American Society of Public Administration, posits that part of the problem may be a lack of public relations savvy within the public works community. "They're just not good at tooting their own horn."

Larry Lux agrees. "Generally speaking, the public works community needs to become more involved in the political process," he says. "We need to take stronger and more affirmative advocacy positions, both locally and on the Hill. It's the only way our voices will be recognized. I've made a career out of [trying to get attention for public works], but I'm only one voice. We need thousands of voices."

Lux, president of Plainfield, Ill.–based Lux Advisors, which counsels communities on emergency and disaster management, is a member of APWA's Emergency Management Board and an adjunct faculty instructor at FEMA's Emergency Management Institute. He calls public works employees "the mop-up guys."

"People are absolutely unaware of the importance of public works" in homeland protection, Lux says. "Public works is not thought of as a first responder. What we do isn't glamorous. Fire and law enforcement people arrive in big red vehicles with their sirens going. After they're finished, public works comes up in their little yellow trucks."

Lux insists that communities need to more seriously pursue homeland protection training opportunities for their public works employees. "Not much in that regard has changed since Sept. 11," he says. "The government is earmarking a lot of money for homeland security, but none of the language and none of the money is targeted at improving public works response and training."

In fact, although public works was never mentioned, the Heritage Foundation, a conservative Washington, D.C., think tank, seemed to target the profession in a backgrounder called "Meeting the Needs of America's First Responders." "From 1996 to 1999, the federal government was able to provide [WMD] response training to only 134,000 of the nation's 9 million first responders," the paper noted. It cited the problems of inadequate information regarding available training programs, expensive and inconvenient programs and lack of coordination as issues that the federal government must address.

Fighting an Out-of-date Image

"Part of the problem," Gordon says, "is how 'homeland protection' is being defined. We need to expand the definition."

To some extent, that is happening. Dust from the World Trade Center still hung in the air as national concern over the safety of the country's water plants, highways and bridges was being ratcheted up.

Much of the early homeland security legislation focused on securing the nation's water supply and other "critical infrastructure." Additionally, in a March 2002 letter to APWA members, FEMA Director Joe Allbaugh noted that "at this time, perhaps more than at any other time, we realize the importance of public works infrastructure, facilities and services."

FEMA and APWA are ironing out the details of a Memorandum of Understanding that will provide the basis for a new cooperative effort between the two groups. And APWA has been active in providing comments on proposed legislation and on budget items, according to Karen Bloodworth, manager of professional development programs for the organization.

Still, Bloodworth concedes that PR is a big part of the problem in APWA's efforts to put the importance of public works on the homeland defense agenda. "We haven't been that good at [public relations]," she says. "The staff agrees that PR has been a shortcoming. We are making an effort to change that."

Bloodworth points out that public works functions in emergency management are all-encompassing and include engineering, health and safety codes, roads and bridges, dams, canals, wastewater collection and treatment, electric generation and distribution, telephone service, garbage collection, debris removal and flood control. "Public

works people are so involved in the whole emergency management process," says Gordon. "It's hard to fathom how they can be overlooked."

"When a disaster occurs, the first people in are law enforcement, fire and medical personnel," Lux says. "After a time, it's all public works. The cleanup and restoration of the community is almost 100% public works. We are critical to first response. We need to make everyone understand that."

Notes

1. For information on the National Response and Rescue Training Center, see http://teexeb.tamu.edu/division.cfm?div=NERRTC.

2. For information on the Center for National Response, see www.wvmemorialtunnel.com.

3. For information on the Center for Domestic Preparedness, see www.ojp.usdoj.gov/odp.

4. For information on the Emergency Management Institute of the Federal Emergency Management Agency, see http://training.fema.gov.

CHAPTER 40

RESPONSIBILITIES FOR HOMELAND SECURITY: FEDERAL AND LOCAL GOVERNMENTS

Roger L. Kemp

On November 25, 2002, President Bush signed the "Homeland Security Act of 2002" into law. The Act restructures and strengthens the executive branch of the Federal government to better meet the threat to our homeland posed by terrorism. In establishing the new Department of Homeland Security, the Act, for the first time, creates a Federal department whose primary mission will be to help prevent, protect against, and respond to acts of terrorism on American soil. This is the newest Federal department in the last half-century. Many historians believe that the passage of this Act is the most significant law to be passed by Congress since the approval of the National Security Act in 1947.

President Truman originally asked Congress to combine the War and Navy Departments into a single Department of Defense in 1945. Two years later, Congress responded by passing the National Security Act of 1947. In addition to creating a new Federal department headed by a civilian secretary appointed by the President, it established the Central Intelligence Agency to coordinate all foreign intelligence activities, and created the National Security Council in the White House to coordinate all foreign and defense policy initiatives. While the National Security Act was necessary to face the Cold War, the Homeland Security Act was required for America's new War on Terrorism.

The National Role

The new Department of Homeland Security is supposed to make Americans safer because our nation now has:

- One department whose primary mission is to protect the American homeland.
- One department to secure our borders, transportation sector, ports, and critical infrastructure.
- One department to synthesize and analyze homeland security intelligence from multiple sources.

- One department to coordinate communications with state and local governments, private industry, and the American people about threats and preparedness.
- One department to coordinate our efforts to protect the American people against bioterrorism and other weapons of mass destruction.
- One department to help train and equip our nation's first responders.
- One department to manage federal emergency response activities.
- More security officers in the field working to stop terrorists.

In order to achieve these goals, this department was organized into four divisions, as follows: Border and Transportation Security; Emergency Preparedness and Response; Chemical, Biological, Radiological and Nuclear Countermeasures; and Information Analysis and Infrastructure Protection. Other key components include increased federal, state, local government, and private sector coordination; the Secret Service was moved to this new department; and the White House Office of Homeland Security and the Homeland Security Council will continue to advise the President. Although not directly related to homeland security, the Federal Emergency Management Agency (FEMA) and the U. S. Coast Guard were also transferred to this new department.

A Slow Start

While Congress approved this new department in November of 2002, some critics felt that the Federal government took too much time to create a national mechanism for responding to possible future terrorist attacks, and is still stumbling over efforts to better coordinate preventative measures at the Federal level. For example, it wasn't until October 2003 that the new Secretary of this department, Thomas Ridge, approved the Initial National Response Plan (INRP), an interim plan designed to help develop a unified approach to domestic incident management across the U.S. The INRP represents a significant first step toward the overall goal of integrating the current family of federal domestic prevention, preparedness, response, and recovery plans into a single all-hazards national response plan.

The initial plan was developed in conjunction with state and local governments, law enforcement officials, and the fire and emergency management agencies, tribal associations, the private sector, and other nongovernmental organizations. The objective of the INRP was for the United States to be better prepared by integrating emergency response plans that cover terrorist attacks, major disasters, and other emergencies. This led to the development of the National Incident Management System (NIMS). NIMS is now the model for all state and local governments in America for responding to significant emergency incidents, including acts of terrorism.

The Homeland Security Act also designated the Secretary of the Department of Homeland Security as the principal Federal official for domestic incident management. The Secretary is responsible for coordinating Federal operations to prepare for and respond to terrorist attacks and to coordinate the use of the Federal government's resources during recovery from terrorist attacks, major disasters, and other emergencies. For this action to take place one of four conditions must apply. They are:

- A Federal department or agency acting under its own authority has requested the assistance of the Secretary of the Department of Homeland Security.
- The resources of state and local authorities have been overwhelmed and the appropriate state and local authorities have requested Federal assistance.
- More than one Federal department or agency has become substantially involved in responding to the incident.

• The Secretary of the Department of Homeland Security has been directed to assume responsibility for managing the domestic incident by the President of the United States.

Local Officials Are First Responders

Federal and state officials have made substantial progress in the field of homeland security since September 2001. City and county managers and their elected officials, however, are at the forefront of this movement. After all, local governments were the first responders to the terrorist acts of September 11. While national and state leadership are essential, the future of homeland security will depend on preparedness initiatives at the local level. Fire, public health, and law enforcement officials have developed new emergency management practices, applied new computer software to this field, and have begun to initiate new security measures and safeguards to protect our citizens.

In only a few years, state law enforcement agencies have standardized many of their practices in emergency management for those cities and counties within their respective boundaries. The national government has responded with a new agency, the first in a half-century, the Department of Homeland Security. As this department evolves, coordination among federal agencies in the area of homeland security will improve. Equally important, federal departments are initiating training programs to educate public safety personnel in the many facets of homeland security.

Against this backdrop of increased security and safeguards comes the loss of personal freedom that Americans commonly take for granted. Many Americans feel their world has changed since the terrorist attack on September 11, 2001. In a less secure world, Americans are re-examining the delicate balance between protecting the public safety while preserving individual civil liberties. Also, government officials are revisiting policies that seemed intrusive or discriminatory only a few months ago. The public's attention has shifted, at least temporarily, to several public policy debates, including racial profiling, Internet privacy, and the rights of noncitizens. These sensitive issues will be sorted out in our state capitols, by the federal government, and in our court systems, as our nation's homeland security practices evolve during the months and years ahead.

Conclusion

As future homeland security practices emerge, the challenge will be to maintain democracy and accountability while attempting to protect the nation and its citizens from future terrorist acts. The challenge is to develop a framework in which liberty and order can coexist while our public officials take steps to increase our domestic security. Many Americans now feel that their world has changed since the events of 2001. In the less secure world we all live in, Americans are now beginning to re-examine that fine line between protecting the public safety and maintaining our individual civil liberties. Evolving homeland security practices should fit our nation's long-standing philosophy of maintaining security while, at the same time, protecting the rights of citizens from the over-zealous actions of their government.

CHAPTER 41

SECURITY AND EMERGENCY RESPONSE IMPROVED THROUGH PUBLIC-PRIVATE COOPERATION

Russell J. Decker

Public- and private-sector organizations working together is nothing new, but an initiative in northwest Ohio called the Lima Area Security & Emergency Response Task Force has been recognized repeatedly as an unusually successful effort.

- Ohio governor Bob Taft has recognized LASER as a "best practice" example of grassroots homeland security.
- The Ohio Chemical Technology Council has pointed to LASER and its chemical industry members as "the model of private/public success."
- The group won the 2003 "Partners In Preparedness" award from the International Association of Emergency Managers.
- Most recently, 4th Dist. Ohio Congressman Michael Oxley wrote to President Bush regarding LASER's success, touting the task force as "a leading example of how local communities should work together to deal with the new challenges of protecting the homeland."

The Targets and the Threat

Allen County is home to the Lima Army Tank Plant, a 390-acre U.S. Army facility operated by General Dynamics where America's main line battle tank, the Abrams MIA2, is built. Across the road from the tank plant are a major oil refinery and several petrochemical plants. These plants all share a common fence line extending for more than 5 miles.

Immediately after the 9-11 attacks, this area became a security concern to local authorities, as well as to the companies operating these critical facilities and the community at large. For decades, these companies had cooperated with local fire, law enforcement and emergency management officials in developing emergency response plans and first-responder training to scenarios involving accidental chemical releases and other emergencies. But deliberate attacks by a terrorist group hadn't been high on the list of likely scenarios during most of these planning and training sessions.

Just days after the attacks on the World Trade Center and Pentagon, a meeting was

Originally published as "Good Fences, Good Neighbors," *Homeland Protection Professional*, Vol. 3, No. 3, April 2004. Published by A. J. Parrino & Associates, Western Springs, Illinois. Reprinted with permission of the publisher.

called of the plant managers of these key facilities, along with local police chiefs, the sheriff, the Army commander for the tank plant and the local emergency management agency director. And while all of these organizations had worked together previously, this became the first time all of the most senior officials for these companies and agencies were together in the same room.

The meeting was a good one. Its most important outcome was a consensus that this group of senior-level officials had to continue to meet. Thus LASER was born and continues to meet regularly to this day.

Since that first meeting, the LASER members have teamed up to tackle issues such as uniformity of security levels at all facilities, cooperative funding of enhanced security measures, intelligence-sharing, emergency planning, joint exercises, collective briefings for elected leaders, and joint information-sharing to the public.

From the very start, LASER has had only 10 members: the five private-sector plant managers, from BP Lima Chemicals, Chemtrade Logistics, Fort Amanda Specialties (Akzo Nobel/BASF), General Dynamics and the Premcor Lima Refinery, and on the public side, the police chiefs from the City of Lima and Shawnee Township, the Allen County sheriff, the U.S. Army commander for the Lima Army Tank Plant, and the director of the Allen County Office of Homeland Security & Emergency Management.

One of the questions that's asked most often about LASER is why there are no fire or EMS agencies in the task force. The answer is that fire, EMS, state agencies, the FBI and other critical players are invited to meetings when issues are being discussed that directly affect them or where their input would be important. However, since the core of the LASER mission is security, the members have opted to keep their number limited to the original 10 members.

What's truly exceptional about the LASER group is the high level of trust that's

been developed among the members. The results of this trust and cooperation speak for themselves.

- Patrols of the perimeter fence line 24/7, paid for 100% by the private sector.
- Logged patrols of external perimeters by local law enforcement.
- Acquisition of a $100,000 communications system to solve interoperability issues among local first responders and industry. The funding was 75% federal grant, 25% local match from private-sector LASER members.
- Consistent inspections of all vehicles entering any LASER facility.
- Ongoing intelligence-sharing.
- Joint terrorism response exercises.
- A joint public information/education program.
- Unified physical enhancement of facilities' security.

Commonality and Candor

Let's take a closer look at a few of these accomplishments. Shortly after the LASER group began meeting, it became apparent that security measures at the plants needed to mirror each other.

As Chuck Treloar, plant manager of BP Lima Chemicals explains, "Because of our shared fence line and close proximity to one another, our plant is only as secure as our neighbor's plant." Soon all facilities began a cooperative program to maintain equal security and plant-entry protocols.

One example of this cooperation came in the matter of vehicle inspections. While soldiers at the Lima Army Tank Plant were experienced in this area, it was new ground for the security forces at the refinery and chemical companies. At the suggestion of the tank plant's commander, Lt. Col. Ted Harrison, soldiers on security detail at his facility trained their counterparts from across the road so the end result was a uniform technique for searching all vehicles entering any LASER property.

Meanwhile, at the request of the plant managers, members of the sheriff's office Selective Enforcement Team began performing 24-hour security checks on all facilities to look for weaknesses. Candid reports of their findings were shared with all LASER members, with the result being a continued upgrading of security techniques and procedures.

"I don't think we could have been as honest and frank with these plant managers if it were not for the relationships developed through LASER," explains Sheriff Dan Beck.

The unprecedented sharing of information and intelligence is another of the many unique benefits resulting from this task force. Initially everyone was a little hesitant to share sensitive information, but as relationships have developed and trust levels increased, this is an area that really stands out. The LASER meetings are regular forums for law enforcement and plant managers to speak openly about security issues at their plants.

"It's a positive that at one time all the concerned parties can hear the exact same information and that we keep everyone on the same page," explains Shawnee Township police chief Richard Kohli.

Money Well Spent

Communications is always a problem, and it's no different here. LASER members quickly realized that should an incident occur, communications between facilities and first responders would be hampered with the systems in place at that time. After careful analysis, it was agreed that enhancements to the county's communications capabilities would benefit everyone concerned.

The public-sector folks agreed to pool their efforts in an application for a Byrne Formula Grant from the Bureau of Justice Assistance to acquire $100,000 worth of improved technology to meet the new needs. The grant required a 25% local funding match. When the five corporate members of LASER learned this, and without being asked, they offered to contribute the local matching money. The grant was awarded, and today Allen County has one of the most advanced and versatile communications systems in northwest Ohio, without the use of any local government funds.

Currently LASER's focus is on improving the perimeter barriers around the complex. BP Lima Chemicals began the effort with a project using rows of boulders to reinforce the fence line. Embassy-style gates are also being installed at a number of locations, the number of video security cameras has more than doubled, and several other enhancements are scheduled for the remainder of 2004 and early 2005.

Recently, the LASER task force briefed local elected leaders and state and federal officials. During this briefing it was disclosed that to date the private-sector members have collectively invested more than $7 million in capital improvements to enhance security at their plants. They also estimate the annual cost of maintaining heightened security levels at $3 million.

So why does LASER work so well? What's the secret? Members say they believe the key to success has been the dedicated involvement of senior-level personnel sharing a single view: that the safety of these key critical assets is essential for their continued success and for the safety of their employees and the community at large.

CHAPTER 42

STATEWIDE GUIDELINES BY THE PRESIDENT'S HOMELAND SECURITY ADVISORY COUNCIL

Joseph J. Grano

Purpose

The Statewide Template Initiative is consistent with and designed to support implementation of the "*National Strategy for Homeland Security.*"

- The primary objective of the Statewide Template Initiative (STI) is to assist state[1] and local and tribal authorities in their development of coordinated and comprehensive Homeland Security plans. The *Template*'s questions, which were developed by leaders of state and local governments and emergency response community, provide a foundation for the preparation of comprehensive and compatible state, local and tribal Homeland Security plans that maximize state and local terrorism prevention and response capabilities.
- The *Template*'s questions (and additional questions posed by state and local officials) will expand and integrate existing homeland security planning to deal with terrorist attacks, no matter how unlikely or catastrophic, as well as all manner of natural disasters and other hazards. The resulting plans will bolster everyday protection and

response capabilities and the states' ability to better serve its citizens in today's environment.

Guiding Principles

- Make America "*Safer, Stronger, and Better.*"
- Recognize the effects of all terrorist attacks occur locally.
- Maximize collective efforts to prevent terrorist attacks, reduce risks, and respond effectively to attacks that do occur.
- Assure that efforts are State based but locally focused and driven —*flexible, scalable, and adaptable*.
- Recognize that our enemy is networked and can only be defeated by a networked system — therefore homeland defense must resemble networked PCs rather than a mainframe computer.
- Ensure that our homeland security efforts do not result in significant alteration of our federalist form of government.
- Empower state and local officials' Homeland Security efforts, leveraging existing

Originally published as *Statewide Template Initiative*, President's Homeland Security Advisory Council, Washington, D.C., March 2003.

emergency preparedness and response programs and capabilities to meet emerging threats to the Nation and its citizens.
- Promote interoperable and reliable telecommunications capabilities nationwide.
- Promote integrated and collective training, exercises and evaluations.
- Facilitate the adoption of best practices from other jurisdictions.
- Enable government and private sector at all levels the ability to carry out its Homeland Security responsibilities.
- Promote citizen participation in state, local, private sector and regional homeland security efforts through volunteer service activities, preparedness, education and awareness.
- Ensure funding follows policy.
- Process matters — specific measures of performance in plans drive clarity, accountability, and success.
- The *Homeland* will be secure when *Hometowns* are secure.

Template Questions

The following questions are *"outcome based"* and designed to assist state and local governments prepare their State Homeland Security Plans. The questions are intended to provide a common understanding of responsibilities of all participants, the scope of issues, authorities, and responsibilities to be addressed, required operational capabilities; and to help provide an interoperable context to the homeland security planning effort.

EXPECTATIONS

- What does the state expect from the federal government?
- What do local governments expect from the state government?
- What should private sector entities expect from federal, state and local governments?
- What should citizens expect from federal, state and local governments?

- What should state and local governments expect from their citizens?

CONTINUITY OF STATE AND LOCAL GOVERNMENT

- Are plans in place to ensure the timely and successful *"Order of Succession"* of state and local leaders?
- What measures exist to ensure the continuity of state and local government?
  * Have alternative locations for state and local government operations been identified?
- What collaborative agreements are in place with private industry to ensure business continuity?
- Do state or local mutual assistance compacts address the continuity issue?

CONTINUITY OF CRITICAL STATE SERVICES

- Have critical state services (e.g., hospitals, emergency medical services, critical infrastructure and associated personnel) been identified?
  * Are contingency plans in place to ensure their reliability, and have they been recently tested?
- What are your plans to include key representatives of the private sector and those specifically responsible for critical infrastructures in the development of plans supporting the continuity of government, business and critical infrastructures?

CRITICAL INFRASTRUCTURE

- What are the critical key assets and infrastructures (cyber and physical)?
- Who owns them and who is responsible for their operation?
- Do regionally located critical infrastructures and infrastructure services have the capacity to impact adjacent regions?
  * Have these infrastructures been identified to all potentially affected regions and Federal Government?
- What are the multi-region critical infra-

structures' single points of failure and interdependencies?

   * How are they being addressed?

- What measures need to be taken to assure state and local critical infrastructure reliability?
- Is state and local government partnering with critical private sector industries and infrastructures to help ensure their protection and survivability?
- Has a method been established to allow critical infrastructure owners to query the backgrounds and help ensure the reliability of new employees and periodically those in sensitive positions?

LAW

- Do you have an active system of law reform to identify and address issues related to terrorism?
- Do you have a system for education of individuals affected by legal reforms related to terrorism?
- Do you have a plan for continuity of your legal system in the event of a terrorist attack?

INFORMATION SHARING AND TECHNOLOGY

- What is the state information-sharing structure?
- What requirements for specific Homeland Security related information have been provided to local, state, and federal authorities and the private sector?
- What policies and mechanisms (beyond law enforcement) are in place to ensure timely and reliable exchange of intelligence and information among and between local, state, and federal authorities and the private sector?
- What communications limitations currently exist that require upgrading to take advantage of emerging Homeland Security related information sharing.
- Are local, state and federal law enforcement agencies aware of the mechanisms

for intelligence sharing that support homeland security efforts (education process)?

- Do local and state plans provide for outreach to the media before, during, and after terrorist incidents, natural disasters, and all matter of hazards?
- Are commercial Information Technology reliability standards sufficient to ensure systems performance in emergency environments?
- Is there a requirement for secure communications?
  - * If so, are there assigned/protected frequencies available for use by the emergency response community?
- Has each sector identified and defined the information needed to carry out its homeland security mission?
- Has each sector identified and defined what information needs to be shared among entities within sector and with other sectors?
- Have the differences between the needs of urban and rural responders been identified and accommodated?
- What are the plans to continue communication with appropriate private sector and critical infrastructure representatives in the event an emergency precludes normal means of communication?

BORDERS

- Do state and local Border Security plans clearly define the roles and responsibilities of federal, state, and local jurisdictions?
- Where do federal and state responsibilities coincide?
- Where do federal and state responsibilities diverge?
- How are different federal/state roles and responsibilities defined?
- Have lines of communication been established with the Department of Homeland Security?
- Are procedures in place to track high-risk interstate traffic/cargo?

First Responders and Emergency Services

- Who are they?
- What do they require/need?
- How are requirements/needs determined and prioritized?
- How is consensus gained for requirements/ needs?
- Is there any process to monitor training and equipment acquisition for responders for standardization and quality?
- How is standardization of equipment purchasing achieved?
- How are requirements tied to capability?
- How are new capabilities obtained and sustained?
- Have protected/exclusive communications paths and command authorities been established?
- Is there a standard, unified system for incident command?
- Are the command systems implemented and trained across city, county, and state agencies?
- Have homeland security information requirements been documented?
- Are public utility services, public health, hospitals and other medical care providers, and emergency medical service providers involved in planning and training?
  * Are their emergency plans tested and training evaluated?

National Guard

- Is the National Guard included in state plans?
- How many Guardsmen are also first responders?
- Are they included in local and multi-state mutual assistance compacts?
- What is the understanding between state and local governments regarding the use of the National Guard to support homeland security operations?
- Are Title 10 and Title 32 US Code authorities and responsibilities clearly understood?

Public Health and Chemical/Biological/ Radiological Terrorism

- Who is responsible for chemical/biological/radiological defense efforts?
  * Do chemical/biological defense efforts include decontamination of humans, livestock, crops, water supplies, and facilities?
  * Are Agricultural products inspected at the borders and ports?
  * Are there laboratories readily available that can quickly test for agents affecting humans as well as vegetable and livestock diseases?
  * Is there a rapid means to communicate critical communicable disease information to appropriate agencies (federal, state and local)?
  * Are chemical/biological/radiological antidotes and prophylaxes, antidotes and other emergency pharmaceuticals readily available?
  * Are distribution systems reliable and in place and are they exercised?
- Is there a comprehensive public health plan that addresses, federal, state and local resources, legal, economic and operational components?
- Are hospital and other medical care providers, emergency medical services, and veterinarian and agricultural inspectors included in the plans?
- What methods are used to ensure timely equipment purchasing?
- Is the public safety community inoculated?
- Have biological, chemical, and nuclear attack exercises been conducted?
- How are new capabilities obtained and sustained?

Private Sector

- How is the Private Sector being incorporated into your planning process?
  * What public/private sector agreements are in place to ensure effective partner-

ships between state and local governments and the private sector?

* Have key private sector leaders been identified?
* Have critical private sector industries been identified in terms of their specialized resource capability or economic value?
* Have private sector resources been identified for potential government use through appropriate agreements and contracts?
* Are small and medium sized enterprises integrated into state and local plans?

VOLUNTEER SERVICE

• Are Private Volunteer Organizations, Non-Governmental Organizations and federally-sponsored volunteer programs (e.g., Civil Air Patrol, Red Cross, community and faith-based, Americorps, and Senior Corps) included in terrorism strategic and operational plans, such as through state and local Citizen Corps Councils?

• Have volunteers with specialized expertise and supplemental equipment (e.g., high-mobility transportation, communication, etc.) been identified?

• Do your state and local communities have Citizen Corps Councils to coordinate citizen participation in homeland security activities (see www.citizenscorps.gov)?

SCHOOLS

• Are homeland security issues factored into public and private school operations?

CITIZENS WITH SPECIAL NEEDS

• How do your plans deal with citizens with special needs?

OPERATIONS AND INFORMATION SECURITY

• What activities are divulging information that could support planning for, conduct of, and enhance the effects of terrorist operations?

* What is being done to correct the practice(s)?

• What resources are required or are being utilized to help improve state, local and private sector operations and information security procedures?

• What mechanisms are used to disseminate secured information?

• What are your priority information systems and how is their performance assured?

HOMELAND SECURITY ADVISORY SYSTEM (HSAS)

• Has the HSAS been adopted by the state and/or local governments?

• Has the HSAS been tailored for regional needs?

• Has the HSAS been integrated into the state's emergency public information plan?

• Has the media been informed of the basic characteristics of the system?

• Have you translated the advisory system into actual operational use?

• Is there a standardized system of tasks for each level?

• What can state and local governments do to tailor the HSAS for their policy-makers, emergency planners, first responders, and public information officers?

PUBLIC INFORMATION AND COMMUNICATIONS

• Does the state's emergency public information plan integrate the public information resources of all state and local agencies?

• Does the emergency public information plan extend to local authorities?

• Are there agreements between state and local jurisdictions regarding who has the lead for various categories of public information?

• Is the media being consulted and included in public information planning?

• Does the emergency public information plan include pre-scripted messages designed for rapid dissemination through the media to inform, reassure, and protect the public?

• Is there specific emergency information training available for elected and appointed officials?

LEXICON

• Is there an accepted, commonly used and universally understood language among the multiple disciplines of the State and local and response communities?
  * Is the lexicon consistent with the Emerging National Incident Management System?

FUNDING

• How are local operational needs identified, developed, prioritized, and presented to state authorities?

• How is bottom-up funding consensus achieved?

• How is the state working with local governments to identify and support local priority needs?

• How is the state ensuring local priorities are met?

• How does consensus support budget priorities?

• Are budget priorities supported by the Governor's Office and State Legislature?

• How are federal funds monitored and distributed to meet operational needs of the state and local jurisdictions?

• What are the roadblocks to the efficient and timely distribution of federal resources?

TRAINING, EXERCISING AND EVALUATING

• Is there an integrated testing/evaluation program?
  * Are Emergency Management Accreditation Program (EMAP) evaluation standards utilized?

• Are "lessons-learned" integrated into new performance standards?

• Have minimum terrorism training, exercise, and evaluation standards been established for state agencies?

• Are those same standards required at the local level?

• How is success determined?

• Will Field Exercises and Tabletop Exercises be a component of the evaluation methodology?

• Have state level documents been refined to reflect the changing response requirements of terror related incidents?
  * Field Operating Guide?
  * Standard Operating Procedures?
  * Modifications to the state Comprehensive Emergency Management Plan?

• Is there a joint training program for responding to acts of terrorism that involve appropriate representatives from critical infrastructures?

• Is there a process to review and provide recommendations to corporate security officials for enhancing security at critical infrastructure sites?

• How is standardization of training/equipment and interoperability both vertically and horizontally assured?

• What training and maintenance programs are in place to sustain new capabilities?

PLANNING AND CHANGE MANAGEMENT

• How are strategic processes adapted to changing capabilities and conditions?

• How are plans adapted to sustain new capabilities and ensure long-term success?

• How are specific goals identified and measures of performance applied to objectively assess and manage existing efforts and track new initiatives in statewide plans?

The primary steps involved in the *Statewide Template Initiative* are shown in Figure 1. This Template supports the National Homeland Security Strategy, the primary components of which are listed in Figure 2.

FIGURE 1

Statewide Template Initiative by the President's Homeland Security Advisory Council

Step	Title
1	Critical Functions and Assets
2	Daily Operations
3	Methods of Effectiveness
4	Outcomes/Execution/Lessons Learned
5	Best Practices

FIGURE 2

The Template Supports the National Homeland Security Strategy

The Template Includes

- Expectations
- Continuity of State and Local Governments
- Continuity of Critical State Services
- Critical Infrastructure
- Law
- Information Sharing and Technology
- Borders
- First Responders and Emergency Services
- National Guard
- Public Health and Chemical/Biological/Radiological Terrorism
- Private Sector
- Volunteer Service
- Schools
- Citizens with Special Needs
- Operations and Information Security
- Homeland Security Advisory System
- Public Information and Communications
- Lexicon
- Funding
- Training, Exercising and Evaluating
- Planning and Change Management

Note

1. The *"National Strategy for Homeland Security"* defines "State" to mean "any state of the United States, the District of Columbia, Puerto Rico, the Virgin Islands, Guam, American Samoa, the Canal Zone, the Commonwealth of the Northern Mariana Islands, or the trust territory of the Pacific Islands." The *Strategy* defines "local government" as "any county, city, village, town, district, or other political subdivision of any state, any Native American tribe or authorized tribal organization, or Alaska native village or organization, and includes any rural community or unincorporated town or village or any other public entity for which an application for assistance is made by a state or political subdivision thereof."

CHAPTER 43

STRESS MANAGEMENT FOR FIREFIGHTERS

Robert L. Smith

The events of Sept. 11 will prove to be pivotal in our nation's history. The shift in behavior and attitude that will take place in American society will have a significant impact on the attitudes and behaviors of firefighters and fire service managers.

In other words, the fire service will never be the same as it was prior to the attacks. As fire chiefs, we'll be forced to examine the way we conduct operations and how we take care of our brothers, sisters and their families. Addressing the psychological and emotional care of our firefighters has become an important aspect of our mission.

The fact that the fire service is a caretaking profession has some bearing on this discussion. Firefighters are trained and socialized to respond to the needs of others, and this mission is an important facet of the firefighter's job. Individuals in other caretaking professions, such as nurses and physicians, also are trained to respond to the needs of others. We know that job stress and burnout are issues that people in these caretaking professions should pay attention to. Consequently, we must place a higher emphasis on the psychological and emotional health of firefighters so they are physically and mentally prepared to serve the public.

New questions have developed and are being asked by fire chiefs in response to the attacks. How will we treat a high-rise fire? How will we ensure safety on the fireground during a suspected terrorist attack? Will we handle hazmat incidents differently? It's important to note that questions like these now are emotionally charged rather than simply tactical. How can we take care of our firefighters' emotional, psychological and stress management needs as these tactical questions are processed?

Traditionally, fire departments have taken a response approach rather than a management approach to stress. Often, we're slow to respond until something goes wrong. We send a firefighter to addictions treatment for a drinking problem, or we mandate employee counseling sessions when behavior is problematic. As a result of this strategy, firefighters are forced to resolve their problems in a time of stress while at odds with their employer.

Instead, a management/prevention approach to stress could better serve the firefighter. Recent events have signaled a need to end the reactive approach. Fire service managers no longer have the luxury of waiting for a problem to occur before responding.

Originally published as "Coping with Catastrophe," *Fire Chief*, Vol. 45, No. 12, December 2001. Published by Primedia Business Magazines & Media, Inc., Overland Park, Kansas. Reprinted with permission of the publisher.

Stress Management Units

The management of firefighter stress is complex and multifaceted. The average firefighter encounters stress, not only from critical incidents, but also from non-critical incidents such as personality conflicts within the firehouse, family problems, common hardships of a long tour of duty or the death of a family member.

My Global Fire Service Stress Management Model strives to focus on all fire department stress rather than only focusing on stress that is encountered by exposure to a critical incident. As stress is cumulative, it doesn't matter if the particular stressor is critical incident stress or other more routine firefighter stress.

For example, firefighters tend to be socialized as task-oriented perfectionists. Firefighters will encounter significant stress over failed equipment that hindered a rescue or a department policy that they do not agree with. In short, stress is stress — we can't overlook any of it. The Global Fire Service Stress Management Model goes beyond Critical Incident Stress Management and other models while integrating CISM as part of the package.

The Washington Township Fire Department Stress Management Unit was developed to address these critical and non-critical issues and to follow the Global Fire Service Stress Management Model. The model seeks to address difficulties early in the problem process, as early treatment is the key to effective management.

Members of the Washington Township Fire Department SMU are trained in CISM; however, the central focus of the unit is the management of multifaceted firefighter stress. The SMU is composed of one clergy member and two firefighters who are licensed as mental health practitioners to act as trainers, supervisors and facilitators.

The SMU operates in a non-intrusive manner, and the call for response is often initiated by the affected firefighter or by their supervisor. The unit's response can provide support, as well as initiate a possible assessment for further mental health assistance.

The model has several areas of concentration, including stress education, mentoring, unit response guidelines, new recruit education, spiritual care, public relations and assessment. Education includes stress awareness/management training for the firefighter as well as relationship skills workshops for spouses and families.

One example of the stress management component is the coaching of the firefighter and spouse around the single-parent phenomenon of the fire service: The spouse can be left to parent the children without assistance from the firefighter during long tours of duty and beyond, especially if a part-time job is included in that time of absence.

Unit Components

Assessment is a function of the department SMU. All members meet for quarterly training and are introduced to basic stress management skills. The SMU in a fire department must address firefighter stress with an open-minded attitude.

However, the SMU must be a conduit to introduce firefighters into a mental health system that understands the specific needs of firefighters and their families. Too often, firefighters gain access to an unfamiliar mental health system that attempts to treat them like non-firefighters and devalues their coping mechanisms and loyalties. The SMU addresses and can improve this problem.

Pastoral care is an important aspect in the model. The Washington Township Fire Department has three chaplains: a rabbi and a minister who are certified firefighters, and a Catholic priest. Members of our pastoral care staff are trained to function in both the pastoral care role and the peer counselor role. The peer training is important for pastors and mental health clinicians to become involved in and be accepted as part of the organization.

It's been shown that firefighters respond best to other firefighters as they understand the built-in coping mechanisms developed by those in the fire service. Individuals who attempt to assist firefighters should understand the nature of the occupation and the cohesion of the group. Too often, firefighters are put off by a mental health professional who fails to understand firefighter coping methods. The helper must know how to enable these socialized methods.

Internal public relations is a very large consideration for the fire department SMU. Firefighters depend on the maintenance of confidentiality, loyalty and prompt service of the unit. The connection firefighters experience with members of the SMU is tantamount to the unit's success. Unit members are very aware of their image with firefighters and are selected on their merits. The unit also functions as a diplomatic arm of the fire department administration. Firefighters soon understand that the administration values their ability to function on the job without stress-related symptoms.

Unit response guidelines are an important consideration in the Global Fire Service Stress Management Model. The SMU has responded to conflicts in fire stations, in addition to being called on to assist hospitalized firefighters or firefighters on light duty. At times, SMU members provide a meal or transportation to another firefighter in need. These examples range from simple acts of kindness to the referral for more complicated mental health intervention. The goal of all responses is to enable proper coping and assist the firefighter in the reduction of stress.

New recruit education and firefighter mentoring are additional aspects of the Global Fire Service Management Model. New recruits at the Washington Township Fire Department receive training in stress management and coping techniques as a part of their fire academy curriculum.

Each new recruit is assigned a mentor from the SMU. The mentors assist with orienting new recruits to their assignments in a manner that promotes development of appropriate coping techniques and good mental health awareness. In addition, they also teach many of the emotional mechanics of the fire service job. These include getting along with other firefighters in the new environment and the introduction of spouses and family members to the fire service circle.

Many interventions exist to assist firefighters in this time of stress. The fire service must begin to recognize stress as a cumulative phenomena. Firefighters should learn in advance how to deal with the stress from critical incidents such as the ones in New York, Washington and Pennsylvania. Firefighters who respond to critical incidents in a lower state of stress have a greater chance of sustaining psychological wellness and avoiding burnout during their career.

Critical Incident Debriefing

A fire department plan for critical incident stress debriefing is essential in the wake of recent events. This should encompass two areas: lower-profile incidents and large-scale critical incidents.

Unfortunately, many departments don't have a plan for handling these types of large-scale incidents. Departments shouldn't depend on outside agencies alone to formulate this plan. A department representative should be involved in the planning stages because fire department managers know their personnel best.

Your department's plan for a large incident should include the following:
1) The lead mental health practitioner should be familiar with the firefighters of your department, their job roles and your organization.

FIGURE 1
Methods of Stress Reduction for Firefighters
~ Dealing with Everyday Stress ~

1) Establish a Stress Management Unit for your organization.

2) Make contact with interested mental health practitioners and employee assistance programs that want to be involved in the stress management process of your organization. Be sure these counselors spend time in the fire stations, riding along on the apparatus and learning about how to work with fire department families based on current research.

3) Have a plan for ongoing stress education for your department. This should include stress management presentations that focus on both critical and non-critical incidents. Current research exists to support the idea that non-critical incident stress also plays a role in cumulative stress.

4) Provide basic stress education to new recruits. Firefighters are socialized or indoctrinated into their jobs. Fire chiefs and departments can supply early messages to recruits by including information about proper coping methods.

5) Provide structured firefighter mentoring for all ranks.

6) Provide good information about stress management to your firefighters. Put information and contact numbers in the stations and provide peer contacts who are accessible to your firefighters. Police departments and industrial plants have had peer support teams for years. These individuals do not practice mental health but assist other firefighters in gathering information about stress, mental health and mental health resources.

7) Create a way for firefighters to enter the mental health system if needed. Contract with licensed mental health practitioners in advance. The counselors and therapists who are most familiar with your department should train other therapists about your department and firefighters.

8) Listen to the new concerns of firefighters since Sept. 11. Start a continual process of assessing the newest concerns of your firefighters. How do they feel about the possibility of future attacks? Find a new way to show support for your firefighters on a regular basis, such as telling them you appreciate their efforts and visiting the stations. Address the needs of your firefighters.

9) Showcase your firefighters — get caught telling the public, the media and elected officials how good they are. Specifically, tell others about how your department is ready for disasters and further attacks.

10) Allow your firefighters to participate in addressing their job concerns. For example, create a safety committee or an advisory committee to formulate new operating guidelines or procedures. This will help your firefighters emotionally by helping them to feel in control of their job situation.

---

2) The counselor or therapist should have exposure to the fire station environment and should build rapport with the firefighters in your department.

3) The lead counselor should have a license to practice mental health and access to the latest research about the mental health care of firefighters.

4) The involvement of a qualified CISM team is essential. The team should be fully

trained, experienced and include other firefighters.

5) Firefighters are most comfortable talking to other firefighters. While others may be well intentioned, they may not have the same credibility as a CISM team composed of firefighters trained in CISM.

6) Department chaplains should be involved in the response to a large-scale incident. Fire chiefs should commission chaplains of firefighter-represented denominations prior to a tragedy.

7) Fire departments should have stress-related material available for both critical incidents and stress prevention. Departments should consider seminars and classes that address stressors other than critical incidents prior to a tragedy. Tragedies can be easier to handle if fire departments adopt a stance of prevention.

8) Protocols should be developed to direct fire departments to assist families in the event of line of duty death or injury. Family care should be considered when long deployments of firefighters are necessary. Families could need extra assistance due to the combination effect of an absent spouse and the emotional hardships of worrying about their firefighter family member.

Your department can make a difference. We'll have better prepared and more effective rescuers if we work to reduce stress before large incidents.

CHAPTER 44

STRESS MANAGEMENT FOR POLICE OFFICERS

Rickey Hargrave

The September 11, 2001, terrorist attacks on the United States remind law enforcement executives not only of the need for prevention and response strategies but also of the tremendous impact events of this magnitude can have on rescue personnel. Chiefs of police all across America are seeking remedies to the extended trauma in their own agencies.

Helping these brave men and women find some normalization after such an extraordinary event is what chaplains attempt to do. Lessons learned by the chaplains and Critical Incident Stress Management (CISM) teams in New York can help relieve the stresses inherent in police work. This is my story of how I responded and the lessons I learned.

Sunday, September 16, 2001

After the terrorist attacks, the International Conference of Police Chaplains (ICPC) requested chaplains and CISM teams to assist the Port Authority of New York/New Jersey. The ICPC requested certified master chaplains and members of the International

Critical Incident Stress Foundation (ICISF) holding advanced certification in critical incident stress management. The assignment was to contact members of the Port Authority Police Department in each of their 13 stations throughout the greater New York area. As a police chaplain with the requested qualifications, I joined in this response.

In the 16 weeks following September 11, a total of 67 ICPC chaplains responded to the PAPD, filling 108 slots. Other CISM members totaled 187. These members consisted of peer support officers from other agencies and mental health professionals trained in CISM. We were sent out in teams of three to five, depending on the vehicles available for transport. Each team had at least one chaplain.

We planned to use defusings and, if possible, debriefings. A defusing is a three-phase, structured small group discussion provided within hours of a crisis for purposes of assessment, triaging, and acute symptom mitigation. A debriefing is a closed confidential discussion of a critical incident relating to the feelings and perceptions of those directly involved before, during, and after a stressful event. Models for group intervention, de-

Originally published as "A Police Chaplain's Perspective on the Aftermath of September 11," Reprinted from *The Police Chief*, Vol. LXIX, No. 2, February 2002. Published by the International Association of Chiefs of Police, Alexandria, VA. Reprinted with permission of the publisher.

briefings are intended to provide support, education, and an outlet for views and feelings associated with the event. Debriefings are not counseling or an operational critique of the incident.

We decided to follow as closely as possible the model of one-to-one debriefing established by Dr. Jeffery Mitchell and Dr. George Everly, presently professors at the University of Maryland and Loyola College, respectively. With the extreme trauma evident on every street and in every set of shock-widened eyes, we knew we would not be able to go into depth with these rescue personnel. Our goal was to let them know that counseling and debriefing help would be available when they needed it and to give a word of encouragement while they performed a task for which no one could prepare them.

Our first briefing at the center came at 10:00 p.m. Saturday, September 15. My assignment was the noon to midnight shift beginning on Sunday. During the week our team was to be moved from point to point to prevent burnout from being in one place all the time.

Our team did not handle buckets, we did not open body bags, and we did not participate in the discovery. We were there to listen, which was initially difficult.

Eventually, we noticed that the rescue workers were more receptive to us. People were talking about their feelings, their hurts, thinking about family and friends they saw last week and who they hadn't seen since. Our local rescue and recovery workers were amazed by all the groups coming from all over the country to assist. New York officers and firefighters are finding they are part of a large family that includes New Jersey, Washington, Pennsylvania, Oklahoma, Texas, and parts beyond. All across this city we are experiencing a warmth and a closeness that is only evident in the most loving of families. And when families hurt, families pull together.

There was a change in the conversa-tions. The stories at the morgue were of those who they knew who had died. It was tough duty to listen to the stories of longtime friends and all the things they used to do on and off duty. It was critical that we listen, especially with a confidential ear. The wall of confidence can be a fragile one. One breach and there may not be another opportunity to regain lost trust.

Tuesday, September 18, 2001

The purpose of crisis counselors in the middle of an emergency such as this is mainly one of laying a foundation and helping to address and lessen the immediate emotional and spiritual needs of the moment. The counselors and stress management professionals who arrive in 2002 will be able to see more progress than we saw. They will work with a full critical incident team using the Mitchell Model of Debriefing (see Figure 1).

We noted the change in emotional expressiveness from one day to the other. We listened as workers spoke of the broken sleep so evident in their faces. We heard of physical problems including nausea, profuse sweating or chills, tremors, or an increased pulse rate. Some confessed to being confused and having difficulty making decisions or remembering orders or procedures. Many suffered from a sense of grief, anger, or fear of the magnitude of the event. Several expressed feelings of numbness and isolation.

The ministry of a chaplain does not predominantly involve long-term counseling. This is the reason most chaplains work well in emergency situations. On Monday between 12:45 p.m. and 3:10 p.m. we listed 187 firefighters, police officers, medical workers, and others who visited with us personally, sometimes one on one, many times four or five on one. But always we had the same purpose to get them to understand how much

FIGURE 1
The Mitchell Model of Debriefing

Critical Incident Stress Management (CISM) is a comprehensive, integrative, multicomponent crisis intervention system. CISM is considered comprehensive because it consists of multiple crisis intervention components, which functionally span the entire temporal spectrum of a crisis. CISM interventions range from the precrisis phase through the acute crisis phase, and into the post-crisis phase. CISM is also considered comprehensive in that it consists of interventions that may be applied to individuals, small functional groups, large groups, families, organizations, and even communities.

A complete CISM would include preventive/educational/informational programs as well as the following:

- On-scene support
- Advice to command
- Demobilization services
- Formal debriefings
- Resource referral services
- Family/loved one support services
- Support to emergency management
- Support to employee assistance programs (EAP)
- Community awareness

The Mitchell model also advances seven core components of critical incident stress management:

1. **Precrisis preparation** occurs during pre-crisis phase planning. It is used in anticipation of a crisis. The goals are to set expectations and improve coping stress management. The typical format is one of group organization and should include decision making staff and personnel.

2. **Demobilization and staff consult** (rescuers) involves a group information briefing for civilians, schools, and businesses. This would occur after the crisis

or at the end of a shift. It is event-driven. The goals are to inform and consult with those affected by the event, allow psychological decompression, and assist in stress management. The format is that of a large group organization.

3. **Defusing** occurs within 12 hours after the crisis. Defusing is usually symptom-driven, with the goals of symptom mitigation and possible closure or triage for those who may need extra help. The format is small group, possibly even one-to-one, interaction.

4. **Critical incident stress debriefing (CISD)** occurs one to seven days after the crisis. It is usually symptom-driven but can be event-driven. The goals are to facilitate psychological closure, mitigate symptoms, or perform triage. The format is small group.

5. **Individual crisis intervention** (one to one) can occur anytime, anywhere. It is symptom-driven, with the goals of symptom mitigation and a return to function, if possible. Referrals are made if needed. The format is individual and was the most often used format for us in New York.

6. **Family CISM or organization consultation** can occur at any time and is either symptom-driven or event-driven. The goals are to foster support, communications, and mitigation of symptoms; attain closure on the event, if possible; and make referrals, if needed. The format is within the organizations or family.

7. **Follow-up and referral** is a final step that can occur any time but most often after the crisis. It is usually symptom-driven. The goals are to assess mental status and access a higher level of care. The format may be either individual or family.

Adapted from Everly and Mitchell, Critical Incident Stress Management (CISM): A New Era and Standard of Care in Crisis Intervention *(Ellicott City, Md.: Chevron Publishing, 1997).*

the families appreciate what they do, how much we appreciate what they do, and how much the nation appreciates what they do.

One young officer leaning on a barricade, telling folks they could not enter this area, said to me, "What good am I serving here away from the main site?" I told him that keeping these folks away from the center of the rescue effort keeps the rescuers' areas clear so they can do their work. This is a tremendous help to the effort. He wanted to do more. Of course, we all want to do more. The key is to do our job and do it well.

As I talked with this young officer about the importance of his job, my purpose became a little clearer. All the men and women with whom we talked desperately needed to know that there is stability in the chaos. We never had to bring up the subject of God or religion. It was raised for us by many of those who were talking and was phrased in their own personal belief systems. Answers were not required but understanding was. The need to express one's own belief was evident as we listened to the hearts of the officers.

Wednesday, September 19, 2001

Each time a transport ambulance arrived at our site we were warned whether the victim wore a uniform. If a uniform was confirmed, then every person in the area formed an honor line. When the transport arrived at its designated space, the ranks closed and snapped to attention. The call of "present arms" brought salutes from every sworn member of the police department or the fire department. Those of us who were auxiliary to this event placed our right hands over our hearts. As the gurney entered the triage station there was the call of "order arms" and we stood down. We all turned to resume our assigned duties. There is something special we were privileged to observe

about the brotherhood of firefighters and police officers.

It's almost like violating a sacred place to write about such things. But the emotions flowing from the soul as we talked to as many of the men and women around there as possible needed to be expressed. As we stood next to a four-foot-by-eight-foot piece of plywood near the trailer trucks in the morgue area, we read these unsigned words:

We are the guardians of the unknown. We see the end result of dastardly deeds and attempt to answer questions that will reveal the true identity of these honored dead. There are no questions concerning sacrifice, courage and bravery for they have been proven by heroic actions. We play a small part in an incident that shall become an inspiration to all those who may come after.

Attention was then directed to the posters with pictures of a father or mother, a son or daughter, a husband or wife begging for information, asking, "Have you seen...?" This place seemed to invite such outpourings of emotion. Earlier that emotion had been suppressed. Now it flowed during break times. Candles, long since burned out, lined the walls leading to the office of the New York medical examiner. Each candle reminded us that people, like flames, eventually die. Flowers, some fresh, many faded, also testified to the fleeting nature of life. Officers asked about a second chance, life after death, preparation for death.

And the people came — all observed by the officers, with me beside them. Many officers would stop to read the message on the signs, many offering prayers, some just standing amid their own sweeping emotions. Some would see me and respond to my questions:

"Yes, I knew someone in the towers who died."

"I barely escaped with my life and I wonder why God would spare me?"

"We can't let terror reign, not in New York, not in America!"

"Thank you, Chaplain. I'll be all right.

Just pray for those families who lost loved ones."

Thursday, September 20, 2001

On the scene, the Disaster Mortuary Officials Response Teams (D-MORT) came in to assist with the "routine" tasks of the medical examiner because death did not take a holiday after Tuesday's tragedy. The state police of New York and New Jersey pulled duty shifts guarding the main entrance to the morgue. Police academy recruits directed traffic at the busy intersection of First Avenue and 30th Street. Visiting departments brought buses full of willing officers ready and able to relieve New York's finest at perimeter checkpoints. All of these groups were glad to see the chaplain rolling down the street pushing a shopping cart full of water and energy bars.

Friday, September 21, 2001

This was the last day of my first tour (I served a second tour in New York City from December 8 through 18). Protocol planned to conduct exit interviews with all the chaplains and CISM team members. The last thing we needed was to send a lot of traumatized people back to their departments. A debriefing was scheduled for me when I returned to Texas with team members not directly affected by the incident. Debriefing the debriefer is paramount in the process. My experience after the bombing in Oklahoma City helps explain why.

Coming home from my 10 days in Oklahoma City following the bombing of the Murrah building, things went well for about three weeks. People were talking to me and asking me about what I saw and did. I was never debriefed. Sometime in June my wife came into my study and urged me to go talk to a mental health expert. That was the first time I had any indication that I had changed. It was clear to her that I was more aloof, generally disinterested in everything. I had dropped out of my church choir and become more irritable. I called some of my chaplain friends who had some CISD skills (remember this was early in 1995) and we had a four-hour session.

That was the first time I really cried. I felt safe enough with them to express thoughts of hatred and anger as well as fear and doubt that had never been part of me before. I did not talk about these things with my wife because I would not allow her to know I was weak (this was a bad decision — she knew it already, and I had just denied it). I would not go to the pastor. I wondered how anyone who had not seen what I had could ever understand what it was like. It took all my courage to approach peers who had seen death firsthand before I started to feel normal again. Stress-related problems are real and curable if trained, concerned individuals approach them in a professional manner. Thankfully, I had some of those people around me.

Thus, I applaud the decision to have exit interviews and encourage each chaplain and team member to have his or her own session when they return home.

We checked in to the command post and were told that we had to be out of town by sundown. We started driving home Friday night. No one can visit Ground Zero and remain the same. My prayer is that I will be stronger, more compassionate, and better able to assist those closest and dearest to me. I pray that I will be better able to understand the unity, hurts, fears, and discouragements of these wonderful "protectors of the gates." I hope I can help them normalize their feelings and frustrations to become better officers of the law.

The emotions and feelings discussed in this chapter are not reserved for major catastrophes. By learning from these major events we are better able to care for our own officers using the same principles of stress management employed in New York City. My intent by this chapter is to provide law enforcement executives with a glimpse of the effectiveness of a chaplaincy and a CISM or peer support team.

If you do not have a program like one of these in place, consider developing one.

The ICPC, ICISF, or numerous other organizations would be delighted to give direction in establishing an effective program for your officers. For more information on these two organizations you may consult the following Web sites: http://www.icpc4cops.org or http://www.icist.org, or you may contact the author at highview@attbi.com.

CHAPTER 45

TELEDOCTOR: A NEW CONCEPT IN EMERGENCY PREPAREDNESS AND RESPONSE

Nancy Ferris

The location: Any U.S. city. The scene: An arena or convention center that has been pressed into service as a hospital for treating hundreds of victims of a virulent, SARS-like disease.

No one knows the exact nature of the epidemic nor how best to treat the stricken. They and the medical professionals who are caring for them are quarantined inside the temporary hospital to prevent the spread of the illness. Blood and tissue samples have been collected in special containers and flown to the Centers for Disease Control and Prevention for analysis, but otherwise the facility is sealed off from the rest of America.

More victims keep arriving. Some of the victims are dying. There aren't enough doctors, nurses and other trained professionals to treat everyone. The nation's premier specialists in infectious diseases are hundreds of miles away in cities like Atlanta and Washington.

In such a crisis, telemedicine could come to the rescue. With telemedicine, the doctor and the patient need not be in the same room, or even the same region. They are linked by audio, video, e-mail and computer networks that obviate some of the need for physical contact in medical treatment.

Several years ago, telemedicine seemed exotic. But in an era when teenagers stroll through the mall with their camera phones, the technology no longer is remarkable. Sophisticated monitoring devices are commonplace in hospital rooms, and linking them to the Internet is not a major challenge.

In an epidemic, videos, X-rays, data on blood pressure and heart rates, lab test results, and other vital information could stream from a temporary hospital to labs and doctors' offices anywhere in the world. Specialists could provide medical advice over two-way TV hookups, and people without much medical training could be performing medical procedures with a virtual doctor at their side, via camera phone.

Slow to Take Off

Although these technologies are almost familiar, telemedicine still isn't, four decades

Originally published as "Is There a Teledoctor in the House?" *Homeland Protection Professional*, Vol. 3, No. 5, June 2004. Published by A. J. Parrino & Associates, Western Springs, Illinois. Reprinted with permission of the publisher.

after a Boston physician conceived of it while stuck in a traffic jam en route to the hospital where his patients awaited him. It has been called a technology in search of a user.

"Change is very slow in health care," says Col. Ronald K. Poropatich, M.D., who heads the telemedicine program at Walter Reed Army Hospital in Washington and also is senior clinical adviser to the Army's respected Telemedicine & Advanced Technology Research Center <www.tatrc.org>.

The fact that telemedicine isn't widely used is a problem for emergency medicine, because the experts say it's too difficult to become accustomed to using new systems once an emergency is under way. Even though the systems are not hard to use, learning to incorporate them into medical treatment simply won't happen during a crisis.

Actually, certain kinds of telemedicine have, in fact, taken off. Teleradiology is the most common use, according to Jay Sanders, M.D., president and chief executive officer of the Global Telemedicine Group, McLean, Va., and a former president of the American Telemedicine Association <www.american telemed.org>. Thousands of X-ray images traverse the Internet on any given day.

For the radiologists at Tripler Army Hospital in Honolulu, 20% of their workload consists of X-rays arriving over the Net from Iraq, Kosovo, Germany, the mainland United States and elsewhere, Poropatich says. Treatment of skin diseases, using photos and specimens analyzed in a lab, is another area where telemedicine is used with some frequency.

In some cases, small rural hospitals that lack specialists in areas such as dermatology or cancer in children have established sophisticated communications links with distant specialists and with larger hospitals. The most widespread use of telemedicine is in prisons. Rather than transport dangerous prisoners to an insecure hospital or clinic, corrections departments often use telemedicine hookups to get expert medical advice at a distance.

The military services also use telemedicine to supplement the doctors and medics in their field hospitals, who don't always have the specialized knowledge to care for certain kinds of wounds and diseases. Soldiers from Afghanistan, for example, are taken to Germany for treatment, but before they're transferred, an Army doctor in Germany may be giving advice via a teleconferencing system on how to stabilize and treat them.

You've Got Mail

It's also quite common for physicians to e-mail one another for advice, perhaps attaching a medical record, an image of something seen in a microscope or a set of test results. "There's a lot of ad hoc consultation going on," Poropatich says.

Except for military telemedicine, these uses have one thing in common: Delayed responses are generally acceptable. Only in rare cases does an X-ray need to be read right away. These arrangements wouldn't work in a disaster or other emergency, when time is of the essence. In addition, the most widely used systems today aren't set up for large-scale service and would be of only limited use in a mass-casualty situation.

Nonetheless, telemedicine advocates and some others who've thought about scenarios like the one laid out at the beginning of this chapter consider telemedicine a promising approach for mounting a response to a medical crisis with mass casualties. Most hospitals today operate nearly at capacity and do not have many empty beds available for an emergency.

The emergency need not be a disease. In a situation such as the bombing of the federal building in Oklahoma City in 1995 or the attacks on the World Trade Center in 2001, hospitals will quickly be overwhelmed.

Telemedicine is one way to achieve the "surge capacity" needed to treat large numbers of sick or injured people who arrive with little warning, extending the capacity of the existing medical resources. Doctors anywhere in the world can be plugged into a network of support for those on the scene. Camera phones, teleconferencing systems and even ordinary telephones can deliver distant medical expertise for those in need of emergency care.

"Because telehealth has not been a major player at the national level, its value to homeland security and healthcare in general has been largely overlooked," says a February 2004 report from the federal Technology Administration, an arm of the U.S. Department of Commerce. The report, "Innovation, Demand and Investment in Telehealth," also says that federal agencies have in the past excluded many healthcare providers from the category of first responder, limiting the providers' role in preparations for emergencies. <www.technology.gov/reports/TechPolicy/Telehealth/2004Report.pdf>

An Interstate for Telemed

Telemedicine advocates such as Sanders have been trying to change that situation. Since 2001, he has been prodding federal and state organizations, including the Federal Communications Commission and the National Governors Association, to link existing telemedicine systems into a single national network that could be an important resource in the event of a major disaster or terrorist attack.

As this issue was going to press, a four-state exercise using telemedicine to respond to a simulated smallpox outbreak was getting under way in Missouri, Virginia, Kentucky and Florida. Sanders hopes it will become a model for the rest of the nation, demonstrating the value of using technology in such cases.

He likens the proposed telemedicine network to the national interstate highway system, built in the mid–20th century to support U.S. defense. "The fundamental reality is that we have limited expertise to deal with these chem-bio situations," Sanders says. "Who has seen smallpox? Who really has taken care of anthrax?"

Because the experts are in only a few centers such as the National Institutes of Health and the Army's Fort Detrick in Maryland, the doctors won't be on the scene of an outbreak right away. "What better way to do it than to do it electronically?" Sanders asks.

In ordinary times, the national telemedicine network would be available so that "a rural hospital in Kentucky can be seen by an expert at NIH or in the University of Miami," he adds.

That makes sense because, as many emergency response experts agree, technology that goes unused can be difficult to put to use in an emergency. Frequent use of a system means that it's up and running and the users are comfortable with it when an emergency occurs.

"Everybody always asks me, what's the toughest part of telemedicine?" Sanders says. "I tell them that it has nothing to do with the technology. It's totally to do with the two people at both ends of the technology, and it's the human factors aspect."

Inadequate Pipelines

However, despite the ready availability of the technology, one element of serious telemedicine remains rare in rural America: high-speed communications capability. While anyone in a major metropolitan area can get high-speed, or broadband, Internet access, that technology has not yet been installed in some sparsely populated regions. Slow communications make telemedicine difficult, if not impossible.

Even in well-wired metropolitan areas, the communications infrastructure will become overloaded in a major emergency. The loss of cellular and conventional telephone service in the area around the World Trade Center on Sept. 11 vividly demonstrated the lack of robustness of the communications systems on which telemedicine and other forms of emergency response depend. Clearly, it would not be advisable to count on telemedicine as a primary element of emergency medical response without an alternative or more robust communications channel.

Responding to this need, the Army has developed a portable telemedicine equipment package that includes a satellite communications terminal. Army teams, known as Special Medical Augmentation Response Teams, Medical Command, Control, Communications and Telemedicine (SMART-AC3T), can arrive at emergency and disaster scenes on short notice and set up telemedicine links.

The equipment kits are deployed in strategic locations around the United States, Poropatich says, and also have been used in overseas missions. The technology hasn't changed much since 1997, indicating that it's tested and reliable. Poropatich puts the cost of each kit at $35,000.

An April 2004 report, "Project Responder: National Technology Plan for Emergency Response to Catastrophic Terrorism," from the Memorial Institute for the Prevention of Terrorism and the Department of Homeland Security calls for creation of a testbed to pursue telemedicine responses to disasters and emergencies. <www.mipt.org/pdf/Project-Responder-National-Technology-Plan.pdf>. It says the testbed could evolve into an intelligent system that would advise caregivers and "will likely enable non-physician practitioner(s) to screen patients."

But so far, there has been no sustained effort to develop such a system.

"The amount of funding that it's getting is not very high," says Dr. Steven Kornguth, an expert in chem/bio countermeasures and an author of the MIPT-DHS report. Kornguth is a visiting professor at the University of Texas at Austin.

Local Success

Instead, there are modest local efforts such as the one the University of Vermont has undertaken with Fletcher Allen Health Care in Burlington. The teletrauma program there gives four rural hospitals the ability to call on specialists at the university hospital for help in caring for emergency-room patients. A videoconferencing system lets a surgeon in Burlington see and hear what's happening in the rural ER and provide advice in real time.

By urban standards, the system is not heavily used, having been employed in 50 cases over the last three to four years, according to Dr. Michael Ricci, who heads the program.

But it has saved lives. In one case, a nurse was unable to insert a breathing tube into a patient with head injuries. A surgeon needed to make a hole in the patient's windpipe to allow him to breathe, but the surgeon was reluctant because he hadn't performed the procedure in over 20 years. With the assistance of the distant trauma surgeon, the ER surgeon did the procedure and the patient survived with minimal permanent damage.

As on the battlefield, such systems can save lives by ensuring that the patient gets the right treatment on the spot, before he or she is transferred to a hospital. The Vermont program is now equipping an ambulance with interactive video.

Still, telemedicine isn't yet a priority for most hospitals. After disaster drills and one potentially real emergency, Sept. 11, 2001, the regional Memorial Medical Center in Springfield, Ill., found that it needs to beef up its communications capabilities, says Dr. Charles Callahan, who's leading its homeland security preparations. Phones were overloaded, and the in-house paging system couldn't be heard in the din of an emergency.

The hospital is buying portable radios for key staff members and using an Internet-based notification system. Although these tools could help in treating disaster victims, the hospital is unlikely to invest heavily in telemedicine as part of its emergency preparations, Callahan says. Instead, it's buying portable toilets and decontamination units.

"Everything we're doing applies to the disasters that are more likely to happen here," he explains.

Few would disagree. Until telemedicine plays a larger role in day-to-day medicine, it won't be ready to solve the tough medical treatment issues posed by large-scale disasters and terrorist attacks.

CHAPTER 46

TERRORISM FACT SHEET BY THE FEDERAL EMERGENCY MANAGEMENT AGENCY

Joe M. Allbaugh

Emergency Information

Before the September 11, 2001 attacks in New York and the Pentagon, most terrorist incidents in the United States have been bombing attacks, involving detonated and undetonated explosive devices, tear gas and pipe and fire bombs.

The effects of terrorism can vary significantly from loss of life and injuries to property damage and disruptions in services such as electricity, water supply, public transportation and communications.

One way governments attempt to reduce our vulnerability to terrorist incidents is by increasing security at airports and other public facilities. The U.S. government also works with other countries to limit the sources of support for terrorism.

What Is Terrorism?

Terrorism is the use of force or violence against persons or property in violation of the criminal laws of the United States for purposes of intimidation, coercion or ran-

som. Terrorists often use threats to create fear among the public, to try to convince citizens that their government is powerless to prevent terrorism, and to get immediate publicity for their causes.

The Federal Bureau of Investigation (FBI) categorizes terrorism in the United States as one of two types — domestic terrorism or international terrorism.

Domestic terrorism involves groups or individuals whose terrorist activities are directed at elements of our government or population without foreign direction.

International terrorism involves groups or individuals whose terrorist activities are foreign-based and/or directed by countries or groups outside the United States or whose activities transcend national boundaries.

Biological and Chemical Weapons

Biological agents are infectious microbes or toxins used to produce illness or death in people, animals or plants. Biological agents can be dispersed as aerosols or air-

Originally published as "Backgrounder: Terrorism" and "Fact Sheet: Terrorism," *Informing the Public About Hazards*, Federal Emergency Management Agency, Washington, D.C., October 2004.

borne particles. Terrorists may use biological agents to contaminate food or water because they are extremely difficult to detect. Chemical agents kill or incapacitate people, destroy livestock or ravage crops. Some chemical agents are odorless and tasteless and are difficult to detect. They can have an immediate effect (a few seconds to a few minutes) or a delayed effect (several hours to several days).

Biological and chemical weapons have been used primarily to terrorize an unprotected civilian population and not as a weapon of war. This is because of fear of retaliation and the likelihood that the agent would contaminate the battlefield for a long period of time. The Persian Gulf War in 1991 and other confrontations in the Middle East were causes for concern in the United States regarding the possibility of chemical or biological warfare. While no incidents occurred, there remains a concern that such weapons could be involved in an accident or be used by terrorists.

More information on Bioterrorism preparedness and response is available online from the Department of Health and Human Services Center for Disease Control.

Facts About Terrorism (Prior to September 11, 2001)

- On February 29, 1993, a bombing in the parking garage of the World Trade Center in New York City resulted in the deaths of five people and thousands of injuries. The bomb left a crater 200 by 100 feet wide and five stories deep. The World Trade Center was the second largest building in the world and housed 100,000 workers and visitors each day.
- The Department of Defense estimates that as many as 26 nations may possess chemical agents and/or weapons and an additional 12 may be seeking to develop them.
- The Central Intelligence Agency reports

that at least ten countries are believed to possess or be conducting research on biological agents for weaponization.

Terrorism in the United States

- In the United States, most terrorist incidents have involved small extremist groups who use terrorism to achieve a designated objective. Local, State and Federal law enforcement officials monitor suspected terrorist groups and try to prevent or protect against a suspected attack. Additionally, the U.S. government works with other countries to limit the sources of support for terrorism.
- A terrorist attack can take several forms, depending on the technological means available to the terrorist, the nature of the political issue motivating the attack, and the points of weakness of the terrorist's target. Bombings have been the most frequently used terrorist method in the United States. Other possibilities include an attack at transportation facilities, an attack against utilities or other public services or an incident involving chemical or biological agents.
- Terrorist incidents in this country prior to the September 11, 2001 attack have included bombings of the World Trade Center in New York City, the United States Capitol Building in Washington, D.C. and Mobil Oil corporate headquarters in New York City.

BEFORE A TERRORIST ATTACK

Before an act of terrorism takes place, citizens should be fully informed about the nature of terrorism, the types of weapons used, as well as how to respond during a crisis situation, regardless of its origin. Citizens should also know how to handle bomb threats.

Learn about the nature of terrorism.

• Terrorists look for visible targets where they can avoid detection before or after an attack such as international airports, large cities, major international events, resorts, and high-profile landmarks.

Learn about the different types of terrorist weapons including explosives, kidnapings, hijackings, arson, and shootings.

Prepare to deal with a terrorist incident by adapting many of the same techniques used to prepare for other crises.

• Be alert and aware of the surrounding area. The very nature of terrorism suggests that there may be little or no warning.

• Take precautions when traveling. Be aware of conspicuous or unusual behavior. Do not accept packages from strangers. Do not leave luggage unattended.

• Learn where emergency exits are located. Think ahead about how to evacuate a building, subway or congested public area in a hurry. Learn where staircases are located.

• Notice your immediate surroundings. Be aware of heavy or breakable objects that could move, fall or break in an explosion.

Preparing for a Building Explosion. The use of explosives by terrorists can result in collapsed buildings and fires. People who live or work in a multi-level building can do the following:

• Review emergency evacuation procedures. Know where fire exits are located.

• Keep fire extinguishers in working order. Know where they are located, and how to use them. Learn first aid. Contact the local chapter of the American Red Cross for additional information.

• Keep the following items in a designated place on each floor of the building.

• Portable, battery-operated radio and extra batteries

• Several flashlights and extra batteries

• First aid kit and manual

• Several hard hats

• Fluorescent tape to rope off dangerous areas

Bomb Threats. If you receive a bomb threat, get as much information from the caller as possible. Keep the caller on the line and record everything that is said. Notify the police and the building management.

After you've been notified of a bomb threat, do not touch any suspicious packages. Clear the area around the suspicious package and notify the police immediately. In evacuating a building, avoid standing in front of windows or other potentially hazardous areas. Do not restrict sidewalk or streets to be used by emergency officials.

During a Terrorist Attack

During an act of terrorism, citizens should know the steps they should take to protect themselves. This includes information about both building explosions as well as the possible dangers caused by fire and smoke.

In a building explosion, get out of the building as quickly and calmly as possible.

If items are falling off of bookshelves or from the ceiling, get under a sturdy table or desk. If there is a fire:

• Stay low to the floor and exit the building as quickly as possible.

• Cover nose and mouth with a wet cloth.

• When approaching a closed door, use the palm of your hand and forearm to feel the lower, middle and upper parts of the door. If it is not hot, brace yourself against the door and open it slowly. If it is hot to the touch, do not open the door — seek an alternate escape route.

• Heavy smoke and poisonous gases collect first along the ceiling. Stay below the smoke at all times.

After a Terrorist Attack

After an act of terrorism takes place, citizens should be fully informed about how to free themselves if they are trapped in debris, as well as how to assist the victims of an incident. Citizens should know how to respond to a possible terrorist attack using both chemical and biological agents.

If you are trapped in debris:

- Use a flashlight.
- Stay in your area so that you don't kick up dust. Cover your mouth with a handkerchief or clothing.
- Tap on a pipe or wall so that rescuers can hear where you are. Use a whistle if one is available. Shout only as a last resort — shouting can cause a person to inhale dangerous amounts of dust.

Assisting victims:

- Untrained persons should not attempt to rescue people who are inside a collapsed building. Wait for emergency personnel to arrive.

Chemical Agents. Chemical agents are poisonous gases, liquids or solids that have toxic effects on people, animals or plants. Most chemical agents cause serious injuries or death.

Severity of injuries depends on the type and amount of the chemical agent used, and the duration of exposure.

Were a chemical agent attack to occur, authorities would instruct citizens to either seek shelter where they are and seal the premises or evacuate immediately. Exposure to chemical agents can be fatal. Leaving the shelter to rescue or assist victims can be a deadly decision. There is no assistance that the untrained can offer that would likely be of any value to the victims of chemical agents.

Biological Agents. Biological agents are organisms or toxins that have illness-producing effects on people, livestock and crops.

Because biological agents cannot necessarily be detected and may take time to grow and cause a disease, it is almost impossible to know that a biological attack has occurred. If government officials become aware of a biological attack through an informant or warning by terrorists, they would most likely instruct citizens to either seek shelter where they are and seal the premises or evacuate immediately.

A person affected by a biological agent requires the immediate attention of professional medical personnel. Some agents are contagious, and victims may need to be quarantined. Also, some medical facilities may not receive victims for fear of contaminating the hospital population.

More information on Bioterrorism preparedness and response is available online from the Department of Health and Human Services Center for Disease Control.

Note

This information was obtained from the FEMA website (http://www.fema.gov), and was last updated on October 22, 2004.

CHAPTER 47

THREAT CONDITION ORANGE: COMMON SENSE MEASURES TO SAFEGUARD YOUR COMMUNITY

Roger L. Kemp

In order to improve coordination and communication among all levels of government and the public in the fight against terrorism, the President signed Homeland Security Presidential Directive 3 on March 12, 2002, creating the *Homeland Security Advisory System* (HSAS). This advisory system serves as a foundation for a common sense approach for a simple communications structure for the dissemination of information regarding the risk of possible terrorist attacks to all levels of government, as well as our nation's citizens.

There are many Federal alert systems in our country, and each is tailored and unique to different sectors of our society: transportation, defense, agriculture, and weather, for example. These alert systems fill vital and specific requirements for a variety of situations in both the government and commercial sectors.

The HSAS provides a national framework for these systems, allowing government officials and citizens to communicate the na-

ture and degree of terrorist threats. This advisory system characterizes appropriate levels of vigilance, preparedness, and readiness, in a series of graduated Threat Conditions.

The Protective Measures that correspond to each Threat Condition will help the local government and its citizens decide upon what actions they should take to help counter and respond to possible terrorist activity. Based on the threat level, Federal agencies will implement appropriate Protective Measures. States and municipalities are encouraged to adopt compatible local response systems.

State and local officials will be informed in advance of national threat advisories whenever possible. The Department of Homeland Security (DHS) will convey relevant information to Federal, State, and local public officials, as well as to the private sector. Heightened Threat Levels can be declared for the entire nation, or for a specific geographic area, functional, or industrial sector. Changes in assigned Threat Conditions will be made whenever necessary by the DHS.

These Threat Conditions characterize the risk of a possible terrorist attack based on the best information available. Protective Measures are the steps that should be taken by government and the private sector to reduce their respective vulnerabilities. The HSAS contains five Threat Conditions with associated suggested Protective Measures. They are:

- Green: Low Condition
- Blue: Guarded Condition
- Yellow: Elevated Condition
- Orange: High Condition
- Red: Severe Condition

Since September 11, 2001, our nation has been at Threat Condition Orange, High Condition, only a few times. Recent HSAS warnings have been regional and/or functional in their scope. When the nation goes to Threat Condition Orange, and this threat level is not limited to specific geographic areas, public officials in cities should take steps so citizens know that their municipal officials are making an effort to protect them.

To achieve this goal, there are several common sense measures that local public officials should take so their citizens and business persons know they are being properly protected against a possible terrorist attack, regardless of its actual likelihood. These public officials include elected officials (mayors and city council members), city managers, police chiefs, fire chiefs, public works directors, and other emergency personnel. The suggested measures they should take include the following:

- Police and Fire personnel should maintain a heightened sense of awareness while responding to, and working at, incident scenes.
- Appropriate City officials (city manager, police chief, fire chief, and public works director) should review local emergency response plans and be prepared to activate their Emergency Operations Center.

- City Managers (as well as police chiefs, fire chiefs, and public works directors) should communicate and coordinate with their respective counterparts at other levels of government in case a coordinated response is needed.
- Police Chiefs should closely monitor all available security and intelligence data from Federal, State, and other local law enforcement agencies.
- Police personnel should inspect building and parking areas for suspicious packages.
- City Managers should ensure that employees should be especially watchful for suspicious or unattended packages and articles received through public and private mail delivery systems.
- City Managers should work closely with their Police Chiefs to consider controlled access to all municipal buildings, other significant facilities, and critical components of the public infrastructure.
- City Managers and Police Chiefs should ensure that appropriate security measures are in place and are functioning properly.
- Police Chiefs should make sure that Police Officers closely monitor all municipal reservoirs and watershed areas, wastewater treatment plants, and other sensitive public facilities.
- Local municipal officials should work closely with their County officials in an attempt to report and detect all transmittable diseases.
- The City Manager should place all emergency management and specialized response teams on call-back alert status. This is also applicable to Police and Fire Chiefs.
- The Police Chief should limit access points at critical facilities to essential personnel only. Entry control procedures should be strictly enforced.
- The Police Chief should ensure the enforcement of the restriction for the parking of vehicles away from sensitive public buildings.
- The Police Chief should increase defensive

measures around key structures and for major public events.

- Both the Police and Fire Chiefs should make sure that critical response vehicles are stored in a secure area or in an indoor parking facility, if one is available.

Municipal officials should also issue recommended precautions for citizens and business persons. These measures should be decided upon in advance of a heightened state of alert. The suggested guidelines for these two groups are highlighted below:

Citizens should be encouraged to:

- Resume normal activities but expect some delays, baggage searches, and restrictions as a result of heightened security at public buildings and other facilities.
- Continue to monitor world events and local circumstances, as well as local government threat advisory warnings.
- Report all suspicious activities at or near critical public facilities to local law enforcement agencies by calling 9-1-1.
- Avoid leaving unattended packages or briefcases in public areas.
- Inventory and organize emergency supply kits and discuss emergency plans with family members. Reevaluate the family meeting location based on the national threat level.
- Consider taking reasonable personal security precautions. Be alert to your surroundings, avoid placing yourself in a vulnerable situation, and closely monitor the activities of your children.
- Maintain close contact with your family and neighbors to ensure their safety and emotional well-being.

Business persons should be encouraged to:

- Announce Threat Condition "High" to all employees, and explain any special actions you require of them as their employer.
- Place company emergency response teams on notice, as appropriate.
- Activate the company's operations center, if suitable to the occasion.

- Monitor world and local events, passing on the latest information to your employees.
- Ensure that appropriate security measures are in place and functioning properly.
- Instruct employees to immediately report suspicious activities, packages, and people to their supervisors.
- Search all personal bags and parcels, and require employees to pass through a metal detector, if one is available.
- Restrict vehicular access and parking close to company-owned buildings.
- Inspect intrusion detection systems, lighting, security fencing, and locking systems, to make sure that they are all working properly.
- Inspect all deliveries and consider accepting shipments only at off-site locations.
- Remind employees of heightened security policies and proper building evacuation procedures.

The time to prepare a response plan, such as the one described above, is before our nation goes on a heightened state of alert. A community's guidelines should be put in written form, and distributed to the mayor and city council, all department managers, emergency management personnel, citizens, as well as the local Chamber of Commerce since procedures for the private sector are included. This information should also be posted on a city's website, published in local newspapers, and placed as a public service message on a city's public-access cable television channel. A City newsletter would also be a good vehicle to promote these community safeguards. These latter vehicles are excellent ways to inform citizens about your state of "readiness."

It is also a good idea to inform citizens and business persons of homeland security-related websites. These would typically include, at the Federal level, the Department of Homeland Security (*http://www.dhs.gov*) and the Federal Emergency Management Agency (*http://www.fema.gov*). At the State level, the State Office of Emergency Services (*http://*

www.oes.ca.gov) and the Department of Health Services (*http://www.dhs.ca.gov*) should be listed. It is also good idea to list the American Red Cross (*http://www.redcross.org*), as well as the city's website. Homeland security updates can easily be provided to everyone on a city's website.

The goal is to spread the word to citizens about your city's state of preparation for the next heightened state of national alert.

Citizens expect their public officials to be looking out for their safety and health under such circumstances. Simple guidelines for communities, citizens, and business persons, such as those described above, represent a common-sense approach to being prepared to safeguard and protect your community during a disaster, whether natural or man-made. Take steps now to make sure your city is prepared!

CHAPTER 48

UNDERSTANDING TERRORISTS AND TERRORISM

Lee Anne Jacobs

In societies throughout the world, people have experienced political frustration, racial and ethnic disputes, even religious persecution, but have not responded with terrorism. Why, in some cases, do these experiences lead to terrorist activity? Why do terrorist acts sometimes occur seemingly without provocation? Is there a fundamental factor that causes some to resort to terrorism while others do not? Perhaps more importantly, can these causal factors, if they do exist, be identified and used to predict and prepare for terrorist activity?

Historians, psychologists and political experts have debated these questions for decades. While it is beyond the scope of this chapter to provide conclusive answers, a framework can be developed to begin teasing apart the motivations behind terrorist activity.

Noted terrorism expert Brian Jenkins, author of *The Terrorist Mindset and Terrorist Decision-making: Two Areas of Ignorance*, posed two questions that provide a useful starting point: How does one become a terrorist, and how do terrorists decide what course of action to take?

Terrorism Scenarios

Terrorist acts may be categorized as defensive or offensive. A common suggested cause of defensive aggression, or aggression in response to a perceived threat, is discontent with inequity, real or perceived. The inequitable distribution of wealth combined with increasingly global communication allows some societies (or segments within societies) to see themselves as deprived of wealth as compared to others. Whether perceived or actual, this inequity can produce aggressive reactions.

Frustration also is suggested as a root cause of defensive aggression. Research does not consistently support frustration itself as a cause of aggression; however, a person's perception of a frustrating experience can lead to an aggressive response. Erich Fromm, noted authority on human aggression, suggests in *The Anatomy of Human Destructiveness* that threats to a person's freedom also may be a strong motivating factor in defensive aggression.

Defensive aggression may be predictable, since it is often possible to see when a person or group of people would be experiencing discontent or frustration, or have their

---

Originally published as "What Makes a Terrorist," *State Government News*, October 2001. Published by The Council of State Governments, Lexington, KY. Reprinted with permission of the publisher.

freedom threatened. However, even these scenarios do not necessarily predict terrorism. People often experience frustration, discontent, or lack of freedom without resorting to terrorism. What drives people into offensive aggression, which is not so much a response to a threat as an effort to promote or advance a particular ideology?

Several conditions may turn an aggressive response into an act of terrorism. A person or group may become impatient with moderate or traditional methods of change, and therefore seek a more drastic course of action. They may want to attract attention to their cause through the media to incite fear in the general population, and few acts attract the media more strongly than terrorism. In fact, terrorism is sometimes defined as an act that produces fear out of proportion with the actual violence of the act. Also, the group may be compensating for low numbers of supporters or lack of power. Terrorism is often called "the weapon of the weak."

Interestingly, in some cases potential terrorists have chosen not to take an extremely violent course of action. Understanding these scenarios may help us understand what other modes of action they might take. The terrorists simply may not want to endanger themselves, or they may not want to offend or estrange potential followers with extremely violent acts. They may want to maintain some bargaining power, or they may want to avoid detection.

Psychological Predictors

There is no clear evidence that terrorism is necessarily the product of psychopathology, but the degree to which a person demonstrates certain personality traits may indicate a predisposition for terrorist behavior.

In his discussion of human aggression and destructiveness, Fromm differentiates between benign and malignant forms of aggression. Benign aggression is generally defined as defensive, and is accepted as a normal part of human nature. Malignant aggression, on the other hand, is generally offensive and is not motivated by the need to protect oneself.

Retaliation or vengeful aggression is one form of malignant aggression, in that it occurs after the damage is done, and so serves no defensive purpose. It does not protect against a threat, but rather responds to an offense already committed. However, even vengeance is considered a common and normal reaction, especially when defined in terms of restoring justice.

However, more extreme forms of malignant aggression extend into psychopathology, and may be of some predictive value. People driven by a need for complete control over others, and more extremely by a desire to destroy others, exhibit these personality traits. Joseph Stalin and Adolf Hitler are prime examples of people who exhibited extreme forms of malignant aggression. It is debatable how close the link is between these personality traits and the ability to predict terrorist activity, but with some particularly threatening people, understanding the degree to which they exhibit these traits may offer some insight into the types of actions they are likely to take.

Methods of Terrorism

By understanding the nature of various methods, we may be able to understand and even predict what method a particular group may choose, and therefore prepare responses against these potential threats.

Hostage-taking. Hostage-taking is generally considered a disruptive rather than a destructive form of terrorism in that the purpose of the act is not violence, but some other outcome. Why would a terrorist not take the most violent course of action immediately? Holding hostages without initially harming them allows the terrorist some bargaining power. The hostages are not the target of the act, but are a means to an end, as opposed to kidnap-assassination scenarios in which the hostages are the intended victims and harm may come to them much more quickly. Hostage situations typically indicate that the terrorist is motivated to achieve a specific goal, rather than to simply cause destruction.

Single-issue terrorism. Similar to hostage situations, single-issue terrorists are not necessarily trying to cause destruction, but instead to achieve a very specific goal. Some common examples are abortion activists, animal-rights supporters and environmental terrorists. Their goals may be somewhat benign, such as affecting legislation or causing companies to change their activities.

Actions toward these goals may include creating negative publicity, such as reporting cruel treatment of animals in testing facilities, or acts may be more drastic, such as contaminating meat to stop consumers from purchasing it, or committing vandalism to slow or stop an industry by costing it valuable time and money. Goals may be more desperate, such as the intention of completely stopping an activity. Acts to achieve these goals are often more violent and very specifically targeted. Examples include tree-spiking, which is potentially fatal to foresters and sawmill workers, and abortion-clinic bombings and assassinations.

Chemical and biological. Chemical and Biological (CB) weapons are quite different from the methods of terrorism discussed above, and use of them indicates very different motivations. The effects of CB weapons are very difficult to control and therefore are indiscriminate, which indicates a much less discrete political agenda of the user. In most cases, especially with the use of biological agents, the goal is to maximize casualties.

CB weapons can pose risks to the user, both in the manufacture of the weapon itself and in the chance that the effect could spread back into the user's population. However, CB weapons offer some benefits that other methods do not. Unlike bombings or other immediate displays of force, CB weapons act silently and relatively slowly. A society may be completely unaware that an attack has taken place until it is too late to respond. Also unlike other forms of attack, CB effects can continue to spread through a population long after the initial attack, especially if first-responders and caregivers are not initially aware of the cause of the illness and do not know to take precautions.

Cyberterrorism. Potentially the most insidious form, cyberterrorism is not only a method in itself, but a mechanism by which to perpetrate other methods of terrorism as well. For example, explosives could be planted throughout a region or even throughout locations of a particular company, then detonated simultaneously, all controlled by a single user. Global-positioning systems can be incorporated into weapons to track location and allow the user to detonate the weapon when it reaches the target. Computer systems that control the formulation of foods, vitamins or medications can be altered to slowly weaken a population, such as by increasing iron to potentially toxic levels or reducing the concentration of antibiotics. More directly, cyberterrorism could be used to control water, power, and natural-gas supplies and communications systems.

Cyberterrorism offers some unique benefits to the user. It can be executed and controlled from any geographic location, even remotely from the intended target. Multiple targets can be hit simultaneously or in sequence from any location. There is no physical danger to the user and no risk of being caught at the scene of the crime. It is quite easy to go unnoticed using a variety of encryption methods. And it also is easy to recruit innocent perpetrators who are unaware of what they may be helping to accomplish. Due to the transparency of cyberterrorism, as with CB weapons, a society may be completely unaware of the attack.

Conclusion

While there is no reliable method of consistently predicting and defusing terrorist activity, perhaps by understanding the motivations behind certain acts and the nature of the methods used, we can identify patterns and prepare to respond to potential situations.

Knowing the motivations of terrorists can indicate what methods they are likely to use, and seeing acts already committed indicates traits of the perpetrator. Did they have a specific target and narrow agenda, or are they aiming to cause mass destruction? Understanding these links can help us prepare for future events.

Predicting the impact of various forms of attack also can help us prepare. For example, training local and state-level first-responders to identify and take appropriate precautions against CB attacks can prevent the effects from spreading uncontrollably. Protecting vital computer systems against attack, and even preparing alternative systems if one is attacked, can help offset the potentially devastating effects of cyberterrorism.

The dilemma of predicting and responding to terrorist acts is difficult to resolve, but one well worth pursuing. As noted expert of international law and policy Robert Friedlander stated in *Terrorism: Theory and Practice*, "The debate over whether it is really possible to give a civilized response to an uncivilized act has yet to be resolved. The issue is one of global survival and its outcome affects us all."

CHAPTER 49

U.S. ATTORNEY'S OFFICE AND THE ANTI-TERRORISM ADVISORY COUNCIL

Roger L. Kemp

It was only a few short years ago that the terrible terrorist attacks took place at two of the primary symbols of America — the World Trade Center in New York City, and the Pentagon in our nation's capitol in Washington, D.C. Since this time, the author has tracked the best practices in homeland security among the various levels of government and reflects on what he believes is one of the finest examples of intergovernmental relations that has evolved in this field.

Cities and counties are at the forefront of forging best practices in this new field. States are doing their best to circle the wagons within their jurisdictions among regions, counties, cities, as well as special districts. The federal government is also grappling with our nation's security, with the assistance of the newest federal agency, the Department of Homeland Security. Even before the formation of this newest agency, the Attorney General, six days after September 11, 2001, directed the U.S. Attorney's Office (USAO) to take immediate steps to prevent future terrorist attacks against the homeland. Each USAO District in the nation was charged with forming an Anti-Terrorism Advisory Council (ATAC) to coordinate efforts to achieve this goal.

Since this time, the efforts of all units of government to enhance intergovernmental cooperation in this new field have been admirable. Every state has a branch of the USAO and a recently formed ATAC, and each office is pulling together the city, county, regional, state, and federal resources necessary to protect the homeland from possible future terrorist attacks. Periodic meetings are held that include, among others, public safety representatives from various public and nonprofit agencies. They meet to discuss precautions, safeguards, and best practices to protect their respective areas from possible future terrorist attacks.

Representatives from the following public, special district, and nonprofit agencies typically meet to discuss topics of mutual interest relative to homeland security for their respective jurisdictions and public service responsibilities.

- Federal Government
- State Government

- Municipal Government
- Military, both state and federal
- Tribal Nations
- United States Postal Service
- Regional Transit Authorities
- Special Service Districts
- Other intelligence and law enforcement agencies

Representatives from federal agencies may include the Bureau of Alcohol, Tobacco, Firearms, and Explosives; the Federal Air Marshal Service; the Federal Emergency Management Agency; the Immigration and Customs Service; and the Transportation Security Administration. Other federal agencies involved in this process include the FBI, EPA, IRS, Marshal Service, Secret Service, and as well as the Social Security Administration. Branches of the national military service are also included on these advisory councils.

State government agency representatives usually include public health and safety, homeland security, emergency management, the Attorney General's Office, other criminal justice administration agencies, as well as the National Guard. Other members often include representatives from public colleges and universities, as well as state and international airports.

Public safety representatives from other nonprofit agencies include independent water and utility districts, nuclear power plant companies, regional transit authorities, special service districts, as well as healthcare professionals from major private hospitals and universities.

During these meetings held by each State USAO's Anti-Terrorism Advisory Council, representatives from all levels of government, as well as special districts and nonprofit agencies, discuss items of mutual concern related to their respective agency's homeland security practices. These meetings provide an invaluable forum for the open exchange of ideas about mitigation, preparedness, response, and recovery practices as they relate to emergencies, such as those brought about by a possible terrorist attack.

Some of the precautions and safeguards examined during these meetings include, but are certainly not limited to, the following components of the public infrastructure. These facilities should be protected from anti-terrorist activities to safeguard our citizens, as well as to ensure the continuity of ongoing governmental operations and public services.

- Train stations, both local and regional
- Nuclear power plants
- Municipal harbors and ports
- State and municipal airports
- National and state military installations
- Tribal nation properties, such as major gambling casinos
- Major post offices and mail handling centers
- The locations of private military contractors
- Major intra- and interstate transportation centers and corridors
- Special districts and their facilities
- Other government properties with "target rich" environments

Having attended some of these meetings, I'm duly impressed by the efforts of the ATAC to promote and enhance intergovernmental cooperation in this important field. In a democratic society, this valuable exchange of ideas and information has helped protect our nation, and its citizens, during these uncertain times. All of the ATACs throughout the nation should be congratulated for their efforts to promote state-of-the-art homeland security practices within their respective states.

Much of these homeland security efforts have been directed at protecting our nation's critical infrastructure, and to ensure that essential public services are provided during an emergency. To help achieve this goal, City and County Managers, as well as their Health and Public Safety Directors, should work closely to obtain all available grant funds so that staffing levels and equipment are sufficient to limit the loss of life and property during a disaster.

CHAPTER 50

VEHICULAR SAFEGUARDS AND HOMELAND SECURITY

Corrina Stellitano

Cars and trucks are an American icon and the basis of the nation's transportation and commerce, but for security professionals, vehicles can represent a distressing threat. Like the Trojan horse, vehicles can carry danger to the front door — or worse yet, through the walls — directly into a facility.

Vehicle deterrence devices have increased in popularity and in sophistication in the past five years, but available products can vary in capabilities, construction and cost.

Bollards and Barriers

Devices created to keep vehicles outside a designated perimeter range from stationary concrete posts or planters to automated hydraulically-powered metal posts and steel plates that rise up against the invading vehicle.

While stationary vehicle obstructions, such as planters or concrete barricades called Jersey barriers, keep unwanted vehicles from restricted areas, they are not suitable as gates for entrances and exits. To supplement the carefully guarded perimeters of their facilities, security professionals need versatile, mobile access control devices — and they must be powerful enough to stop a speeding vehicle.

Bollards (or vehicle deterrents in the form of heavy-duty posts) are a balance of function and aesthetics. Even the sturdiest types, those able to repel a speeding tractor-trailer — are offered in ornamental or architecturally-consistent sleeves or finishes. Others can be painted.

Experts say bollards are less disruptive to pedestrian traffic, and are easily accepted by the public.

Bollards are available in several varieties:

- **Fixed bollards** are cost-effective ways to protect large areas permanently, and serve the same purpose as concrete planters, for example, protecting the perimeter at airports. Some decorative planters even have a bollard built in to add strength.
- **Removable bollards** are effective for creating an emergency passage. These bollards may include a mechanism to lock them in place when in use, and caps to cover the holes when the bollards are removed. These devices may not fulfill U.S. State Department safety requirements because the bollard base and foundation may not reach far enough below ground. How-

Originally published as "Roadblocks to Disaster," *Government Security*, Vol. 2, No. 5, May 2003. Published by PRIMEDIA Business Magazines & Media Inc., Atlanta, GA. Reprinted with permission of the publisher.

ever, adding diameter will increase stopping capability.

- **Retractable or automatic bollards**, operated by hydraulic or pneumatic power units, can be lowered below ground to allow entry. Special emergency settings allow the posts to return to an upright setting in case of a security threat. These units are available with a self-contained hydraulic power unit, or more commonly, multiple bollards with internal pneumatic or hydraulic workings can be controlled by an external hydraulic power unit.
- **Manual retractable/semi-automatic bollards** are suitable for less-used entrances and exits and are more cost-effective. Manual bollards are counter-balanced, allowing ease of movement up or down, and the devices lock in either position. When semi-automatic bollards are in the upright position, a key may be inserted and turned to unlock, allowing the operator to press the bollard until it locks in the down position. Then when unlocked by key again, a compressed gas cylinder raises the bollard to an upright, locked position. The ascent may also be completed with a manual screw crank or pull system.

Many facility managers choose to pair bollards with high-security gates or barricades.

- **Crash gates** are steel rods or pickets that slide across a roadway on a track. Cantilevered versions avoid the potential difficulties of a track (which must be kept free of ice or large amounts of sand) by sliding the gate through a stanchion which borders the roadside.
- **Wedge barriers** are steel rectangles that raise a formidable edge above the surface of the road. Steel plate barriers also rise from the road to a 45-degree angle. When raised, the barrier's angle, along with the barrier's foundation pad, deflects the vehicle's force.
- **Drop arm barriers** look much like a parking lot drop arm, with crash or cable beams

rising to allow vehicles to enter, but stopping an unauthorized vehicle when in the lowered position.

A similar version of the drop arm employs a one-inch steel cable to lasso any vehicle attempting to drive under a U-shaped gate, thus destroying the front of the vehicle.

- **Portable (or mobile) barriers** are praised for their speed of installation and mobility. With a swift set-up time — from 15 minutes to a few hours — portable barriers offer less strength than barriers set in concrete, but they allow perimeters to be created quickly when security issues require a larger area of safety around a facility. Portable barriers also require no excavation, thus allowing installation on existing roads or even level compacted soil.

Some portable barriers consist of a crash beam or a rising plate barrier, set on both sides with buttresses — boxes filled with a heavy substance, or 55-gallon drums filled with concrete and placed in ornamental crates. In the 55-gallon drum version, the drums can be removed, allowing the barrier to be easily moved and reinstalled. If the boxes are filled with concrete, they may become a one-time-use-only device. Water, sand and gravel may be more easily removable. A portable plate barrier on wheels can be towed into place and installed in 20 minutes.

While some of these portable solutions pass crash tests, positioning must be carefully considered, as they tend to move when hit with a vehicle. However, movement can be somewhat limited with the addition of support buttresses.

What to Consider When Purchasing

For first-time buyers, the array of vehicle access control products can be overwhelming. Security professionals working for government facilities, or businesses which

Perimeter Case Study

SECURITY ON THE HILL

As one of Washington, D.C.'s most historic districts, Capitol Hill — referring to the area encompassing the U.S. Capitol Building, the U.S. Senate Buildings, and the Capitol Police headquarters — has a myriad of sensitive areas requiring protection.

When Clinton, Md.–based Nasatka Barriers first began helping with ongoing security upgrades in the district, the site required a variety of vehicle access control measures, recalls John Scolaro, Nasatka's international sales director.

Security measures on Capitol Hill have not only been inspired by the terrorist events of Sept. 11, 2001, but also by the shooting of two Capitol Hill officers in July 1998.

"They needed a large range of stopping abilities, depending on the location at Capitol Hill," he says. Entire roadways, parking lots, and various entrances and exits needed to be protected.

One solution requiring minimum excavation and a relatively short installation time was the steel plate barrier. "They needed something that wasn't going to affect the environment drastically, so they didn't want a lot of excavation in roadways," Scolaro says. The steel barriers' hot dip galvanized finish was also helpful in protecting against harsh conditions caused by weather and frequent construction.

Because many areas have been under construction during the last few years, changing entrances and exits in need of protection, mobile steel plate barriers were also used. The barriers-on-wheels enabled flexible perimeters, and could be moved and re-deployed in 30 minutes.

One common factor that was of less concern to the security staff at Capitol Hill was aesthetics. "They weren't really looking at the aesthetic features because they wanted people to know they were serious about unwanted vehicles not entering," Scolaro says.

Over the last several years, the extensive site has employed 60 percent of Nasatka's steel plate barrier models. Like most government entities, Capitol Hill's security professionals knew what they needed, Scolaro says.

"Really what they're looking at is which product best fits the application, and they're looking at durability," he says. "These sort of agencies do a lot of research. They know who they're looking for and they have an idea what they're looking for, but they do value our suggestions as to what product best fits their need."

often work with the government, must know the difference between crash-rated products and crash-tested products.

Crash rating describes an engineering analysis. Vehicle deterrence devices that are described as "crash tested" have actually met a vehicle in an independent test lab. While there are many commercial labs in operation, the U.S. State Department and Department of Defense only approve certain labs.

Careful consideration of each site's needs is important, suppliers say. Most will ask several key questions as they help buyers match products to security demands.

- **What type of vehicle are you trying to stop and how fast can that vehicle travel when approaching vulnerable areas of your facility?** A major measurement of a vehicle's hitting power is its kinetic energy — derived from its velocity and its weight. Upon impact, some of the vehicle's energy is converted to heat, sound and permanent deformation of the vehicle. But the barrier must absorb the remainder of this energy.

The amount of kinetic energy presented by a vehicle changes as a square of its velocity. Therefore, an armored car weighing 30 times as much as a Volkswagen and moving at 10 mph would have less hitting power than the Volkswagen moving at 60 mph. Because velocity weighs so heavily into the damaging power of a vehicle, security engineers often design entrances to force a vehicle to slow down before it reaches the barrier.

If a vehicle approaching a facility must make a 90-degree turn, its velocity will be decreased, and the use of a less invasive barrier might be suggested. However, if the vehicle entrance is at the end of a long straightaway, barrier manufacturers may suggest their strongest-rated devices. The types of vehicles typically entering the site are also considered; a business that has tractor-trailers entering and exiting frequently will require different security measures than a site where the only visitors are cars and pedestrians.

• **How often will the entrance/exit be used?** If the barrier will operate only a few cycles per day or week, a manual option would be acceptable. Automatic barriers can open and close more than 100 times a day, but some options are slower than others.

More to Consider

Other environmental factors must also be evaluated before a final selection is made. If excavation is impossible, shallow-mount barriers would be necessary. If the area is prone to colder conditions, strip heaters would be needed to keep equipment above 32 degrees. Warning signage and signal lights are also helpful to alert visitors to the presence of barriers.

Manufacturers say vehicular access control devices work best when operating as part of a larger access control system. To this end, most can be operated by a combination of methods, including radio, remote control, card readers, keyswitch, numeric keypad, or manually on a push-button panel. Most hydraulic units will also have back-up provisions in case of power failure.

Manufacturers also suggest that bollards and barriers be kept in the closed or upright position until an approaching vehicle has been cleared for entry.

Many suggest installing additional warning systems. A velocity sensor, consisting of digital wire loops embedded in the roadway a distance away from the facility entrance or guard booth, will trigger an early warning alarm or raise barriers if a vehicle is approaching at high speeds.

Vehicle-sensing loops placed in the roadway directly in front of and behind the barricade stop the raising of barricades or bollards while an authorized vehicle is in the way. The coupled loop detector suppresses accidental operation, while an emergency mode allows the safety loop to be overridden in a crisis.

An Open Door for Innovation

While many barriers are similar across the industry, manufacturers continue to produce creative variations. One company offers concrete barriers in the form of precast animals; with optional water spray attachments for water park use.

Another manufactures its bollards separate from its casings. End-users can buy and install the casings now, and purchase the bollards with their decorative finishes after construction, and any changes to the architectural appearance, have been completed.

While most barriers and bollards have traditional push-button operating systems, some now include flat-screen monitors with touch-screen buttons. Operators can view graphic representations of the actions being commanded, with colors representing closed or open positions.

For areas where hydraulics and the

Perimeter Case Study

TERROR ON TRIAL

Vehicle anti-terrorism devices become most important, perhaps, when the formidable institution of terrorism itself is being challenged.

When the federal case of the United States vs. Osama bin Laden was slated to begin in New York City's Daniel Patrick Moynahan U.S. Courthouse and the old Foley Square U.S. Courthouse in Feb. 2001, construction crews hastened to install a safe perimeter around the courthouses. Safety was of the highest priority and concern: bin Laden's alleged followers were on trial for the 1998 bombings of the U.S. embassies in Kenya and Tanzania that killed 224 people.

In the two months preceding the trial, barriers and bollards were installed, cordoning off the entire block housing the two courthouses.

Hydraulically-operated barricades, manufactured by Valencia, Calif.–based Delta Scientific Corp., blocked each end of the street.

Designed to stop a 7.5-ton truck moving at 80 mph, the thick steel plates would pop out of the ground within 1.5 seconds during an emergency. The barriers were accompanied by bulletproof guard booths.

A series of Delta bollards also guarded the front of the U.S. courthouse. The bollards were designed to destroy the front suspension, steering linkage, engine crankcase and portions of the drive train of any 15,000-pound non-armored vehicle that collided with them at 62 mph. The bollards were also intended to stop a 15-ton vehicle traveling at 44 mph, raising and lowering into the ground in one second.

Hours before the trials began each day, the bollards and barriers were raised to create a secure area. Cameras and ground surveillance contributed to the overall security precautions.

Perimeter Case Study

CRASH RATINGS

Government agencies, and the companies who contract with them, typically use products certified in approved labs.

As the State Department's crash rating system is the most widely used, manufacturers will often explain the capabilities of their products using the following ratings.

A K4-rated barrier can stop a 15,000-lb. vehicle traveling at 30 mph.

A K8-rated barrier will stop the same vehicle going 40 mph, and K12 refers to 50 mph.

Ratings of L1 through L3 describe the distance any part of the vehicle will travel past the barrier upon impact.

(For instance, L3 means that the vehicle or major components of a vehicle will travel no more than three feet after striking the barrier.

---

trenching and installation of electrical wiring are impractical, one bollard model runs on a city's water supply. Approximately 60–90 psi will lift the 750-pound bollard — the only byproduct is water.

Sometimes security is needed on the

water, as well. One manufacturer is perfecting a water-borne barrier. Two buoys connected with chains and a 1-inch stainless steel cable can stop a 21-ft. boat from approaching a dam or other sensitive area.

Another manufacturer has designed electromechanical versions of bollards and crash gates, as electromechanical operating systems are more suitable and safer for high-traffic areas such as public or commercial facilities. While many hydraulic units must be housed close to the barriers they operate, an electromechanical power unit can be positioned in a closet 1,000 feet away.

While the options may seem endless, the goal remains the same. With unauthorized vehicle deterrence systems in place, security professionals are once again backed by technology in their pursuit of safety.

Note

The following people and companies were helpful in explaining the technologies described in this article:

David Dickinson, senior vice president, Delta Scientific Corp., Valencia, Calif. Delta Scientific manufactures vehicle barricades, parking control equipment and guard booths.

Mark Perkins, national sales manager, Automatic Control Systems, Port Washington, N.Y. The Automatic Control Systems Group manufactures pedestrian and vehicle access control devices, including six models of electromechanical vehicle barriers.

Scott Rosenbloom, vice-president, ARMR Services Corp., Fairfax, Va. ARMR Services Corp. manufactures crash-rated vehicle barriers and parking control equipment.

Paul Schumacher, sales manager, Petersen Manufacturing Co., Denison, Iowa. Petersen Mfg. manufactures fixed bollards and planters in a variety of shapes and sizes.

John Scolaro, international sales director, Nasatka Barrier, Clinton, Md. Nasatka Barrier specializes in vehicle access control barriers.

R. Shelton Vandiver, product manager, bollards and barriers, Norshield Security Products, Montgomery, Ala. Norshield Security Products manufactures bullet-resistant doors, windows and enclosures, and vehicle access control barriers.

CHAPTER 51

VOLUNTEERISM AND EMERGENCY PREPAREDNESS

William C. Basl and Karin Frinell-Hanrahan

Individuals in public service careers, who see the value associated with this type of career, often wonder how the general public can become better orientated to the work we do every day. One of the positive outcomes of the tragic events of September 11, 2001, is the array of activities under Citizen Corps, which receive federal funds from the Department of Homeland Security. States administer these funds and close to one million new volunteers have answered the president's call to volunteer 4,000 hours of their time to their community through Citizen Corps activities.

Washington State has 51 Citizen Corps Councils, which represents close to 96 percent of the population being represented by a regional, local or tribal Citizen Corps Council. The Council's responsibility is to recruit, train and exercise citizen volunteers who can support emergency responders performing mission central activities. The Citizen Corps programs include Community Emergency Response Training, Volunteers in Police Service, Medical Reserve Corps, USA onWatch.org/Neighborhood Watch and Fire Corps. Each for these activities offers a unique volunteer experience.

Citizen Corps Councils

Citizen Corps Councils have the responsibility as the local organizing group with action items including:

- Creating an action plan to involve the community in prevention, preparedness and response activities and to mobilize the community in a large-scale event.
- Identifying ways that the community's volunteer resources can help meet the needs of its emergency responders.
- Working with existing neighborhood leaders, or creating a neighborhood leadership structure, to design a systematic approach to educate the public and encourage Citizen Corps participation throughout the community.
- Spearheading efforts to offer citizens new and existing volunteer opportunities, educational information and training courses to address crime, terrorism, public health issues and natural disaster risks.
- Recognizing all activities that promote prevention, preparedness and response training as a part of Citizen Corps and encouraging new endeavors.
- Organizing special projects and commu-

Originally published as "Emergency Preparedness Brings Volunteers to Serve," *PA Times*, Vol. 28, No. 3, March 2005. Published by the American Society for Public Administration, Washington, D.C. Reprinted with permission of the publisher.

nity events to promote Citizen Corps activities and recruiting volunteers to participate.

- Fostering a spirit of mutual support by working with Citizen Corps Councils in neighboring communities and jurisdictions to be able to share resources in times of need.
- Capturing innovative practices and reporting accomplishments to the state coordinator for Citizen Corps.
- Surveying your community to assess increased awareness and Citizen Corps participation.

USAonWatch

USAonWatch.org/Neighborhood Watch Programs have the responsibility to support local law enforcement agencies with action items including:

- Arrange for home security inspections by crime prevention officers to identify security vulnerabilities.
- Upgrade locks, security hardware and lighting.
- Train family members to keep valuables secure and to lock windows when leaving home.
- Train family members on identifying suspicious behaviors that could indicate terrorist activity.
- Ask neighbors to watch for suspicious activity when the house is vacant.
- Organize block watch groups to assist children, the elderly and other especially vulnerable persons if they appear to be in distress, in danger, or lost.
- Obtain and study informative materials from the National Sheriffs' Association, the National Crime Prevention Council and local law enforcement agencies.

Community Emergency Response Training (CERT) Programs have the responsibility to support all emergency responder agencies with action items including:

- Staff a community education booth at community events.
- Identify safety needs and vulnerable individuals in your neighborhood.
- Distribute disaster education material in your neighborhood, in multiple languages if appropriate.
- Assist with writing and distributing a CERT newsletter.
- Help organize drills, activities and supplemental training.
- Participate in a speaker's bureau to schools and clubs.
- Assist emergency responders with special projects.
- Help with CERT administrative duties by maintaining databases, helping with class registration and assisting with class logistics.
- Organize recognition activities for volunteers.
- After CERT training, assist in evacuation, shelter management, donations management, care of responders at fires or emergencies, mass care of victims from a large event, damage assessment and perimeter control.

Volunteers in Public Service

Volunteers in Police Service (VIPS) have the responsibility to support local law enforcement agencies with action items including:

- Take police reports
- Make follow-up telephone calls to victims
- Conduct fingerprinting
- Engage in crowd/parking control at special events
- Participate in search and rescue missions
- Participate in mounted patrols in parking lots at high school football games
- Serve subpoenas

Medical Reserve Corps

Medical Reserve Corps have the responsibility to support public health with action items including:
- Assess and monitor the condition of patients
- Counsel patients
- Perform support and management activities (e.g., facilitate patient transfers, inventory and distribute pharmaceuticals, supplies and food)
- Administer and distribute medication. In non-emergency situations, local agencies could request volunteers to assist them in performing their routine duties. Volunteers could:
- Distribute educational materials about the need for immunizations
- Give immunizations
- Assist with health education
- Provide additional support for community

Fire Corps

Fire Corps have the responsibility to support local fire departments and districts with action items including:
- Offer to help the fire department in its fundraising efforts. Help with bingo, bake sales, or other department fundraising programs.
- Help the department with its financial matters if you have a business background or special skills in this area.
- Help with correspondence, public outreach and records management.
- Assist the fire department and fire prevention experts with fire prevention education

in your neighborhood, place of business, schools and community organizations.

Neighbors Helping Neighbors

While the news media commonly depicts the traditional first responder as individuals who will respond immediately to a call, what would happen if that system was incapable of handling the volume of requests for help? The common response is "That cannot happen here," from those not familiar with the operations of our emergency response systems. But ask the people who had to deal with the destruction caused by the hurricanes last fall in Florida, or the recent mud slides in California. It does not take much to overload the calls for emergency response. The situation could quickly become one that will need neighbor helping neighbor in order to survive.

Each household should have an emergency kit that would enable them to survive on their own without receiving emergency assistance. Could you do that today at home and at work? Who would help your neighbors if a sudden earthquake struck your community? Do you have the ability to turn off the natural gas at your house?

Citizen Corps activities enable all of us to become more interdependent and become more civically involved in our community. Information on the various Citizen Corps activities can be found at *www.citizencorps.gov*. It just might be the way to educate your neighbors on the broader role of public service and the need for all to help build our nation.

Part III

The Future of Homeland Security

CHAPTER 52

HOMELAND SECURITY, CIVIL LIBERTIES, AND THE FUTURE

Laurie Clewett

Americans feel their world was changed on Sept. 11, 2001. The terrorist attacks on the World Trade Center and Pentagon disrupted our normal routines and sense of security, as well as the nation's political agenda.

In this less-secure world, Americans are re-examining the balance between protecting public safety and individual civil liberties. Government officials are revisiting policies that seemed intrusive or discriminatory just one month ago, but that now could be considered reasonable strategies for uncovering and deterring terrorist activities. Momentum has shifted, at least temporarily, on several public-policy debates, including racial profiling, Internet privacy and the rights of noncitizens.

"This is going, to some degree I'm afraid, affect our freedom," Louisiana Gov. Mike Foster told *The Times-Picayune*. "I think there's going to be an insistence that law enforcement have the ability to do things that today would be considered intrusive."

Similarly, Vermont Gov. Howard Dean told the *Rutland Herald*, "I think there are going to be debates about what can be said

where, what can be printed where, what kind of freedom of movement people have and whether it's OK for a policeman to ask you for your ID just because you're walking down the street."

The federal government already is implementing anti-terrorism policies. New York has passed a package of strong anti-terrorism measures, and other states likely will increase efforts to detect, prevent and respond to such public-safety threats.

Although the direction and duration of this trend are uncertain, one thing is clear: Public-safety and other measures implemented now could have profound implications for individual privacy and civil liberties for years to come.

Shifting Perspectives

In response to terrorism concerns since Sept. 11, the Bush administration has enacted and proposed several new policies.

On Sept. 18, the administration announced a rule change that extended the

Originally published as "Protecting Freedom: Public Safety vs. Civil Liberty," *State Government News*, October 2001. Published by The Council of State Governments, Lexington, KY. Reprinted with permission of the publisher.

length of time the government may detain immigrants. Previously, officials could hold immigrants suspected of a crime or immigration-status violations for 24 hours before making any charges. Now, immigrants can be detained for 48 hours under normal circumstances and indefinitely during national emergencies.

This policy change reflects a shift in the ongoing debate over detaining immigrants. Detention was "a huge debate in the government" before Sept. 11, said Juliette Kayyem, executive director of Harvard University's Executive Session on Domestic Preparedness, a task force devoted to terrorism and emergency management issues. The question has been "how long we as a nation [are] willing to detain people and actually deport them based on evidence we can't see," she said.

Before the recent terrorist attacks, Kayyem said, many people thought Congress would pass legislation to curtail the government's ability to hold immigrants based on secret evidence. Now, "I think that legislation is dead in the water," she said. "I think that there's going to be a movement toward the kind of powers that England had during the worst parts of the battle with the IRA to detain people for periods of time."

The Bush administration reportedly is considering other anti-terrorism measures, including allowing the U.S. attorney general to arrest and deport suspected terrorists without presenting evidence in court; trying suspects in military tribunals rather than courts; allowing prosecutors to use as evidence information collected by foreign governments in ways that are unconstitutional in the United States; and expanding law-enforcement officials' electronic surveillance, wiretap and search powers. The New York Legislature is considering similar wiretap legislation.

The need to detect terrorist conspiracies is overshadowing previous concerns about high-tech, intrusive technologies eroding personal privacy. Some Internet service providers and computer users now seem more receptive to once contentious computer-surveillance methods, including the FBI's DCS 1000 hardware (formerly known as Carnivore), which can be installed on commercial Internet systems to monitor consumers' e-mail.

Defending Freedom

Some people are concerned about the potential erosion of individual privacy and civil liberties in the name of public safety. They argue that these freedoms are at the heart of what it means to be an American, and if we give them up, the terrorists have won.

More than 150 political, professional, religious and other organizations from across the political spectrum have formed a new coalition called In Defense of Freedom. On Sept. 20, the coalition issued a 10-point declaration urging policy-makers to "consider proposals calmly and deliberately with a determination not to erode the liberties and freedoms that are at the core of the American way of life."

In its press conference, the coalition advised, "We should resist the temptation to enact proposals in the mistaken belief that anything that may be called anti-terrorist will necessarily provide greater security."

Then there is the question of how to define terrorism, which has implications for traditional American freedoms. Is bombing an abortion clinic terrorism? What about "eco-terrorism"? Could anti-terrorism measures be used to justify increased surveillance of certain political groups within the United States?

Let History Be the Judge

Historians, constitutional scholars and civil libertarians agree that during times of war individual rights and privacy tend to take

FIGURE 1
Maintaining a Balance

In Defense of Freedom, a coalition of more than 150 organizations, 300 law professors and 40 computer scientists, issued a declaration that insisted those who committed the Sept. 11 terrorist acts be held accountable, but urged the government to uphold the principles of a democratic society as it considers steps to reduce the risk of future terrorist attacks. Highlights of the coalition's suggestions to Americans are:

• Resist the temptation to enact proposals in the belief that anything that may be called anti-terrorist will necessarily provide greater security. Affirm the right of peaceful dissent, protected by the First Amendment, now, when it is most at risk.

• Applaud our political leaders who in the days ahead have the courage to say that our freedoms should not be limited.

• Have faith in our democratic system, our Constitution, and our ability to protect both the freedom and security of all Americans.

Source: www.indefenseoffreedom.org

a back seat to national security. Government officials are far more likely to approve policies they normally would reject as violations of individuals' fundamental rights.

But is the war on terrorism comparable to other wars? With prime suspects, but no easily defined enemy, and no foreseeable end to the conflict, how temporary will this war's sacrifices really be?

"It's easy for Americans to say, 'Well, we're willing to give up something in terms of our privacy to catch these guys and to address this threat,'" Kayyem said. "The question will be two or three or four years from now, whether we'll want that."

Moreover, 20th-century American history contains several widely criticized cases in which individual rights have been sacrificed for what at the time officials thought was the greater public good. The internment of Japanese-Americans after the bombing of Pearl Harbor is perhaps the most infamous example.

"However hard it is to do, we need to take a deep breath and really question what kind of laws we want to put in place right now, because those laws will be with us forever," Kayyem said. "It's hard to imagine right now a time when this is not story No. 1, issue No. 1, drama No. 1, tragedy No. 1, but there will come a time. And I think it's really a challenge for the people in charge right now to try to balance the obvious need to try to fix something with the traditions of privacy in our country."

Internet Resource

Executive Session on Domestic Preparedness (www.ksgnotes1.harvard.edu/BCSIA/ESDP.nsf/www/Home). This standing task force of leading practitioners and academic specialists offers online resources on terrorism and emergency management.

Homeland
Security Acronyms

AMS . . . . . . Aerial Measuring System

ARAC . . . . . Atmospheric Release Advisory Capability

ARC . . . . American Red Cross

ATAC . . . . . Anti-Terrorism Advisory Council

ATF . . . . Bureau of Alcohol, Tobacco, and Firearms

CBRN . . . . . Chemical/biological/radiation/ nuclear

CB-RRT . . . Chemical and Biological Rapid Response Team

CBW . . . . . . Chemical and Biological Weapons

CCC . . . . . . Citizen Corps Council

CDC . . . . . . Centers for Disease Control and Prevention

CEPPO . . . . Chemical Emergency Prepared- ness and Prevention Office

CERT . . . . . Community Emergency Response Team

CID . . . . Criminal Investigations Division

DEST . . . . . Domestic Emergency Support Team

DHHS . . . . . Department of Health and Human Services

DHS . . . . . . Department of Homeland Security

DOD . . . . . . Department of Defense

DOE . . . . . . Department of Energy

DOJ . . . . Department of Justice

DMAT . . . . . Disaster Medical Assistance Team

D-MORT . . Disaster Mortuary Response Team

DRC . . . . . . Disaster Recovery Center

EAS . . . . Emergency Alert System

EMPG . . . . . Emergency Management Performance Grant

EOC . . . . . . Emergency Operations Center

EPA . . . . Environmental Protection Agency

EPCRA . . . . The Environmental Protection & Community Right-to- Know Act

ERRS . . . . . . Emergency and Rapid Response Team

ERT . . . . Environmental Response Team

FBI . . . . Federal Bureau of Investigation

FCC . . . . . . Federal Coordination Center

FCO . . . . . . Federal Coordinating Office

FDA . . . . . . Food and Drug Administration

FEMA . . . . . Federal Emergency Management Agency

FRMAC . . . Federal Radiological Monitoring Assessment Center

GIS . . . . Geographic Information System

HAN . . . . . . Health Area Network

HAZMAT . . Hazardous Materials Team

HHS . . . . . . Health and Human Services

HSAS . . . . . . Homeland Security Advisory System

HSOC . . . . . Homeland Security Operations Center

HSPD . . . . . Homeland Security Presidential Directive

IIMG . . . . . . Interagency Incident Manage- ment Group

INRP . . . . . . Initial National Response Plan

IRZ . . . . Immediate Response Zone

JFO . . . . Joint Field Office

JIC . . . . Joint Information Center

JOC . . . . Joint Operations Center

JTOT . . . . . . Joint Technical Operations Team

LAN . . . . . . Local Area Network

LEO . . . . . . Law Enforcement Online

LEPC . . . . . . Local Emergency Planning
Committees

LETPP . . . . . Law Enforcement Terrorism
Prevention Program

LFA . . . . Lead Federal Agency

LGAT . . . . . Lincoln Gold Augmentation
Team

LODD . . . . . Line of Duty Deaths

MAG . . . . . . Mutual Aid Agreement

MMRS . . . . Metropolitan Medical Response
System

MMST . . . . Metropolitan Medical Strike
Team

MRC . . . . . . Medical Reserve Corps

MSU . . . . . . Medical Support Units

NDMS . . . . National Disaster Medical System

NDPO . . . . . National Domestic Preparedness Office

NECC . . . . . National Emergency Coordination Center (FEMA)

NEIC . . . . . . National Enforcement Investigations Center

NEST . . . . . Nuclear Emergency Search Team

NIMS . . . . . National Incident Management
System

NIRP . . . . . . National Incidence Response
Plan

NNSA . . . . . National Nuclear Security
Administration

NRAT . . . . . Nuclear Radiological Support
Team

NRS . . . . National Response System

NRST . . . . . Nuclear Radiological Support
Team

NRT . . . . . . National Response Team

ODP . . . . . . Office for Domestic Preparedness

OEM . . . . . . Office of Emergency Management

OEP . . . . Office of Emergency Preparedness

OERR . . . . . Office of Emergency and Reme-
dial Response

ORIA . . . . . . Office of Radiation and Indoor
Air

OSC . . . . . . On-Scene Coordinators

PCCIP . . . . . Presidential Commission on
Critical Infrastructure
Protection

PPE . . . . Personal Protective Equipment

RAID . . . . . . Rapid Assessment and Initial
Detection

RAP . . . . Radiation Assistance Program

REAC/TS . . Radiation Emergency Assistance
Center/Training Site

RERT . . . . . Radiological Emergency
Response Team

ROC . . . . . . Regional Operations Center

RRT . . . . Regional Response Teams

SAC . . . . Special Agent in Charge

SAT . . . . Search Augmentation Team

SBS . . . . Suicide Bomber Suspect

SHSAS . . . . . State Homeland Security
Assessment and Strategy
Program

SHSP . . . . . . State Homeland Security Program

SHSWG . . . State Homeland Security Working Group

SIOC . . . . . . Strategic Information Operations
Center

SRT . . . . Search Response Team

START . . . . Superfund Technical Assessment
and Response Team

SSC . . . . Scientific Support Coordinators

USPHS . . . . United States Public Health
Service

VIPS . . . . . . Volunteers in Police Service

WANS . . . . . Wide Area Notification System

WMD . . . . . Weapons of Mass Destruction

HOMELAND SECURITY INTERNET RESOURCES

Agency for Toxic Substances and Disease Registry
U.S. Department of Health and Human Services
http://www.atsdr.cdc.gov/atsdrhome.html

American Institute of Architects
http://www.aia.org/

American Red Cross
http://www.redcross.org/

America Responds to Terrorism
Office of Citizen Services and Communications
U.S. General Services Administration
http://www.firstgov.gov/

American Society of Civil Engineers
http://www.asce.org/

ANSER Institute for Homeland Security
http://www.homelandsecurity.org/

Bureau of Alcohol, Tobacco, and Firearms
U.S. Department of the Treasury
http://www.atf.treas.gov/

Centers for Disease Control and Prevention
U.S. Department of Health and Human Services
http://www.cdc.gov/

Chemical Emergency Preparedness and Prevention Office
Environmental Protection Agency
http://www.epa.gov/swercepp/

Counterterrorism Office
U.S. Department of State
http://www.state.gov/s/ct/

Domestic Terrorism Research Center
John F. Kennedy School of Government
Harvard University
http://www.ksg.harvard.edu/terrorism/

Emergency Management Institute
Federal Emergency Management Agency
http://www.training.fema.gov/emiweb/

Federal Bureau of Investigation
http://www.fbi.gov/

Federal Emergency Management Agency
http://www.fema.gov/

International Association of Fire Chiefs
http://www.ichiefs.org/

International City/County Management Association
Emergency Readiness Center
http://www.icma.org/issueintersections/er.cfm/

International Critical Incident Stress Foundation
http://www.icisf.org/

National Association of Counties
http://www.naco.org/

National Disaster Medical System
Office of Emergency Preparedness
U.S. Department of Health and Human Services
http://www.oep-ndms.dhhs.gov/NDMS/ndms.html

National Domestic Preparedness Office
Federal Bureau of Investigation
U.S. Department of Justice
http://www.fas.gov/irp/agency/doj/fbi/ndpo/

National Fire Academy
Federal Emergency Management Agency
http://www.usfa.fema.gov/

National Infrastructure Protection Center
http://www.nipc.gov/

National Institute of Justice
U.S. Department of Justice
http://www.ojp.usdoj.gov/nij

National Disaster Medical System
Office of Emergency Preparedness
U.S. Public Health Service
http://www.ndms.dhhs.gov/

National Security Agency
http://www.nsa.gov/

Office for Victims of Crime
U.S. Department of Justice
http://www.ojp.usdoj.gov/ovc/

Office of Domestic Preparedness
Office of Justice Programs
U.S. Department of Justice
http://www.osldps.ncjrs.org/

Office of Homeland Security
Office of the President
U.S. Federal Government
http://www.whitehouse.gov/homeland/

Operation Noble Eagle
U.S. Air Force
http://www.af.mil/news/efreedom/

Public Entity Risk Institute
http://www.riskinstitute.org/

**Public Health Emergency Preparedness &
  Response**

Centers for Disease Control and Prevention
U.S. Department of Health and Human Services
http://www.bt.cdc.gov/

The Terrorism Research Center
http://www.terrorism.com/

The War on Terrorism
Central Intelligence Agency
http://www.odci.gov/terrorism/

U.S. Conference of Mayors
http://www.usmayors.org/

U.S. Department of Defense
http://www.defenselink.mil/

U.S. Department of Energy
http://www.energy.gov/

**U.S. Department of Health and Human Ser-
  vices**
http://www.hhs.gov/

U.S. Department of Justice
http://www.usdoj.gov/

U.S. Department of State
http://www.state.gov/

U.S. Environmental Protection Agency
http://www.epa.gov/

AMERICAN RED CROSS, HOMELAND SECURITY ADVISORY SYSTEM RECOMMENDATIONS

INDIVIDUAL

Risk of Attack	Recommended Actions
Severe Condition (Red)	• *Complete recommended actions at lower levels* • Listen to radio/TV for current information/instructions • Be alert to suspicious activity and report it to proper authorities immediately • Contact business to determine status of work day • Adhere to any travel restrictions announced by local governmental authorities • Be prepared to shelter in place or evacuate if instructed to do so by local governmental authorities • Provide volunteer services only as requested
High Condition (Orange)	• *Complete recommended actions at lower levels* • Be alert to suspicious activity and report it to proper authorities • Review your personal disaster plan • Exercise caution when traveling • Have shelter in place materials on hand, and review procedures in *Terrorism: Preparing for the Unexpected* brochure • If a need is announced, donate blood at designated blood collection center • Prior to volunteering, contact agency to determine their needs
Elevated Condition (Yellow)	• *Complete recommended actions at lower levels* • Be alert to suspicious activity and report it to proper authorities • Ensure disaster supplies kit is stocked and ready • Check telephone numbers and e-mail addresses in your personal communication plan and update as necessary • Develop alternate routes to/from work/school and practice them • Continue to provide volunteer services
Guarded Condition (Blue)	• *Complete recommended actions at lower level* • Be alert to suspicious activity and report it to proper authorities • Review stored disaster supplies and replace items that are outdated • Develop emergency communication plan with family/neighbors/friends

Source: American Red Cross, 2025 "E" Street, N.W., 10th Floor, Washington, D.C. 20006

> • Provide volunteer services and take advantage of additional volunteer train-
> ing opportunities

Low Condition (Green)

> • Obtain copy of *Terrorism: Preparing for the Unexpected* brochure from your
> local Red Cross chapter
> • Develop a personal disaster plan and disaster supplies kit using Red Cross
> brochures *Your Family Disaster Plan* and *Your Family Disaster Supplies Kit*
> • Examine volunteer opportunities in your community; choose an agency to
> volunteer with and receive initial training

FAMILY

Risk of Attack   *Recommended Actions*

Severe Condition (Red)

> • *Complete recommended actions at lower levels*
> • Listen to radio/TV for current information/instructions
> • Be alert to suspicious activity and report it to proper authorities immedi-
> ately
> • Contact business/school to determine status of work/school day
> • Adhere to any travel restrictions announced by local governmental author-
> ities
> • Be prepared to shelter in place or evacuate if instructed to do so by local
> governmental authorities
> • Discuss children's fears concerning possible/actual terrorist attacks

High Condition (Orange)

> • *Complete recommended actions at lower levels*
> • Be alert to suspicious activity and report it to proper authorities
> • Review disaster plan with all family members
> • Ensure communication plan is understood/practiced by all family members
> • Exercise caution when traveling
> • Have shelter in place materials on hand, and review procedures in *Terror-
> ism: Preparing for the Unexpected* brochure
> • Discuss children's fear concerning possible terrorist attacks
> • If a need is announced, donate blood at designated blood collection cen-
> ter

Elevated Condition (Yellow)

> • *Complete recommended actions at lower levels*
> • Be alert to suspicious activity and report it to proper authorities
> • Ensure disaster supplies kit is stocked and ready
> • Check telephone numbers and e-mail addresses in your family emergency
> communication plan and update as necessary
> • If not known to you, contact school to determine their emergency notifi-
> cation and evacuation plans for children
> • Develop alternate routes to/from work/school and practice them

Guarded Condition (Blue)

> • *Complete recommended actions at lower level*
> • Be alert to suspicious activity and report it to proper authorities
> • Review stored disaster supplies and replace items that are outdated
> • Develop an emergency communication plan that all family members un-
> derstand
> • Establish an alternate meeting place away from home with family/friends

Low Condition (Green)

> • Obtain copy of *Terrorism: Preparing for the Unexpected* brochure from your
> local Red Cross chapter
> • Develop a personal disaster plan and disaster supplies kit using Red Cross
> brochures *Your Family Disaster Plan* and *Your Family Disaster Supplies Kit*

SCHOOLS

Risk of Attack   *Recommended Actions*

Severe Condition
(Red)

- *Complete recommended actions at lower levels*
- Listen to radio/TV for current information/instructions
- Be alert to suspicious activity and report it to proper authorities immediately
- Close school if recommended to do so by appropriate authorities
- 100% identification check (i.e. — driver's license retained at front office) and provide an escort for anyone entering school other than students, staff and faculty
- Continue offering lessons from Masters of Disaster "Facing Fear: Helping Young People Deal with Terrorism and Tragic Events" curriculum
- Ensure mental health counselors available for students, staff and faculty

High Condition
(Orange)

- *Complete recommended actions at lower levels*
- Be alert to suspicious activity and report it to proper authorities
- Review emergency plans
- Offer Masters of Disaster "Facing Fear: Helping Young People Deal with Terrorism and Tragic Events" lessons in grades K–12
- Prepare to handle inquiries from anxious parents and media
- Discuss children's fears concerning possible terrorist attacks

Elevated Condition
(Yellow)

- *Complete recommended actions at lower levels*
- Be alert to suspicious activity and report it to proper authorities
- Ensure all emergency supplies stocked and ready
- Obtain copies of *Terrorism: Preparing for the Unexpected* brochure from your local Red Cross chapter and send it home with students in grades K–12, staff and faculty

Guarded Condition
(Blue)

- *Complete recommended actions at lower level*
- Be alert to suspicious activity and report it to proper authorities
- Conduct safety training/emergency drills following the school's written emergency plan for all grades
- Ensure emergency communication plan updated and needed equipment is purchased
- Continue offering lessons from "Masters of Disaster" curriculum for grades K–8 regarding emergency preparedness for natural disasters

Low Condition
(Green)

- Use Red Cross *Emergency Management Guide for Business and Industry* to develop written emergency plans to address all hazards including plans to maintain the safety of students, staff, and faculty, as well as an emergency communication plan to notify parents in time of emergency. Disseminate relevant information to families of children, staff and faculty.
- Initiate offering "Masters of Disaster" curriculum for grades K–8 regarding emergency preparedness for natural disasters

NEIGHBORHOOD

Risk of Attack   *Recommended Actions*

Severe Condition
(Red)

- *Complete recommended actions at lower levels*
- Listen to radio/TV for current information/instructions
- Be alert to suspicious activity and report it to proper authorities immediately
- Adhere to any travel restrictions announced by local governmental authorities

- Be prepared to shelter in place/evacuate and assist neighbors who are elderly or have special needs to do the same

High Condition (Orange)
- *Complete recommended actions at lower levels*
- Be alert to suspicious activity and report it to proper authorities
- Check on neighbors who are elderly or have special needs to ensure their well-being. Review disaster plan with them.
- If a need is announced, contact nearest blood collection agency and offer to organize a neighborhool blood drive

Elevated Condition (Yellow)
- *Complete recommended actions at lower levels*
- Be alert to suspicious activity and report it to proper authorities
- Have neighborhood meeting in order to identify neighbors who are elderly or have special needs. Assist them in development of a personal disaster plan and disaster supplies kit if requested.

Guarded Condition (Blue)
- *Complete recommended actions at lower level*
- Be alert to suspicious activity and report it to proper authorities

Low Condition (Green)
- Have neighborhood meeting to discuss emergency plans and establish a 'Neighborhood Watch'
- Obtain copies of *Terrorism: Preparing for the Unexpected* brochure from your local Red Cross chapter and distribute at neighborhood meeting

Note: Your local American Red Cross chapter has materials available to assist you in developing preparedness capabilities.

FEDERAL EMERGENCY MANAGEMENT AGENCY REGIONAL OFFICES

FEMA Region I
442 J.W. McCormack
POCH
Boston, MA 02109
(617) 223-9540

FEMA Region II
26 Federal Plaza #1337
New York, NY 10278
(212) 225-7209

FEMA Region III
615 Chestnut Street
One Independence
Mall, Sixth Floor
Philadelphia, PA 19106
(215) 931-5608

FEMA Region IV
3003 Chamblee-Tucker Rd.
Atlanta, GA 30341
(770) 220-5200

FEMA Region V
536 South Clark St., 6th Floor
Chicago, IL 60605
(312) 408-5500

FEMA Region VI
FRC 800 North Loop 288
Denton, TX 76201
(940) 898-5399

FEMA Region VII
2323 Grand Blvd., Suite 900
Kansas City, MO 64108
(816) 283-7061

FEMA Region VIII
Federal Center Building 710
Box 25267
Denver, CO 80255
(303) 235-4800

FEMA Region IX
Presidio, Bldg. 105
PO Box 29998
San Francisco, CA 94129
(415) 923-7100

FEMA Region X
Federal Reg. Center
130 228th Street, SW
Bothell, WA 98021
(425) 487-4600

Source: Federal Emergency Management Agency (FEMA), Federal Center Plaza, 500 "C" Street, S.W., Washington, D.C. 20472

STATE OFFICES AND AGENCIES OF EMERGENCY MANAGEMENT

A

Alabama Emergency Management Agency
5898 County Road 41
P.O. Drawer 2160
Clanton, Alabama 35046-2160
(205) 280-2200
(205) 280-2495 FAX
http://www.ema.alabama.gov/

Alaska Division of Emergency Services
P.O. Box 5750
Fort Richardson, Alaska 99505-5750
(907) 428-7000
(907) 428-7009 FAX
http://www.ak-prepared.com

American Samoa Territorial Emergency Management Coordination
(TEMCO)
American Samoa Government
P.O. Box 1086
Pago Pago, American Samoa 96799
(011) (684) 699-6415
(011) (684) 699-6414 FAX

Arizona Division of Emergency Management
5636 E. McDowell Road
Phoenix, Arizona 85008
(602) 244-0504 or 1-800-411-2336
www.azdema.gov

Arkansas Department of Emergency Management
P.O. Box 758
Conway, Arkansas 72033
(501) 730-9750
(501) 730-9754 FAX
http://www.adem.state.ar.us/

C

California Governor's Office of Emergency Services
P.O. Box 419047
Rancho Cordova, California 95741-9047
(916) 845-8510
(916) 845-8511 FAX
http://www.oes.ca.gov/

Colorado Office of Emergency Management
Division of Local Government
Department of Local Affairs
9195 East Mineral Avenue
Suite 200
Centennial, Colorado 80112
(720) 852-6600
(720) 852-6750 Fax
www.dola.state.co.us/oem/oemindex.htm

Connecticut Office of Emergency Management
Military Department
360 Broad Street
Hartford, Connecticut 06105
(860) 566-3180
(860) 247-0664 FAX
http://www.mil.state.ct.us/OEM.htm

D

Delaware Emergency Management Agency
165 Brick Store Landing Road
Smyrna, Delaware 19977
(302) 659-3362
(302) 659-6855 FAX
http://www.state.de.us/dema/index.htm

District of Columbia Emergency Management
Agency

Source: Federal Emergency Management Agency (FEMA), Federal Center Plaza, 500 "C" Street, S.W., Washington, D.C. 20472

2000 14th Street, NW, 8th Floor
Washington, D.C. 20009
(202) 727-6161
(202) 673-2290 FAX
http://www.dcema.dc.gov

F

Florida Division of Emergency Management
2555 Shumard Oak Blvd.
Tallahassee, Florida 32399-2100
(850) 413-9969
(850) 488-1016 FAX
www.floridadisaster.org

G

Georgia Emergency Management Agency
P.O. Box 18055
Atlanta, Georgia 30316-0055
(404) 635-7000
(404) 635-7205 FAX
http://www.State.Ga.US/GEMA/

Office of Civil Defense
Government of Guam
P.O. Box 2877
Hagatna, Guam 96932
(011) (671) 475-9600
(011) (671) 477-3727 FAX
http://ns.gov.gu/

Guam Homeland Security/Office of Civil
   Defense
221B Chalan Palasyo
Agana Heights, Guam 96910
Tel: (671) 475-9600
Fax: (671) 477-3727
http://www.guamhs.org

H

Hawaii State Civil Defense
3949 Diamond Head Road
Honolulu, Hawaii 96816-4495
(808) 733-4300
(808) 733-4287 FAX
http://www.scd.hawaii.gov

I

Idaho Bureau of Disaster Services
4040 Guard Street, Bldg. 600
Boise, Idaho 83705-5004
(208) 334-3460
(208) 334-2322 FAX
http://www.2.state.id.us/bds/

Illinois Emergency Management Agency
110 East Adams Street

Springfield, Illinois 62701
(217) 782-2700
(217) 524-7967 FAX
http://www.state.il.us/iema

Indiana State Emergency Management Agency
302 West Washington Street
Room E-208 A
Indianapolis, Indiana 46204-2767
(317) 232-3986
(317) 232-3895 FAX
http://www.ai.org/sema/index.html

Iowa Homeland Security & Emergency Management Division
Department of Public Defense
Hoover Office Building
Des Moines, Iowa 50319
(515) 281-3231
(515) 281-7539 FAX
www.Iowahomelandsecurity.org.

K

Kansas Division of Emergency Management
2800 S.W. Topeka Boulevard
Topeka, Kansas 66611-1287
(785) 274-1401
(785) 274-1426 FAX
http://www.ink.org/public/kdem/

Kentucky Emergency Management
EOC Building
100 Minuteman Parkway Bldg. 100
Frankfort, Kentucky 40601-6168
(502) 607-1682
(502) 607-1614 FAX
http://kyem.dma.ky.gov

L

Louisiana Office of Emergency Preparedness
7667 Independence Blvd.
Baton Rouge, Louisiana 70806
(225) 925-7500
(225) 925-7501 FAX
http://www.ohsep.louisiana.gov

M

Maine Emergency Management Agency
45 Commerce Drive, Suite #2
#72 State House Station
Augusta, Maine 04333-0072
(207) 624-4400
(207) 287-3180 (FAX)
http://www.state.me.us/mema/memahome.htm

CNMI Emergency Management Office
Office of the Governor

Commonwealth of the Northern Mariana Islands
P.O. Box 10007
Saipan, Mariana Islands 96950
(670) 322-9529
(670) 322-7743 FAX
http://www.cnmiemo.org/

National Disaster Management Office
Office of the Chief Secretary
P.O. Box 15
Majuro, Republic of the Marshall Islands
96960-0015
(011) (692) 625-5181
(011) (692) 625-6896 FAX

Maryland Emergency Management Agency
Camp Fretterd Military Reservation
5401 Rue Saint Lo Drive
Reistertown, Maryland 21136
(410) 517-3600
(877) 636-2872 Toll-Free
(410) 517-3610 FAX
http://www.mema.state.md.us/

Massachusetts Emergency Management Agency
400 Worcester Road
Framingham, Massachusetts 01702-5399
(508) 820-2000
(508) 820-2030 FAX
http://www.state.ma.us/mema

Michigan Division of Emergency Management
4000 Collins Road
P.O. Box 30636
Lansing, Michigan 48909-8136
(517) 333-5042
(517) 333-4987 FAX
http://www.msp.state.mi.us/division/emd/
emdweb1.htm

National Disaster Control Officer
Federated States of Micronesia
P.O. Box PS-53
Kolonia, Pohnpei — Micronesia 96941
(011) (691) 320-8815
(001) (691) 320-2785 FAX

Minnesota Division of Emergency Management
Department of Public Safety
Suite 223
444 Cedar Street
St. Paul, Minnesota 55101-6223
(651) 296-2233
(651) 296-0459 FAX
http://www.dps.state.mn.us/emermgt/

Mississippi Emergency Management Agency
P.O. Box 4501— Fondren Station
Jackson, Mississippi 39296-4501
(601) 352-9100
(800) 442-6362 Toll Free
(601) 352-8314 FAX
http://www.www.msema.org
http://www.msema.org/mitigate/mssaferoominit.
htm

Missouri Emergency Management Agency
P.O. Box 116
2302 Militia Drive
Jefferson City, Missouri 65102
(573) 526-9100
(573) 634-7966 FAX
http://www.sema.state.mo.us/semapage.htm

Montana Division of Disaster & Emergency
Services
1100 North Main
P.O. Box 4789
Helena, Montana 59604-4789
(406) 841-3911
(406) 444-3965 FAX
http://www.state.mt.us/dma/des/index.shtml

N

Nebraska Emergency Management Agency
1300 Military Road
Lincoln, Nebraska 68508-1090
(402) 471-7410
(402) 471-7433 FAX
http://www.nebema.org

Nevada Division of Emergency Management
2525 South Carson Street
Carson City, Nevada 89711
(775) 687-4240
(775) 687-6788 FAX
http://dem.state.nv.us/

Governor's Office of Emergency Management
State Office Park South
107 Pleasant Street
Concord, New Hampshire 03301
(603) 271-2231
(603) 225-7341 FAX
http://www.nhoem.state.nh.us/

New Jersey Office of Emergency Management
Emergency Management Bureau
P.O. Box 7068
West Trenton, New Jersey 08628-0068
(609) 538-6050 Monday–Friday
(609) 882-2000 ext 6311 (24/7)
(609) 538-0345 FAX
http://www.state.nj.us/oem/county/

New Mexico Department of Public Safety
Office of Emergency Management
P.O. Box 1628
13 Bataan Boulevard
Santa Fe, New Mexico 87505
(505) 476-9600
(505) 476-9635 Emergency
(505) 476-9695 FAX
http://www.dps.nm.org/emergency/index.htm

Emergency Management Bureau
Department of Public Safety
P.O. Box 1628
13 Bataan Boulevard
Santa Fe, New Mexico 87505
(505) 476-9606
(505) 476-9650
http://www.dps.nm.org/emc.htm

New York State Emergency Management
   Office
1220 Washington Avenue
Building 22, Suite 101
Albany, New York 12226-2251
(518) 457-2222
(518) 457-9995 FAX
http://www.nysemo.state.ny.us/

North Carolina Division of Emergency Management
116 West Jones Street
Raleigh, North Carolina 27603
(919) 733-3867
(919) 733-5406 FAX
http://www.dem.dcc.state.nc.us/

North Dakota Division of Emergency Management
P.O. Box 5511
Bismarck, North Dakota 58506-5511
(701) 328-8100
(701) 328-8181 FAX
http://www.state.nd.us/dem

O

Ohio Emergency Management Agency
2855 W. Dublin Granville Road
Columbus, Ohio 43235-2206
(614) 889-7150
(614) 889-7183 FAX
http://www.state.oh.us/odps/division/ema/

Office of Civil Emergency Management
Will Rogers Sequoia Tunnel 2401 N. Lincoln
Oklahoma City, Oklahoma 73152
(405) 521-2481

(405) 521-4053 FAX
http://www.odcem.state.ok.us/

Oregon Emergency Management
Department of State Police
P.O. Box 14370
Salem, Oregon 97309-5062
(503) 378-2911
(503) 373-7833 FAX
http://egov.oregon.gov/OOHS/OEM

P

Palau NEMO Coordinator
Office of the President
P.O. Box 100
Koror, Republic of Palau 96940
(011) (680) 488-2422
(011) (680) 488-3312

Pennsylvania Emergency Management Agency
2605 Interstate Drive
Harrisburg, Pennsylvania 17110-9463
(717) 651-2001
(717) 651-2040 FAX
http://www.pema.state.pa.us/

Puerto Rico Emergency Management Agency
P.O. Box 966597
San Juan, Puerto Rico 00906-6597
(787) 724-0124
(787) 725-4244 FAX

R

Rhode Island Emergency Management Agency
645 New London Avenue
Cranston, Rhode Island 02920-3003
(401) 946-9996
(401) 944-1891 FAX
http://www.riema.ri.gov

S

South Carolina Emergency Management Division
2779 Fish Hatchery Road
West Columbia, South Carolina 29172
(803) 737-8500
(803) 737-8570 FAX
http://www.scemd.org/

South Dakota Division of Emergency Management
118 West Capitol
Pierre, South Dakota 57501
(605) 773-3231
(605) 773-3580 FAX
http://www.state.sd.us/dps/sddem/home.htm

T

Tennessee Emergency Management Agency
3041 Sidco Drive
Nashville, Tennessee 37204-1502
(615) 741-4332
(615) 242-9635 FAX
http://www.tnema.org

Texas Division of Emergency Management
5805 N. Lamar
Austin, Texas 78752
(512) 424-2138
(512) 424-2444 or 7160 FAX
http://www.txdps.state.tx.us/dem/

U

Utah Division of Emergency Services and
   Homeland Security
1110 State Office Building
P.O. Box 141710
Salt Lake City, Utah 84114-1710
(801) 538-3400
(801) 538-3770 FAX
http://www.des.utah.gov

V

Vermont Emergency Management Agency
Department of Public Safety
Waterbury State Complex
103 South Main Street
Waterbury, Vermont 05671-2101
(802) 244-8721
(802) 244-8655 FAX
http://www.dps.state.vt.us/

Virgin Islands Territorial Emergency Management — VITEMA
2-C Contant, A-Q Building
Virgin Islands 00820

(340) 774-2244
(340) 774-1491

Virginia Department of Emergency Management
10501 Trade Court
Richmond, Virginia 23236-3713
(804) 897-6502
(804) 897-6506
http://www.vdem.state.va.us

W

State of Washington Emergency Management
   Division
Building 20, M/S: TA-20
Camp Murray, Washington 98430-5122
(253) 512-7000
(253) 512-7200 FAX
http://www.emd.wa.gov/

West Virginia Office of Emergency Services
Building 1, Room EB-80 1900 Kanawha
   Boulevard, East
Charleston, West Virginia 25305-0360
(304) 558-5380
(304) 344-4538 FAX
http://www.state.wv.us/wvoes

Wisconsin Emergency Management
2400 Wright Street
P.O. Box 7865
Madison, Wisconsin 53707-7865
(608) 242-3232
(608) 242-3247 FAX
http://emergencymanagement.wi.gov/

Wyoming Office of Homeland Security
122 W. 25th Street
Cheyenne, Wyoming 82002
(307) 777-4900
(307) 635-6017 FAX
http://wyohomelandsecurity.state.wy.us

About the Editor
and Contributors

Editor (and Contributor)

Roger L. Kemp, **PhD**   has been the Chief Executive Officer of cities on both the West and East Coasts. He is presently City Manager of Vallejo, one of the largest cities in Northern California with the council-manager form of government. Dr. Kemp has also been an adjunct professor at the University of California, California State University, Golden Gate University, Rutgers University, and the University of Connecticut. Roger holds BS, MPA, MBA, and PhD degrees and is a graduate of the Program for Senior Executives in State and Local Government at Harvard University. Dr. Kemp is listed in *Who's Who in America* (since 2003) and *Contemporary American Authors* (since 1997). He is also a Founder and Lifetime Benefactor of the California City Management Foundation, as well as an Honorary Member of Phi Alpha Alpha, a national public administration honor society. Roger has also served on national editorial advisory boards, contributed entries to several encyclopedias, written and edited numerous books, and has authored many articles on topics related to America's cities.

Contributors

Affiliations are as of the times the articles were written

Joe M. Allbaugh   Director, Federal Emergency Management Agency, Washington, DC.

Anne Louise Bannon   Freelance Writer, Los Angeles, California.

William C. Basl   Executive Director, Commission for National and Community Service, State of Washington, Olympia, Washington.

Kevin Baum   Assistant Chief, Fire Department, City of Austin, Texas.

Russell Bennett   Doctoral Student, Department of Public Policy and Administration, Jackson State University, Jackson, Mississippi.

David R. Blossom   Vice Chairman, Fire and Life Safety Code Board of Adjustments and Appeals, Orange County, Florida; and Member, Building and Fire Code Appeals Board, Orlando, Florida.

Paul Bockelman   Operations Manager, Massachusetts Interlocal Insurance Association, Boston, Massachusetts.

Colin A. Campbell   Freelance Writer, Annandale, Virginia.

Laurie Clewett   Information Specialist, The Council of State Governments, Lexington, Kentucky.

Dan Cook   Founding Editor, *Military Aerospace Technology*, Rockville, Maryland.

Deborah J. Daniels   Assistant Attorney General, Office of Justice Programs, U.S. Department of Justice, Washington, DC.

Chris DeChant   Firefighter and Paramedic, Fire Department, City of Glendale, Arizona.

Russell J. Decker   Director, Office of Homeland Security and Emergency Management, Allen County, Lima, Ohio.

Jacqueline Emigh   Freelance Writer, New York, New York.

Marsha J. Evans   President and Chief Executive Officer, American Red Cross, Washington, DC.

Nancy Ferris   Technology Correspondent, *Homeland Protection Professional*, A. J. Parrino & Associates, Western Springs, Illinois.

Jon Fleischman   Deputy Director for Public Affairs, Sheriff's Department, Orange County, Santa Ana, California.

Karin Frinell-Hanrahan   Coordinator, Citizens Corps Program, Commission for National and Community Service, State of Washington, Olympia, Washington.

Joseph J. Grano   Chairman, President's Homeland Security Advisory Council, Washington, DC.

Rickey Hargrave   Police Chaplain, Police Department, City of McKinney, Texas.

Lee Anne Jacobs   Research Associate, The Council of State Governments, Lexington, Kentucky.

Russ Johnson   Public Safety Manager, ESRI, Redlands, California.

Randall D. Larson   Dispatch Supervisor and Field Communications Manager, Fire Department, City of San Jose, California.

Philip Leggiere   Journalist and Business Analyst, Northern New Jersey.

Trudi Matthews   Health Policy Analyst, The Council of State Governments, Lexington, Kentucky.

Stephen McGrail   Director, Emergency Management Agency, State of Massachusetts, Boston, Massachusetts.

John Nicholson   Associate Editor, *NFPA Journal*, National Fire Protection Association, Quincy, Massachusetts.

Robert T. O'Connor   Chief Information Officer, USI Hastings-Tapley, Woburn, Massachusetts.

W. Ronald Olin   Chief of Police, City of Lawrence, Kansas.

John Ouellette   Editor, *Municipal Advocate*, Massachusetts Municipal Association, Boston, Massachusetts.

Jennifer Pero   Assistant Editor, *Government Security*, PRIMEDIA Business Magazines and Media Inc., Atlanta, Georgia.

Thomas E. Poulin   Battalion Chief, Fire Department, City of Virginia Beach, Virginia.

John R. Powers   Former Commissioner and Executive Director, Presidential Commission on Critical Infrastructure Protection, Washington, DC.

Gary Raymer   Chief of Police, City of Bowling Green, Kentucky.

Thomas Ridge   Secretary, Department of Homeland Security, U.S. Government, Washington, DC.

Joseph F. Russo   Director, Fire Safety Engineering, Polytechnic University, Brooklyn, New York.

Robert L. Smith   Lieutenant, Stress Management Unit, Fire Department, Washington Township, Indianapolis, Indiana.

Corrina Stellitano   Freelance Writer, Mobile, Alabama.

David Wagman, Contributing Editor, *Homeland Protection Professional*, A. J. Parrino & Associates, Western Springs, Illinois.

Janet Ward   Senior Editor, *Homeland Protection Professional*, A. J. Parrino & Associates, Western Springs, Illinois.

Roger Williams   Vice President, JPS Communications, Inc., Raleigh, North Carolina.

Rick Wimberly   Public Safety Director, Dialogue Communications Corporation, Franklin, Tennessee.

Robert Yates   Freelance Writer, Evanston, Illinois.

INDEX